SMALL STEPS

SMALL STEPS

LOUIS SACHAR

WORKBOOK

Contents

'아동 도서계의 노벨상!' 미국 최고 권위의 아동 문학상

뉴베리 상(Newbery Award)은 미국 도서관 협회에서 해마다 미국 아동 문학 발전에 가장 크게 이바지한 작가에게 수여하는 아동 문학상입니다. 1922년에 시작된 이 상은 미국에서 가장 오랜 역사를 지닌 아동 문학상이자, '아동 도서계의 노벨상'이라 불릴 만큼 높은 권위를 자랑하는 상입니다.

뉴베리 상은 그 역사와 권위만큼이나 심사 기준이 까다롭기로 유명한데, 심사단은 책의 주제 의식은 물론 정보의 깊이와 스토리의 정교함, 캐릭터와 문체의 적정성 등을 꼼꼼히 평가하여 수상작을 결정합니다.

그해 최고의 작품으로 선정된 도서에게는 '뉴베리 메달(Newbery Medal)'이라고 부르는 금색 메달을 수여하며, 최종 후보에 올랐던 주목할 만한 작품들에게는 '뉴베리 아너(Newbery Honor)'라는 이름의 은색 마크를 수여합니다.

뉴베리 상을 받은 도서는 미국의 모든 도서관에 비치되어 더 많은 독자들을 만나게 되며, 대부분 수십에서 수백만 부가 판매되는 베스트셀러가 됩니다. 뉴베리 상을 수상한 작가는 그만큼 필력과 작품성을 인정받게 되어, 수상 작가의 다른 작품들 또한 수상작 못지않게 커다란 주목과 사랑을 받습니다.

왜 뉴베리 수상작인가?
쉬운 어휘로 쓰인 '검증된' 영어원서!

뉴베리 수상작들은 '검증된 원서'로 국내 영어 학습자들에게 큰 사랑을 받고 있습니다. 뉴베리 수상작이 원서 읽기에 좋은 교재인 이유는 무엇일까요?

1. 아동 문학인 만큼 어휘가 어렵지 않습니다.
2. 어렵지 않은 어휘를 사용하면서도 '문학상'을 수상한 만큼 문장의 깊이가 상당합니다.
3. 적당한 난이도의 어휘와 깊이 있는 문장으로 구성되어 있기 때문에 초등 고학년부터 성인까지, 영어 초보자부터 실력자까지 모든 영어 학습자들이 읽기에 좋습니다.

실제로 뉴베리 수상작은 국제중 · 특목고에서는 입시 필독서로, 대학교에서는 영어 강독 교재로 다양하고 폭넓게 활용되고 있습니다. 이런 이유로 뉴베리 수상작은 한국어 번역서보다 오히려 원서가 훨씬 많이 판매되는 기현상을 보이고 있습니다.

'베스트 오브 베스트'만을 엄선한 「뉴베리 컬렉션」

「뉴베리 컬렉션」은 뉴베리 메달 및 아너 수상작, 그리고 뉴베리 수상 작가의 유명 작품들을 엄선하여 한국 영어 학습자들을 위한 최적의 교재로 재탄생시킨 영어 원서 시리즈입니다.

1. 어휘 수준과 문장의 난이도, 분량 등 국내 영어 학습자들에게 적합한 정도를 종합적으로 검토하여 선정하였습니다.
2. 기존 원서 독자층 사이의 인기도까지 감안하여 최적의 작품들을 선별하였습니다.
3. 판형이 좁고 글씨가 작아 읽기 힘들었던 원서 디자인을 대폭 수정하여, 판형을 시원하게 키우고 읽기에 최적화된 영문 서체를 사용하여 가독성을 극대화하였습니다.
4. 함께 제공되는 워크북은 어려운 어휘를 완벽하게 정리하고 이해력을 점검하는 퀴즈를 덧붙여 독자들이 원서를 보다 쉽고 재미있게 읽을 수 있도록 구성하였습니다.
5. 기존에 높은 가격에 판매되어 구입이 부담스러웠던 오디오북을 부록으로 제공하여 리스닝과 소리 내어 읽기에까지 원서를 두루 활용할 수 있도록 했습니다.

루이스 새커(Louis Sachar)는 현재 미국에서 가장 인기 있는 아동 문학 작가 중 한 사람입니다. 그는 1954년 미국 뉴욕에서 태어났으며 초등학교 보조 교사로 일한 경험을 바탕으로 쓴 「웨이사이드 스쿨(Wayside School)」 시리즈로 잘 알려져 있습니다. 그 외에도 그는 「마빈 레드포스트(Marvin Redpost)」 시리즈, 「There's a Boy in the Girls' Bathroom」, 「The Boy Who Lost His Face」 등 20여 권의 어린이책을 썼습니다. 그가 1998년에 발표한 「Holes」는 독자들의 큰 사랑을 받으며 National Book Award 등 많은 상을 수상하였고, 마침내 1999년에는 뉴베리 메달을 수상하였습니다. 2006년에는 「Holes」의 후속편 「Small Steps」를 출간하였습니다. 그는 현재 텍사스에서 딸과 아내와 함께 살고 있습니다.

「스몰 스텝스(Small Steps)」는 Camp Green Lake에서 나온 지 2년 후, Theodore Armpit이 텍사스주 오스틴에서 새로운 삶을 살아가기 위해 발버둥치는 이야기를 담고 있습니다. Armpit의 노력에도 불구하고 그의 전과 기록 때문에 사람들은 그에게 아무것도 기대하지 않습니다. 오직 한 사람, 그의 옆집에 사는 10살된 백인 장애인 Ginny만이 그의 유일한 말동무이자 그에게 믿음을 주는 친구입니다. 그들은 함께 그들의 삶을 위해, 그리고 세상을 향해 한걸음씩 내딛습니다.
Armpit은 올바른 길을 가는 듯이 보입니다. X-Ray가 나타나기 전까진 말이죠. X-Ray는 일확천금의 기회를 노린 계획을 가지고 Armpit에게 접근합니다. 이 계획은 Armpit이 팝스타 Kaira DeLeon을 만나게 되는 엄청난 기회를 가져다 주는데, 이것이 한순간에 Armpit의 운명을 바꿔놓습니다.
인종 문제, 유명인의 사생활, 그리고 한 사람의 삶을 좌지우지하는 보이지 않는 연결들. 앞으로의 인생을 설계해야 하는 사춘기 10대들에게 전하는 작가 루이스 새커의 메시지가 이 책을 통해 전해집니다.

이 책의 구성

원서 본문

내용이 담긴 원서 본문입니다.

원어민이 읽는 일반 원서와 같은 텍스트지만, 암기해야 할 중요 어휘들은 볼드체로 표시되어 있습니다. 이 어휘들은 지금 들고 계신 워크북에 챕터별로 정리되어 있습니다.

학습 심리학 연구 결과에 따르면, 한 단어씩 따로 외우는 단어 암기는 거의 효과가 없다고 합니다. 단어를 제대로 외우기 위해서는 문맥(context) 속에서 단어를 암기해야 하며, 한 단어당 문맥 속에서 15번 이상 마주칠 때 완벽하게 암기할 수 있다고 합니다.

이 책의 본문에서는 중요 어휘를 볼드체로 강조하여, 문맥 속의 단어들을 더 확실히 인지(word cognition in context)하도록 돕고 있습니다. 또한 대부분의 중요 단어들은 다른 챕터에서도 반복해서 등장하기 때문에 이 책을 읽는 것만으로도 자연스럽게 어휘력을 향상시킬 수 있습니다.

또한 본문 하단에는 내용 이해를 돕기 위한 '각주'가 첨가되어 있습니다. 각주는 굳이 암기할 필요는 없지만, 알아 두면 도움이 될 만한 정보를 설명하고 있습니다. 각주를 참고하면 스토리를 더 깊이 있게 이해할 수 있어 원서를 읽는 재미가 배가됩니다.

워크북(Workbook)

Check Your Reading Speed

해당 챕터의 단어 수가 기록되어 있어, 리딩 속도를 측정할 수 있습니다. 특히 리딩 속도를 중시하는 독자들이 유용하게 사용할 수 있습니다

Build Your Vocabulary

본문에 볼드 표시되어 있는 단어들이 정리되어 있습니다. 리딩 전·후에 반복해서 보면 원서를 더욱 쉽게 읽을 수 있고, 어휘력도 빠르게 향상될 것입니다.

단어는 〈스펠링 – 빈도 – 발음기호 – 품사 – 한글 뜻 – 영문 뜻〉 순서로 표기되어 있으며 빈도 표시(★)가 많을수록 필수 어휘입니다. 반복해서 등장하는 단어는 빈도 대신 '복습'으로 표기되어 있습니다. 품사는 아래와 같이 표기했습니다.

n. 명사 | a. 형용사 | ad. 부사 | vi. 자동사 | vt. 타동사 | v. 자·타동사 모두 쓰이는 동사

conj. 접속사 | prep. 전치사 | int. 감탄사 | phrasal v. 구동사 | idiom 숙어 및 관용구

Comprehension Quiz

간단한 퀴즈를 통해 읽은 내용에 대한 이해력을 점검해 볼 수 있습니다.

「뉴베리 컬렉션」 이렇게 읽어 보세요!

아래와 같이 프리뷰(Preview) → 리딩(Reading) → 리뷰(Review) 세 단계를 거치면서 읽으면, 더욱 효과적으로 영어 실력을 향상할 수 있습니다.

1. 프리뷰(Preview) : 오늘 읽을 내용을 먼저 점검하자!

- 워크북을 통해 오늘 읽을 챕터에 나와 있는 단어들을 쭉 훑어봅니다. 어떤 단어들이 나오는지, 내가 아는 단어와 모르는 단어는 어떤 것들이 있는지 가벼운 마음으로 살펴봅니다.
- 평소처럼 하나하나 쓰면서 암기하려고 하지는 마세요! 익숙하지 않은 단어들을 주의 깊게 보되, 어차피 리딩을 하면서 점차 익숙해질 단어라는 것을 기억하며 빠르게 훑어봅니다.
- 뒤 챕터로 갈수록 '복습'이라고 표시된 단어들이 늘어나는 것을 알 수 있습니다. '복습' 단어인데도 여전히 익숙하지 않다면 더욱 신경을 써서 봐야겠죠? 매일매일 꾸준히 읽는다면, 익숙한 단어들이 점점 많아진다는 것을 몸으로 느낄 수 있습니다.

2. 리딩(Reading) : 내용에 집중하며 빠르게 읽어 나가자!

- 프리뷰를 마친 후 바로 리딩을 시작합니다. 방금 살펴봤던 어휘들을 문장 속에서 다시 만나게 되는데, 이 과정에서 단어의 쓰임새와 어감을 자연스럽게 익히게 됩니다.
- 모르는 단어나 이해되지 않는 문장이 나오더라도 멈추지 말고 전체적인 맥락을 파악하면서 속도감 있게 읽어 나가세요. 이해되지 않는 문장들은 따로 표시를 하되, 일단 넘어가고 계속 읽는 것이 좋습니다. 뒷부분을 읽다 보면 자연히 이해가 되는 경우도 있고, 정 이해가 되지 않는 부분은 리딩을 마친 이후에 따로 리뷰하는 시간을 가지면 됩니다. 문제집을 풀듯이 모든 문장을 분석하면서 원서를 읽는 것이 아니라, 리딩을 할 때는 리딩에만, 리뷰를 할 때는 리뷰에만 집중하는 것이 필요합니다.
- 볼드 처리된 단어의 의미가 궁금하더라도 워크북을 바로 펼치지 마세요. 정 궁금하다면 한 번씩 참고하는 것도 나쁘진 않지만, 워크북과 원서를 번갈아 보면서 읽는 것은 리딩의 흐름을 끊고 단어 하나하나에 집착하는 좋지 않은 리딩 습관을 심어 줄 수 있습니다.
- 같은 맥락에서 번역서를 구해 원서와 동시에 번갈아 보는 것도 좋은 방법이 아닙니다. 한글 번역을 가지고 있다고 해도 일단 영어로 읽을 때는 영어에만 집중하고 어느 정도 분량을 읽은 후에 번역서와 비교하도록 하세요. 모든 문장을 일일이 번역해서 완벽하게 이해하려는 것은 오히려 좋지 않은 리딩 습관을 심

어 주어 장기적으로는 바람직하지 않은 결과를 얻을 수 있습니다. 처음부터 완벽하게 이해하려고 하는 것보다는 빠른 속도로 2~3회 반복해서 읽는 방식이 실력 향상에 더 도움이 됩니다. 만일 반복해서 읽어도 내용이 전혀 이해되지 않아 곤란하다면 책 선정에 문제가 있다고 할 수 있습니다. 그럴 때는 좀 더 쉬운 책을 골라 실력을 다진 뒤 다시 도전하는 것이 좋습니다.

- 초보자라면 분당 150단어의 리딩 속도를 목표로 잡고 리딩을 합니다. 분당 150 단어는 원어민이 말하는 속도로, 영어 학습자들이 리스닝과 스피킹으로 넘어가기 위해 가장 기초적으로 달성해야 하는 단계입니다. 분당 50~80단어 정도의 낮은 리딩 속도를 가지고 있는 경우는 대부분 영어 실력이 부족해서라기보다 '잘못된 리딩 습관'을 가지고 있어서 그렇습니다. 이해력이 조금 떨어진다고 하더라도 분당 150단어까지는 속도에 대한 긴장감을 놓치지 말고 속도감 있게 읽어 나가도록 하세요.

3. 리뷰(Review) : 이해력을 점검하고 꼼꼼하게 다시 살펴보자!

- 해당 챕터의 Comprehension Quiz를 통해 이해력을 점검해 봅니다.
- 오늘 만난 어휘들을 다시 한번 복습합니다. 이때는 읽으면서 중요하다고 생각했던 단어를 연습장에 써 보면서 꼼꼼하게 외우는 것도 좋습니다.
- 이해가 되지 않는다고 표시해 두었던 부분도 주의 깊게 분석해 봅니다. 다시 한번 문장을 꼼꼼히 읽고, 어떤 이유에서 이해가 되지 않았는지 생각해 봅니다. 따로 메모를 남기거나 노트를 작성하는 것도 좋은 방법입니다.
- 사실 꼼꼼히 리뷰하는 것은 매우 고된 과정입니다. 원서를 읽고 리뷰하는 시간을 가지는 것이 영어 실력 향상에 많은 도움이 되기는 하지만, 이 과정을 철저히 지키려다가 원서 읽기의 재미를 반감시키는 것은 바람직하지 않습니다. 그럴 때는 차라리 리뷰를 가볍게 하는 것이 좋을 수 있습니다. '내용에 빠져서 재미있게', 문제집에서는 상상도 못할 '많은 양'을 읽으면서, 매일매일 조금씩 꾸준히 실력을 키워 가는 것이 원서를 활용하는 기본적인 방법이며, 영어 공부의 왕도입니다. 문제집 풀듯이 원서 읽기를 시도하고 접근해서는 실패할 수밖에 없습니다.
- 이런 방식으로 원서를 끝까지 다 읽었다면, 다시 반복해서 읽거나 오디오북을 활용하는 등 다양한 방식으로 원서 읽기를 확장해 나갈 수 있습니다. 이에 대한 자세한 안내가 워크북 말미에 실려 있습니다.

1. What kind of work did Armpit do?
   A. Accounting
   B. Cooking
   C. Landscaping
   D. Delivery

2. How did Armpit get his nickname?
   A. A scorpion stung him in the arm and the pain hit his armpit.
   B. A doctor had given him a shot in the armpit and he cried.
   C. He sweat a lot from his armpits and his friends teased him.
   D. He had a tattoo of a scorpion on his armpit.

3. Which of the following was NOT included in the five goals Armpit set for himself?
   A. Graduate from high school
   B. Save his money
   C. Lose the name armpit
   D. Quit his job

4. How did Armpit and X-Ray meet?
   A. Armpit met X-Ray while working at his current landscaping job.
   B. Armpit met X-Ray at Camp Green Lake.
   C. Armpit met X-Ray while buying a Kaira DeLeon CD.
   D. Armpit met X-Ray in elementary school.

5. How did X-Ray plan on making more money with Armpit?
   A. They were going to invest in the stock market.
   B. They were going to start their own hole digging business.
   C. They were going to resell tickets to Kaira's concert.
   D. They were going to use X-Ray's car as a taxi.

6. Which of the following did NOT describe El Genius?
   A. He had almost died in Iraq.
   B. He was Kaira's business manager.
   C. He was Kaira's mother's husband.
   D. His real name was Jerome Paisley.

7. What did Fred do with the letter and photograph Kaira received and why?
   A. He burned them in order to destroy them completely.
   B. He threw them in the trash because Kaira received so many others.
   C. He framed them because he admired Kaira's fans.
   D. He put them in a plastic bag to send to the FBI.

1분에 몇 단어를 읽는지 리딩 속도를 측정해보세요.

$$\frac{2{,}573 \text{ words}}{\text{reading time (} \quad \text{) sec}} \times 60 = (\qquad) \text{ WPM}$$

Build Your Vocabulary

shovel[*]
[ʃʌvəl]

n. 삽; v. ~을 삽으로 뜨다[파다], 삽으로 일하다
A shovel is a tool with a long handle that is used for lifting and moving earth, coal, or snow.

irrigate
[írəgèit]

v. (땅에) 물을 대다, 관개하다 (irrigation n. 관개)
To irrigate land means to supply it with water in order to help crops grow.

landscape[*]
[lǽndskeip]

v. (나무를 심거나 지형을 바꾸어) 미화[조경]하다; n. 풍경, 경치, 조망 (landscaping n. 조경)
If an area of land is landscaped, it is changed to make it more attractive, for example by adding streams or ponds and planting trees and bushes.

process[**]
[práses]

n. 과정, 진행; v. (정보 · 데이터를) 처리하다; (식품을) 가공하다
A process is a series of actions which are carried out in order to achieve a particular result.

trench
[trentʃ]

n. 깊은 도랑; 방어 전선; v. 도랑을 파다, (홈 따위를) 새기다
A trench is a long narrow channel that is cut into the ground, for example in order to lay pipes or get rid of water.

mayor[*]
[méiər]

n. 시장(市長); (지방 자치단체의) 행정장관
The mayor of a town or city is the person who has been elected to represent it for a fixed period of time or, in some places, to run its government.

unusual[**]
[ùnjú:ʒuəl]

a. 보통이 아닌, 드문
If you describe someone as unusual, you think that they are interesting and different from other people.

dirt[**]
[də:rt]

n. 흙, 진흙, 먼지; 가십, 스캔들
You can refer to the earth on the ground as dirt, especially when it is dusty.

sod
[sad]

n. 잔디(밭); (이식용으로 사각형 또는 직사각형으로 떠낸) 뗏장
Sod is the surface of the ground, especially when covered with grass.

intact
[intǽkt]

a. 손상되지 않은, 온전한
Something that is intact is complete and has not been damaged or changed.

replace[**]
[ripléis]

v. (원래 장소 · 지위로) 돌려놓다; 대신하다, 대체하다
If you replace something, you put it back where it was before.

14

rectangular*
[rektǽŋgjulər]

a. 직사각형의; 직각의
Something that is rectangular is shaped like a rectangle.

blade*
[bleid]

n. 칼날; (프로펠러 등의) 날개; 잎
The blade of a knife, ax, or saw is the edge, which is used for cutting.

juvenile*
[dʒúːvənl]

n. 청소년; a. 유치한, 미숙한; 젊은, 나이 어린
A juvenile is a child or young person who is not yet old enough to be regarded as an adult.

correct***
[kərékt]

v. 나무라다, 벌주다; 정정하다, 고치다; a. 옳은 (correctional a. 처벌의)
If you correct someone, you scold or punish them in order to improve.

facility*
[fəsíləti]

n. 기관, 시설; 편의, 쉬움
A facility is a building or place that provides a particular service or is used for a particular industry.

bead*
[biːd]

n. (땀·이슬 등의) 방울; 구슬; vt. 구슬로 장식하다
A bead of liquid or moisture is a small drop of it.

perspire*
[pərspáiər]

vi. 땀을 흘리다, 땀이 나다 (perspiration n. 땀)
When you perspire, a liquid comes out on the surface of your skin, because you are hot or frightened.

drench
[drentʃ]

vt. 흠뻑 젖게 하다; 담그다
To drench something or someone means to make them completely wet.

sweat*
[swet]

n. 땀; v. 땀 흘리다; 습기가 차다
Sweat is the salty colorless liquid which comes through your skin when you are hot, ill, or afraid.

have something to do with

idiom ~와 관계가 있다
To have something to do with another thing means to be connected or concerned with it.

scorpion
[skɔ́ːrpiən]

n. 전갈
A scorpion is a small creature which looks like a large insect. Scorpions have a long curved tail, and some of them are poisonous.

sting*
[stiŋ]

vt. (stung-stung) 찌르다, 쏘다; n. 찌름, 쏨
If a plant, animal, or insect stings you, a sharp part of it, usually covered with poison, is pushed into your skin so that you feel a sharp pain.

armpit
[áːrmpit]

n. 겨드랑이
Your armpits are the areas of your body under your arms where your arms join your shoulders.

twist**
[twist]

v. 감기다, 비틀다, 돌리다, 꼬다; n. 뒤틀림, 엉킴
If you twist something, you turn it so that it moves around in a circular direction.

complain**
[kəmpléin]

v. 불평하다, 투덜거리다
If you complain about a situation, you say that you are not satisfied with it.

eventually**
[ivéntʃuəli]

ad. 결국, 마침내
Eventually means at the end of a situation or process or as the final result of it.

stick**
[stik]

① v. (stuck–stuck) 달라붙다, 붙이다; 내밀다; 고수하다 ② n. 막대기, 지팡이
If one thing sticks to another, it becomes attached to it and is difficult to remove.

approach**
[əpróutʃ]

v. 접근하다, 다가오다; n. 접근, 가까움
When you approach something, you get closer to it.

ponytail
[póunitèil]

n. 포니테일(뒤에서 묶어 아래로 드리운 머리)
A ponytail is a hairstyle in which someone's hair is tied up at the back of the head and hangs down like a tail.

reputation*
[repjutéiʃən]

n. 평판, 명성
Something's or someone's reputation is the opinion that people have about how good they are.

weird*
[wiə:rd]

a. 이상한, 기묘한; 수상한
If you describe something or someone as weird, you mean that they are strange.

extend**
[iksténd]

v. (손·발 등을) 뻗다, 늘이다; 넓히다, 확장하다
If someone extends their hand, they stretch out their arm and hand to shake hands with someone.

stand***
[stænd]

v. 키[높이]가 ~이다; 서다, 일어서다; 참다, 견디다; n. 가판대, 좌판; 관람석
You can describe how tall or high someone or something is by saying that they stand a particular height.

broad**
[brɔ:d]

a. 넓은, 광대한; (웃음·빛이) 가득한, 환한
Something that is broad is wide.

muscular*
[mʌskjulə:r]

a. 근육으로 된, 근육이 발달한; 늠름한, 강건한
If a person or their body is muscular, they are very fit and strong, and have firm muscles which are not covered with a lot of fat.

overweight
[óuvərwèit]

a. 지나친 비만의, 중량 초과의
over (접두사: 과도한) + weight (명사: 무게)

excess*
[iksés]

a. 여분의, 제한 초과의; n. 초과, 과잉
Excess is used to describe amounts that are greater than what is needed, allowed, or usual.

sweaty
[swéti]

a. 땀이 나는, 땀투성이의
If parts of your body or your clothes are sweaty, they are soaked or covered with sweat.

grip**
[grip]

v. 꽉 잡다, 움켜잡다; n. 꽉 붙잡음, 움켜쥠; 손잡이
If you grip something, you take hold of it with your hand and continue to hold it firmly.

elder**
[éldər]

n. 연장자, 웃어른; a. 나이가 더 많은 (elderly a. 나이가 지긋한)
A person's elder is someone who is older than them, especially someone quite a lot older.

16

be taken aback
idiom ~에 당황하다, 놀라다
If you are taken back, you are shocked or surprised by someone or something.

firm***
[fə:rm]
① a. 굳은, 단단한; 견고한 (firmness n. 견고) ② n. 회사
If someone's grip is firm or if they perform a physical action in a firm way, they do it with quite a lot of force or pressure but also in a controlled way.

terrible*
[térəbl]
a. 심한, 지독한; 무서운, 소름끼치는
A terrible experience or situation is very serious or very unpleasant.

admire**
[ædmáiər]
v. 감탄하다, 칭찬하다, 존경하다
If you admire someone or something, you like and respect them very much.

get through
phrasal v. (곤란 등을) 벗어나다, 극복하다; 끝내다, 해결하다
If you get through something, you survive a difficult or unpleasant experience or period in your life.

environmentalist
[invàiərənméntəlist]
n. 환경 운동가
An environmentalist is a person who is concerned with protecting and preserving the natural environment, for example by preventing pollution.

occasion***
[əkéiʒən]
n. 경우, 기회; 특별한 일, 행사
An occasion is a time when something happens, or a case of it happening.

rolling
[róuliŋ]
a. 완만하게 경사진, 구릉으로 된
Rolling hills are small hills with gentle slopes that extend a long way into the distance.

preserve*
[prizə́:rv]
n. 보호구; 보존하는 것; v. 보호하다, 보존하다, 유지하다
(nature preserve n. 자연 보존구)
A nature preserve is an area of land or water where animals are protected from hunters.

trail*
[treil]
n. 길; 지나간 자국, 흔적; v. 뒤쫓다; 끌(리)다
A trail is a route along a series of paths or roads, often one that has been planned and marked out for a particular purpose.

flatland
[flǽtlæ̀nd]
n. 평지, 평탄한 토지
flat (형용사: 편평한) + land (명사: 땅, 대지)

mosquito*
[məskí:tou]
n. 모기
Mosquitos are small flying insects which bite people and animals in order to suck their blood.

buzz*
[bʌz]
v. 윙윙거리다; 분주하게 돌아다니다; n. 윙윙거리는 소리; 소문, 수군거림
If something buzzes or buzzes somewhere, it makes a long continuous sound, like the noise a bee makes when it is flying.

swat
[swɑt]
v. (파리 따위를) 찰싹 치다; n. 찰싹 때림, 강타
If you swat something such as an insect, you hit it with a quick, swinging movement, using your hand or a flat object.

bucket *
[bʌ́kit]

n. 버킷, 양동이
A bucket is a round metal or plastic container with a handle attached to its sides.

ease **
[iːz]

v. 살짝 움직이다[옮기다]; (고통 · 고민 등을) 진정[완화]시키다; n. 편함, 안정
If you ease your way somewhere or ease somewhere, you move there slowly, carefully, and gently.

row *
[rou]

① n. 열, (좌석) 줄 ② vi. (노를 써서) 배를 젓다; (배가) 저어지다
A row of things or people is a number of them arranged in a line.

senior **
[síːnjər]

n. 선배, 연장자; a. 최고 학년의, 상위의; 손위의
Seniors are students in a high school, university, or college who are the oldest and who have reached an advanced level in their studies.

stick out

phrasal v. 불쑥 내밀다[나오다], 돌출하다
If you stick something out, you make it, especially part of your body, come through a hole.

yell *
[jel]

v. 소리치다, 고함치다; n. 고함소리, 부르짖음
If you yell, you shout loudly, usually because you are excited, angry, or in pain.

spill *
[spil]

v. 엎지르다, 흘리다; n. 엎지름, 유출
If a liquid spills or if you spill it, it accidentally flows over the edge of a container.

cruel **
[krúːəl]

a. 끔찍한, 잔인한, 잔혹한
A situation or event that is cruel is very harsh and causes people distress.

bed ***
[bed]

n. (바다 · 강 등의) 바닥; 침대
The sea bed or a river bed is the ground at the bottom of the sea or of a river.

apply **
[əplái]

v. 지원하다, 신청하다; 적합하다; 적용하다, 응용하다
If you apply for something such as a job or membership of an organization, you write a letter or fill in a form in order to ask formally for it.

fair **
[fɛər]

a. 상당한; 공평한, 공정한; n. 박람회, 전시회
A fair amount, degree, size, or distance is quite a large amount, degree, size, or distance.

counsel *
[káunsəl]

v. 상의하다; 조언[충고]하다; n. 상담; 조언, 권고 (counseling n. 카운슬링, 상담)
If you counsel people, you give them advice about their problems.

recidivism
[risídəvìzm]

n. 재범; 상습적 범행 (recidivism rate n. 재범률)
Recidivism is the chronic tendency toward repetition of criminal or antisocial behavior patterns.

statistics *
[stətístiks]

n. 통계; 통계학
Statistics are facts which are obtained from analysing information expressed in numbers, for example information about the number of times that something happens.

18

arrest[**]
[ərést]
vt. 체포하다, 저지하다; (주의 · 이목 · 흥미 등을) 끌다; n. 체포, 검거, 구속
If the police arrest you, they take charge of you and take you to a police station, because they believe you may have committed a crime.

prison[**]
[prizn]
n. 교도소, 감옥
A prison is a building where criminals are kept as punishment or where people accused of a crime are kept.

upstream
[ʌ́pstri:m]
ad. 상류로; a. 상류의
Something that is moving upstream is moving toward the source of a river, from a point further down the river.

rush[**]
[rʌʃ]
v. 급히 움직이다, 서두르다, 돌진하다 (rushing a. 격한, 성급한)
If air or liquid rushes somewhere, it flows there suddenly and quickly.

current[**]
[kɔ́:rənt]
n. 흐름, 해류, 기류; a. 지금의, 현재의; 유행하는
A current is a steady and continuous flowing movement of some of the water in a river, lake, or sea.

knock off
phrasal v. ~을 쳐서[두드려서] 떨어뜨리다
If you knock off someone or something, you make them fall off by hitting them.

downstream
[dáunstrí:m]
ad. 하류로; a. 강 아래의
Something that is moving downstream is moving toward the mouth of a river, from a point further up the river.

graduate[**]
[grǽdʒueit]
vi. 졸업하다; n. 졸업생; 대학원생
When a student graduates, they complete their studies successfully and leave their school or university.

violent[**]
[váiələnt]
a. 난폭한, 폭력적인; 격렬한, 맹렬한
If someone is violent, or if they do something which is violent, they use physical force or weapons to hurt, injure, or kill other people.

site[*]
[sait]
n. 장소, 위치; (건축) 부지, 용지; vt. 위치하게 하다, 두다
A site is a piece of ground that is used for a particular purpose or where a particular thing happens.

exclaim[*]
[ikskléim]
v. 외치다, 소리치다
If you exclaim, you say or shout something suddenly because of surprise, fear and pleasure.

wiggle
[wigl]
v. (몸을) 뒤흔들다, (좌우로) 움직이다; n. 뒤흔듦
If you wiggle something or if it wiggles, it moves up and down or from side to side in small quick movements.

1분에 몇 단어를 읽는지 리딩 속도를 측정해보세요.

$$\frac{2{,}573 \text{ words}}{\text{reading time ( ) sec}} \times 60 = (\quad) \text{ WPM}$$

Build Your Vocabulary

rust[*]
[rʌst]
v. (금속 등이) 녹슬(게 하)다, 부식하다; n. 녹
When a metal object rusts, it becomes covered in a brown substance and often loses its strength.

mayor^{복습}
[méiər]
n. 시장(市長); (지방 자치단체의) 행정장관
The mayor of a town or city is the person who has been elected to represent it for a fixed period of time or, in some places, to run its government.

trench^{복습}
[trentʃ]
n. 깊은 도랑; 방어전선; v. 도랑을 파다, (홈 따위를) 새기다
A trench is a long narrow channel that is cut into the ground, for example in order to lay pipes or get rid of water.

attach[*]
[ətǽtʃ]
vt. 붙이다, 달다
If you attach something to an object, you connect it or fasten it to the object.

bash
[bæʃ]
vt. 후려갈기다, 강타하다; n. 세게 때림, 강타
If you bash something, you hit it hard in a rough or careless way.

worth^{**}
[wə:rθ]
a. 가치가 있는; n. 가치, 값어치
If you say that something is worth having, you mean that it is pleasant or useful, and therefore a good thing to have.

stick^{복습}
[stik]
① n. 막대기, 지팡이 ② v. 달라붙다, 붙이다; 내밀다; 고수하다
A stick is a long thin piece of wood which is used for a particular purpose.

shift[*]
[ʃift]
n. 변속 장치; 변화, 전환; 교대 근무; v. (차의 기어를) 바꾸다; 옮기다, 이동하다
If you shift gears in a car, you put the car into a different gear.

exit[*]
[égzit]
v. 나가다, 퇴장하다; n. 퇴장; 출구
If you exit from a room or building, you leave it.

passenger^{**}
[pǽsəndʒər]
n. 승객, 여객 (passenger side n. 조수석)
A passenger in a vehicle such as a bus, boat, or plane is a person who is traveling in it, but who is not driving it or working on it.

personalize
[pɔ́:rsənəlàiz]
v. (개인 소유물임을 나타내는) 표시를 하다, (개인의 필요에) 맞추다
(personalized a. 이름이 들어간)
If an object is personalized, it is marked with the name or initials of its owner.

license[*]
[láisəns]
n. 면허(증), 허가(증); v. 면허를 주다 (license plate n. (자동차의) 번호판)
A license plate is a sign on the front and back of a vehicle that shows its license number.

20

shut someone up	phrasal v. (〜을) 입 다물게 하다 To shut someone up means to make them stop talking or making a noise.
sweat^{복습} [swet]	v. 땀 흘리다; 습기가 차다; n. 땀 When you sweat, sweat comes through your skin.
dirt^{복습} [dəːrt]	n. 흙, 진흙, 먼지; 가십, 스캔들 You can refer to the earth on the ground as dirt, especially when it is dusty.
last^{**} [læst]	vi. (시간적으로) 계속하다, 이어지다; 충분하다, 오래가다; a. 최후의 If an event, situation, or problem lasts for a particular length of time, it continues to exist or happen for that length of time.
lifetime^{**} [láiftàim]	n. 일생, 생애 A lifetime is the length of time that someone is alive.
ashamed^{**} [əʃéimd]	a. 부끄러워하는 If someone is ashamed, they feel embarrassed or guilty because of something they do or they have done.
annoy^{**} [ənɔ́i]	v. 성가시게 굴다, 괴롭히다; 불쾌하다 If someone or something annoys you, it makes you fairly angry and impatient.
skinny [skíni]	a. 바싹 여윈, 깡마른 A skinny person is extremely thin, often in a way that you find unattractive.
shade^{**} [ʃeid]	n. (pl.) 선글라스; 그늘, 음영; 색조; vt. 그늘지게 하다 Shades are sunglasses.
shovel^{복습} [ʃʌ́vəl]	n. 삽; v. 〜을 삽으로 뜨다[파다], 삽으로 일하다 A shovel is a tool with a long handle that is used for lifting and moving earth, coal, or snow.
leverage [lévəridʒ]	n. 지레 장치; 지레 작용 Leverage is the force that is applied to an object when something such as a lever is used.
shrug[*] [ʃrʌg]	v. (어깨를) 으쓱하다; n. (양 손바닥을 내보이면서 어깨를) 으쓱하기 If you shrug, you raise your shoulders to show that you are not interested in something or that you do not know or care about something.
paycheck [péitʃèk]	n. 급료, 봉급 Paycheck is salary or wages.
make up for (something)	idiom 만회하다, 보충하다; 보상하다 To make up for something means to do or provide something good to balance or reduce the effects of something bad.
tax^{**} [tæks]	n. 세금; 부담, 과중한 요구; vt. 세금을 부과하다 Tax is an amount of money that you have to pay to the government so that it can pay for public services.

stuff
[stʌf]

n. 일[것](일반적으로 말하거나 생각하는 것); 물건, 물질 vt. 채워 넣다, 속을 채우다
You can use stuff to refer to things such as a substance, a collection of things, events, or ideas, or the contents of something in a general way without mentioning the thing itself by name.

propose^{**}
[prəpóuz]

v. 제안하다, 제의하다; 결혼 신청하다 (proposition n. 제의)
If you propose something such as a plan or an idea, you suggest it for people to think about and decide upon.

guarantee[*]
[gærəntíː]

vt. 보증하다, 단언하다; n. 보증
If you guarantee something, you promise that it will definitely happen, or that you will do or provide it for someone.

keep it cool

idiom 안정을 유지하다, 침착성을 잃지 않다
If you keep it cool in a difficult situation, you manage to remain calm. If you lose your cool, you get angry or upset.

hear out

phrasal v. ~의 말을 끝까지 들어주다
If you hear someone out, you listen until they has finished saying what they want to say.

assure[*]
[əʃúəːr]

vt. 단언하다, 보증하다
If you assure someone that something is true or will happen, you tell them that it is definitely true or will definitely happen, often in order to make them less worried.

release[*]
[rilíːs]

vt. 해방하다, 석방하다, 놓아주다; n. 석방
If a person or animal is released from somewhere where they have been looked after, they are set free or allowed to go.

screw up

phrasal v. 망치다, 엉망으로 만들다
To screw something up means to cause it to fail or be spoiled.

offer^{***}
[ɔ́ːfər]

v. 제공하다, 제의[제안]하다; n. 제공
If you offer something to someone, you ask them if they would like to have it or use it.

opportunity^{**}
[àpərtjúːnəti]

n. 기회
An opportunity is a situation in which it is possible for you to do something that you want to do.

century^{**}
[séntʃəri]

n. 1세기, 100년
A century is any period of a hundred years.

get it

idiom (구어) 알다, 이해하다
You can say get it when you understand or get the right answer immediately.

curious^{**}
[kjúəriəs]

a. 궁금한, 호기심이 많은; 별난, 특이한
If you are curious about something, you are interested in it and want to know more about it.

pause^{**}
[pɔːz]

vi. 중단하다, 잠시 멈추다; n. 멈춤, 중지
If you pause while you are doing something, you stop for a short period and then continue.

22

for effect

idiom 효과를 노리고, 상대의 주의를 끌려고
If you say that someone is doing something for effect, you mean that they are doing it in order to impress people and to draw attention to themselves.

pillow*
[pílou]

n. 베개; 머리 받침대
A pillow is a rectangular cushion which you rest your head on when you are in bed.

oomph
[umf]

n. 특별한 매력
If you say that someone or something has oomph, you mean that they are energetic and exciting.

stuffing
[stʌ́fiŋ]

n. (쿠션 · 장난감 등의 안에 넣는) 속
Stuffing is material that is used to fill things such as cushions or toys in order to make them firm or solid.

edge**
[edʒ]

n. 끝, 가장자리, 모서리
The edge of something is the place or line where it stops, or the part of it that is furthest from the middle.

fray
[frei]

① v. 닳게 하다, 닳아서 해지다; 소모시키다 ② n. 소동, 난투; 경쟁
If something such as cloth or rope frays, or if something frays it, its threads or fibers start to come apart from each other and spoil its appearance.

fade*
[feid]

vi. 희미해지다, 바래다; 시들(게 하)다
When a colored object fades or when the light fades it, it gradually becomes paler.

visible*
[vízəbl]

a. 알아볼 수 있는, 뚜렷한; 눈에 보이는
If something is visible, it can be seen.

groggy
[grɔ́gi]

a. (질병 · 심한 피로로) 비틀거리는, 몸을 가누지 못하는 (groggily ad. 비틀거리면서)
If you feel groggy, you feel weak and rather ill.

boxer shorts
[bάksər ʃɔ́:rts]

n. (남성용) 사각 팬티
Boxer shorts are loose-fitting men's underpants that are shaped like the shorts worn by boxers.

pajama
[pədʒάːmə]

n. (pl.) 파자마, 잠옷; a. 파자마 같은
A pair of pajamas consists of loose trousers and a loose jacket that people wear in bed.

shriek*
[ʃri:k]

v. 비명을 지르다, 새된 소리를 지르다; n. 비명
When someone shrieks, they make a short, very loud cry.

couch*
[kautʃ]

n. 소파, 긴 의자
A couch is a long, comfortable seat for two or three people.

clutch*
[klʌtʃ]

v. 움켜쥐다, 꽉 잡다; 잡으려고 하다; n. 붙잡음, 움켜쥠
If you clutch at something or clutch something, you hold it tightly, usually because you are afraid or anxious.

slam*
[slæm]

v. (문 따위를) 탕 닫다; 세게 치다; 털썩 내려놓다; n. 쾅 (하는 소리)
If you slam a door or window or if it slams, it shuts noisily and with great force.

bounce*
[bauns]

v. 튀다, 튀게 하다; 급히 움직이다, 뛰어다니다; n. 튐, 바운드
If something bounces off a surface or is bounced off it, it reaches the surface and is reflected back.

doofus
[dúːfəs]

n. (비격식) 멍청이, 얼간이
Doofus is a slow-witted or stupid person.

latch
[lætʃ]

v. 걸쇠를 걸다, 잠그다; n. 걸쇠, 빗장
If you latch a door or gate, you fasten it with a metal bar.

privacy*
[práivəsi]

n. 사생활, 비밀, 은밀
If you have privacy, you are in a place or situation which allows you to do things without other people seeing you or disturbing you.

opposite**
[ápəzit]

a. 반대편의, 맞은편의; 정반대의; ad. 정반대의 위치에
If one thing is opposite another, it is on the other side of a space from it.

suite*
[swiːt]

n. 호텔의 스위트 룸; (물건의) 한 벌
A suite is a set of rooms in a hotel or other building.

suspect*
[səspékt]

v. 짐작하다, 의심하다, 혐의를 두다; n. 용의자
If you suspect that something dishonest or unpleasant has been done, you believe that it has probably been done.

psychiatrist*
[sikáiətrist]

n. 정신과 의사
A psychiatrist is a doctor who treats people suffering from mental illness.

purpose**
[pə́ːrpəs]

n. 목적, 의도; vt. 의도하다, 꾀하다 (on purpose idiom 고의로, 일부러)
The purpose of something is the reason for which it is made or done.

be better off

idiom (~하는 것이) 더 낫다
Be better off is used to say that someone would be happier or more satisfied if they were in a particular position or did a particular thing.

therapy*
[θérəpi]

n. 치료, 요법
Therapy is the treatment of someone with mental or physical illness without the use of drugs or operations.

session*
[séʃən]

n. (어느 활동을 위한) 기간; (의회 등의) 회의; 학기, 수업
A session of a particular activity is a period of that activity.

confidential*
[kànfədénʃəl]

a. 은밀한, 비밀의
Information that is confidential is meant to be kept secret or private.

parrot*
[pǽrət]

n. [동물] 앵무새; v. 흉내 내다, 따라하다
A parrot is a tropical bird with a curved beak and brightly-colored or grey feathers. Some parrots are able to copy what people say.

snot
[snat]

n. 콧물; 코흘리개 (snot-nosed a. 애송이의, 건방진)
Snot is the substance that is produced inside your nose.

resent*
[rizént]

vt. 분개하다, 불쾌하게 생각하다
If you resent someone or something, you feel bitter and angry about them.

swing^{**}
[swiŋ]

n. 짧은 여행, (정치인의) 유세; 그네; 휘두르기; v. 흔들다, 빙 돌다; 휘두르다
A swing of a long journey is one part of it.

original^{**}
[ərídʒənl]

a. 본래의, 최초의; 독창적인, 신기한; n. 원형, 원작 (originally ad. 원래는)
You use original when referring to something that existed at the beginning of a process or activity, or the characteristics that something had when it began or was made.

due^{***}
[dju:]

a. ~로 인한, ~ 때문에; ~하기로 되어 있는; n. ~에게 마땅히 주어져야 하는 것
If an event is due to something, it happens or exists as a direct result of that thing.

rally[*]
[ræli]

n. (자동차·오토바이 등의) 경주 대회; 집회; v. 규합하다, 모집하다, 결집하다
A rally is a competition in which vehicles are driven over public roads.

accidental[*]
[æksədéntl]

a. 우연한; 부수적인 (accidentally ad. 우연히)
An accidental event happens by chance or as the result of an accident, and is not deliberately intended.

coordinator
[kouɔ́:rdənèitər]

n. 제작 진행 책임자, 코디네이터
A coordinator is someone whose task is to see that work goes harmoniously.

personal^{**}
[pə́rsənl]

a. 자신이 직접 하는; 개인의, 사사로운 (personally ad. 몸소, 개인적으로)
If you give something your personal care or attention, you deal with it yourself rather than letting someone else deal with it.

laundry[*]
[lɔ́:ndri]

n. 세탁물; 세탁소
Laundry is used to refer to clothes, sheets, and towels that are about to be washed, are being washed, or have just been washed.

emerge[*]
[imɔ́:rdʒ]

vi. 나오다, 나타나다
To emerge means to come out from an enclosed or dark space such as a room or a vehicle, or from a position where you could not be seen.

robe[*]
[roub]

n. 길고 헐거운 겉옷(실내복이나 휴식 때의 옷); 예복, 관복
A robe is a piece of clothing, usually made of toweling, which people wear in the house, especially when they have just got up or had a bath.

puke
[pju:k]

v. 토하다
When someone pukes, they vomit.

go through

idiom 자세히 검토하다; 통과하다; 겪다
To go through something means to look at, check or examine it closely and carefully, especially in order to find something.

fire^{***}
[faiər]

v. 해고하다; 발사하다; 불을 지르다; n. 불; 정열, 흥분
If an employer fires you, they dismiss you from your job.

station^{***}
[stéiʃən]

n. 방송 채널, 방송국; 역, 정류장; 지역 본부, 사업소; 부, 부서
If you talk about a particular radio or television station, you are referring to the programes broadcast by a particular radio or television company.

agent[**]
[éidʒənt]

n. 대리인, 중개인; 행위자
An agent is a person who looks after someone else's business affairs or does business on their behalf.

sarcastic[*]
[sɑːrkǽstik]

a. 빈정대는, 비꼬는, 풍자적인
Someone who is sarcastic says or does the opposite of what they really mean in order to mock or insult someone.

compliment[*]
[kámpləmənt]

n. 찬사, 칭찬의 말; (pl.) 존경을 나타내는 인사말; v. 경의를 표하다, 칭찬하다
A compliment is a polite remark that you say to someone to show that you like their appearance, appreciate their qualities, or approve of what they have done.

come up with

idiom ~을 제안하다, 생각하다
If you come up with a plan or idea, you think of it and suggest it.

genius[*]
[dʒíːnjəs]

n. 천재; 특수한 재능
A genius is a highly talented, creative, or intelligent person.

title[**]
[taitl]

v. 제목을 붙이다; 직함을 주다; n. 표제, 제목; 직함
When a writer, composer, or artist titles a work, they give it a name.

fountain[*]
[fáuntən]

n. 분수; 샘
A fountain is an decorative feature in a pool or lake which consists of a long narrow stream of water that is forced up into the air.

youth[**]
[juːθ]

n. 젊음, 청춘; 청년(층), 젊은이들
Youth is the quality or state of being young.

classy
[klǽsi]

a. 세련된, 멋진; 고급의
If you describe someone or something as classy, you mean they are stylish and sophisticated.

capital[**]
[kǽpətl]

n. 대문자; 자본, 자산; 수도, 중심지; a. 자본의; 주요한
Capitals or capital letters are written or printed letters in the form which is used at the beginning of sentences or names.

entire[*]
[intàiər]

a. 전체의; 완전한
You use entire when you want to emphasize that you are referring to the whole of something, for example, the whole of a place, time, or population.

charm[**]
[ʧɑːrm]

v. 매력이 있다; 황홀하게 하다; n. 매력, 마력; 마술 (charming a. 매력 있는)
If you say that something is charming, you mean that it is very pleasant and attractive.

hilarious
[hiléəriəs]

a. 아주 우스운, 재미있는
If something is hilarious, it is extremely funny and makes you laugh a lot.

hire[*]
[haiər]

vt. 고용하다; 빌리다, 빌려주다; n. 고용
If you hire someone, you employ them or pay them to do a particular job for you.

confine[*]
[kənfáin]

vt. 가두다, 틀어박히게 하다; 제한하다 (confined a. ~에 틀어박힌)
If someone is confined to a mental institution, prison, or other place, they are sent there and are not allowed to leave for a period of time.

freak
[fri:k]

n. 열광자, 괴짜; 희한한 것; v. 기겁하(게 하)다
(control freak n. 만사를 자기 뜻대로 하려는 사람, 지배광)
If you say that someone is a control freak, you mean that they want to be in control of every situation they find themselves in.

proposal**
[prəpóuzəl]

n. 결혼 신청, 청혼; 신청, 제안
A proposal is the act of asking someone to marry you.

plastic bag
[plǽstik bæg]

n. 비닐봉지
A plastic bag is a bag made of thin plastic material.

point out

phrasal v. ~을 지적하다
If you point out a fact or mistake, you tell someone about it or draw their attention to it.

glance*
[glæns]

v. 흘끗 보다, 잠깐 보다; n. 흘끗 봄
If you glance at something or someone, you look at them very quickly and then look away again immediately.

profound*
[prəfáund]

a. 심오한, 깊이가 있는
You use profound to emphasize that something is very great or intense.

muscular*복습
[mʌ́skjulə:r]

a. 근육으로 된, 근육이 발달한; 늠름한, 강건한
If a person or their body is muscular, they are very fit and strong, and have firm muscles which are not covered with a lot of fat.

wavy
[wéivi]

a. 웨이브가 있는, 물결 모양의
Wavy hair is not straight or curly, but curves slightly.

screwup
[skrú:ʌ̀p]

n. 중대한 실수; 늘 실수하는 사람
Screwup is something mishandled or done badly.

row*복습
[rou]

① n. 열, (좌석) 줄 ② vi. (노를 써서) 배를 젓다; (배가) 저어지다
A row of things or people is a number of them arranged in a line.

sassy
[sǽsi]

a. 멋진, 근사한
Sassy is used to describe things that are smart and stylish.

critique
[krití:k]

n. 비평, 평론; vt. 비평하다
A critique is a written examination and judgment of a situation or of a person's work or ideas.

critic*
[krítik]

n. 비평가, 평론가
A critic is a person who writes about and expresses opinions about things such as books, films, music, or art.

consider***
[kənsídər]

v. 고려하다, 숙고하다
If you consider something, you think about it carefully.

split**
[split]

v. 분배하다; 쪼개다, 찢다, 째다; n. 쪼개기, 분열
If something splits or if you split it, it is divided into two or more parts.

profit**
[práfit]

n. 이익, 수익; v. 이익을 얻다; 득이 되다
A profit is an amount of money that you gain when you are paid more for something than it cost you to make, get, or do it.

exhale
[ekshéil]

v. (숨 등을) 내쉬다; (증기 · 향기 등을) 발산[방출]하다
When you exhale, you breathe out the air that is in your lungs.

risk***
[risk]

n. 위험; vt. 위험을 무릅쓰다
If there is a risk of something unpleasant, there is a possibility that it will happen.

replace복습
[ripléis]

v. (원래 장소 · 지위로) 돌려놓다; 대신하다, 대체하다
If you replace something, you put it back where it was before.

sod복습
[sad]

n. 잔디(밭); (이식용으로 사각형 또는 직사각형으로 떠낸) 뗏장
Sod is the surface of the ground, especially when covered with grass.

stomp
[stamp]

v. 짓밟다; 발을 구르다, 쿵쿵거리며 걷다
If you stomp somewhere, you walk there with very heavy steps, often because you are angry.

buck*
[bʌk]

① n. (속어) 달러 ② n. 수사슴, 수컷
A buck is a US or Australian dollar.

dude
[dju:d]

n. 사내, 녀석; (구어) 형씨, 친구
A dude is a man.

think outside of the box

idiom (문제 · 상황 등을) 새로운 관점에서 생각하다
To think ouside of the box means to think about something, or how to do something, in a new, different or creative way.

siren
[sáiərən]

n. (신호 · 경보 따위를 나타내는) 사이렌
A siren is a warning device which makes a long, loud noise.

blare
[blɛər]

v. 크게 울리다, 울려 퍼지다
If something such as a siren or radio blares or if you blare it, it makes a loud, unpleasant noise.

exclaim복습
[ikskléim]

v. 외치다, 소리치다
If you exclaim, you say or shout something suddenly because of surprise, fear and pleasure.

fumble
[fʌmbl]

v. 손으로 더듬어 찾다, 만지작거리다; (말을) 더듬거리다
If you fumble for something or fumble with something, you try and reach for it or hold it in a clumsy way.

electric*
[iléktrik]

a. 전기의; 전기를 이용하는
An electric device works by means of electricity, rather than using some other source of power.

wind down

phrasal v. 서서히 끝나다, 점차 감소하다
If a machine winds down, it goes slowly and then stops.

transform*
[trænsfɔ́:rm]

v. 변형하다, 바꾸다; n. 변형
To transform something into something else means to change or convert it into that thing.

flurry
[flə́:ri]

n. (잠시 한바탕 벌어지는) 소동, 부산; 질풍, 돌풍
A flurry of something such as activity or excitement is a short intense period of it.

note[***]
[nout]

n. (악기의) 음; (짧은) 기록; 짧은 편지; v. 주목하다, 알아채다; 메모하다
In music, a note is the sound of a particular pitch, or a written symbol representing this sound.

chord
[kɔ́:rd]

n. 코드, 화음; (악기의) 현; vi. 가락이 맞다, 화음을 연주하다
A chord is a number of musical notes played or sung at the same time with a pleasing effect.

intro
[íntrou]

n. (음악 작품·글의) 도입부
The intro to a song, programe, or book is the first part, which comes before the main part.

threaten[**]
[θretn]

v. 위협하다, 협박하다; 조짐을 보이다
If something or someone threatens a person or thing, they are likely to harm that person or thing.

security[*]
[sikjúərəti]

n. 안전, 보호; 보안, 경비
A feeling of security is a feeling of being safe and free from worry.

alert[*]
[əlɔ́:rt]

n. 경보, 경계; a. 방심하지 않는; v. 경고하다
An alert is a situation in which people prepare themselves for something dangerous that might happen soon.

stomach[**]
[stʌ́mək]

n. 배, 위
You can refer to the front part of your body below your waist as your stomach.

ache[*]
[eik]

vi. 쑤시다, 아프다; n. 아픔, 쑤심
If you ache or a part of your body aches, you feel a steady, fairly strong pain.

quake
[kweik]

v. (땅·건물이) 마구 흔들리다, 진동하다; (공포·긴장감으로) 몸을 떨다, 전율하다
A quake is a shaking of the ground caused by movement of the earth's crust.

scowl
[skaul]

vi. 얼굴을 찌푸리다, 싫은 기색을 하다; n. 찌푸린 얼굴
When someone scowls, an angry or hostile expression appears on their face.

gripe
[graip]

vi. 불평하다, 투덜대다; 괴롭히다; n. 불평
If you say that someone is griping, you mean they are annoying you because they keep on complaining about something.

dial[*]
[dáiəl]

n. 다이얼; v. 전화를 걸다, 다이얼을 돌리다
On some telephones, especially older ones, the dial is the disc on the front that you turn with your finger to choose the number that you want to call. telephone in order to phone someone.

compete[**]
[kəmpíːt]

vi. 겨루다, 경쟁하다
If you compete with someone for something, you try to get it for yourself and stop the other person getting it.

shut down

phrasal v. (기계가) 멈추다, 정지하다
If a machine shuts down, or someone shuts it down, it stops working.

pat[*]
[pæt]

v. 톡톡 가볍게 치다, (애정을 담아) 쓰다듬다; n. 쓰다듬기
If you pat something or someone, you tap them lightly, usually with your hand held flat.

1. Which of the following is NOT true about where Armpit
   lived?
   A. He lived in a duplex.
   B. He lived in west Austin.
   C. He lived with just his parents.
   D. Interstate 35 divided his city in half.

2. How did Armpit feel about Ginny in his life?
   A. He felt nervous around her due to her disability.
   B. He felt burdened by having to take care of her.
   C. He felt that she helped him by giving his life meaning.
   D. He felt that she could help him get a better job.

3. What kind of sample did Armpit's parents want and why
   do they want it?
   A. They wanted a sample of cake because they are hungry.
   B. They wanted a urine sample to test for drugs.
   C. They wanted a sample of Kaira's music because they heard it was
      good.
   D. They wanted a sample of Armpit's deodorant because he smells.

4. Why did Armpit use so much deodorant and even spray his feet?

    A. He wanted to be careful of smelling since his name was Armpit.

    B. He had a big problem with foot odor.

    C. It stopped his body from sweating so much.

    D. He won a whole case of deodorant in a radio contest.

5. What was the next major assignment in Armpit's speech class?

    A. Recording a video of oneself giving a speech at home

    B. Writing a paper about a famous public speaker

    C. Giving a campaign speech for a stuffed animal in class

    D. Memorizing a famous speech and delivering it in class

6. Why did Armpit want Coach Simmons to think he would join the football team?

    A. Armpit was determined to be a great football player.

    B. Armpit wanted to go to college on a football scholarship.

    C. Coach Simmons would let him skip classes to practice.

    D. Coach Simmons gave better grades to football players.

7. Why did Kaira feel foolish about the show in Philadelphia?

    A. The ticket prices were actually exaggerated by El Genius.

    B. Her equipment had broken and embarrassed her on stage.

    C. The show sold out and her fans were disappointed.

    D. She was not prepared for the weather and caught a cold.

$$\frac{1{,}319 \text{ words}}{\text{reading time ( ) sec}} \times 60 = (\quad) \text{ WPM}$$

Build Your Vocabulary

border**
[bɔ́:rdə:r]

n. 국경선, 경계선; 테두리, 가장자리; v. 테를 두르다; 접경하다, 인접하다
The border between two countries or regions is the dividing line between them.

traffic**
[tráefik]

n. 교통(량), 통행, 왕래; 거래, 무역; v. 매매하다, 거래하다
Traffic refers to all the vehicles that are moving along the roads in a particular area.

stretch**
[stretʃ]

n. (특히 길게 뻗은) 길, 구간; 뻗침; v. 늘이다, 쭉 펴다, 뻗다
A stretch of road, water, or land is a length or area of it.

flow***
[flou]

n. 흐름, 유입, 유출; v. 흐르다, 흘리다; 넘치다, 풍부하다
If a number of people or things flow from one place to another, they move there steadily in large groups, usually without stopping.

geographical*
[dʒi:əgráefikəl]

a. 지리(학)적인, 지리학(상)의 (geographically ad. 지리적으로)
Geographical or geographic means concerned with or relating to the way that features such as rivers, mountains, towns, or streets are arranged within a place.

economic**
[èkənámik]

a. 경제(상)의, 경제적인; 경제학의 (economically ad. 경제적으로)
Economic means concerned with the organization of the money, industry, and trade of a country, region, or society.

extent**
[ikstént]

n. 범위, 정도; 넓이, 크기 (to some extent idiom 다소, 어느 정도는)
You use expressions such as to a large extent, to some extent, or to a certain extent in order to indicate that something is partly true, but not entirely true.

racial*
[réiʃəl]

a. 인종[민족]간의 (racially ad. 인종적으로)
Racial describes things relating to people's race.

identical*
[aidéntikəl]

a. 동일한, 꼭 같은
Things that are identical are exactly the same.

porch*
[pɔ:rtʃ]

n. (본 건물 입구에 달린 지붕이 있는) 현관, 포치
A porch is a sheltered area at the entrance to a building, which has a roof and sometimes has walls.

serve***
[sə:rv]

v. (교도소에서) 복역하다; 근무하다, 복무하다; 시중들다, 접대하다; 제공하다
If you serve something such as a prison sentence, you spend a period of time doing it.

32

occupy
[ákjupài]

vt. 차지하다, 점령하다, 거주하다; 주의를 끌다
If a room or something such as a seat is occupied, someone is using it, so that it is not available for anyone else.

skinny^{복습}
[skíni]

a. 바싹 여윈, 깡마른
A skinny person is extremely thin, often in a way that you find unattractive.

stay up

phrasal v. 무너지지 않고 견디다; 자지 않고 일어나 있다
If something stays up, it remains in a standing or higher position where it has been put or built.

concentrate^{**}
[kánsəntrèit]

v. 집중하다, 전념하다
If you concentrate on something, you give all your attention to it.

tell me about it

idiom (나도 같은 경험을 해 봐서) 무슨 말인지 잘 안다
Tell me about it is used to say that you understand what someone is talking about and have had the same experience.

block^{***}
[blak]

n. (도시의) 블록, 한 구획; 덩어리; 방해물; vt. 막다, 방해하다
A block in a town is an area of land with streets on all its sides.

bend^{**}
[bend]

v. (bent-bent) 굽히다, 굽혀지다; n. (도로 · 강의) 굽이
When you bend a part of your body such as your arm or leg, or when it bends, you change its position so that it is no longer straight.

rigid[*]
[rídʒid]

a. 굳은, 단단한; 엄격한, 완고한 (rigidly ad. 단단하게)
A rigid substance or object is stiff and does not bend, stretch, or twist easily.

aware^{**}
[əwéər]

a. 알고 있는, 의식하고 있는, 알아차린
If you are aware of something, you know about it.

remind^{**}
[rimáind]

vt. 생각나게 하다, 상기시키다, 일깨우다
If someone reminds you of a fact or event that you already know about, they say something which makes you think about it.

glance^{복습}
[glæns]

v. 흘끗 보다, 잠깐 보다; n. 흘끗 봄
If you glance at something or someone, you look at them very quickly and then look away again immediately.

separate^{**}
[sépərèit]

a. 별개의, 독립된; 개개의; v. 가르다, 떼다, 분리하다
If you refer to separate things, you mean several different things, rather than just one thing.

being^{**}
[bí:iŋ]

n. 존재, 생명체
You can refer to any real or imaginary creature as a being.

figure out

phrasal v. ~을 생각해내다, 발견하다
If you figure out a solution to a problem or the reason for something, you succeed in solving it or understanding it.

string^{**}
[striŋ]

n. 끈, 실; (악기의) 현[줄]; 일련, 한 줄; v. 묶다, 매달다
String is thin rope made of twisted threads, used for tying things together or tying up parcels.

retard
[rítɑːrd]

n. 모자라는 사람, 저능아; 지연, 지체; v. 더디게 하다
If you describe someone as a retard, you mean that they have not developed normally, either mentally or socially.

respect**
[rispékt]

n. 존중, 주의, 관심; v. 존경하다, 소중히 여기다
If you have respect for someone, you have a good opinion of them.

taunt
[tɔːnt]

n. 조롱, 비웃음; vt. 조롱하다, 비아냥거리다
A taunt is a sarcastic challenge or insult.

bleed*
[bliːd]

v. 피가 나다, 출혈하다 (bleeding n. 출혈)
When you bleed, you lose blood from your body as a result of injury or illness.

violent**ᵇ
[váiələnt]

a. 난폭한, 폭력적인; 격렬한, 맹렬한
If someone is violent, or if they do something which is violent, they use physical force or weapons to hurt, injure, or kill other people.

criminal**
[krímənl]

n. 범죄자, 범인; a. 범죄의
A criminal is a person who regularly commits crimes.

hit it off

idiom 잘 해나가다, 타협하다
If two people hit it off with each other, they like each other and become friendly immediately.

pity**
[píti]

v. 동정하다, 불쌍히 여기다; n. 동정, 연민
If you feel pity for someone, you feel very sorry for them.

brace*
[breis]

n. 버팀대; 치아 교정기; v. 떠받치다, 보강하다; 재빨리 대비하다
(leg brace n. 다리 보조기)
A brace is a device attached to a part of a person's body, for example to a weak leg, in order to strengthen or support it.

claim***
[kleim]

v. 주장하다; 요구[청구]하다; n. 요구, 청구; 권리
If you say that someone claims that something is true, you mean they say that it is true but you are not sure whether or not they are telling the truth.

pinch*
[pintʃ]

v. (신발 등이) 너무 끼다; 꼬집다, 끼워서 조이다; n. 꼬집기
If you pinch a part of someone's body, you take a piece of their skin between your thumb and first finger and give it a short squeeze.

walker*
[wɔ́ːkər]

n. 보행 보조기, 보행기; 보행자
A walker is a special kind of frame which is designed to help babies or disabled or ill people to walk.

recess*
[risés]

n. 휴식 시간, 휴식, 휴게; vi. 휴게하다, 휴업[휴교]하다
A recess is a break between the periods of work of an official body such as a committee, a court of law, or a government.

look up to

idiom ~를 우러러보다, 존경하다
If you look up to someone, you admire or respect them.

extend**ᵇ
[iksténd]

v. (손·발 등을) 뻗다, 늘이다; 넓히다, 확장하다
If someone extends their hand, they stretch out their arm and hand to shake hands with someone.

34

delicate
[délikət]

a. 섬세한, 고운; 예민한, 민감한 (delicately ad. 섬세하게)
Something that is delicate has a color, taste, or smell which is pleasant and not strong or intense.

have nothing to do with

idiom ~와 관계가 없다
To have nothing to do with something means not to be connected or concerned with it.

disability
[dìsəbíləti]

n. 신체 장애; 무능력, 불능
A disability is a permanent injury, illness, or physical or mental condition that tends to restrict the way that someone can live their life.

puberty
[pjú:bərti]

n. 사춘기
Puberty is the stage in someone's life when their body starts to become physically mature.

giggle[*]
[gigl]

vi. 낄낄 웃다; n. 낄낄 웃음
If someone giggles, they laugh in a childlike way, because they are amused, nervous, or embarrassed.

crack^{**}
[kræk]

v. 금이 가다, 깨다, 부수다; n. 갈라진 금[틈]; 갑작스런 날카로운 소리
(cracked a. 갈라진, 금이 간)
If something hard cracks, or if you crack it, it becomes slightly damaged, with lines appearing on its surface.

weed[*]
[wi:d]

n. 잡초; v. 잡초를 없애다
A weed is a wild plant that grows in gardens or fields of crops and prevents the plants that you want from growing properly.

poke[*]
[pouk]

v. 삐져나오다; 찌르다, 쑤시다; 들이대다; n. 찌름, 쑤심
If something pokes out of or through another thing, you can see part of it appearing from behind or underneath the other thing.

plant^{***}
[plænt]

v. (나무 · 씨앗 등을) 심다; n. 식물, 초목; 공장
When you plant a seed, plant, or young tree, you put it into the ground so that it will grow there.

shrub[*]
[ʃrʌb]

n. 키 작은 나무, 관목
A shrub is a small bush with several woody stems.

install^{**}
[instɔ́:l]

vt. 설치하다, 장치하다
If you install a piece of equipment, you fit it or put it somewhere so that it is ready to be used.

irrigate^{복습}
[írəgèit]

v. (땅에) 물을 대다, 관개하다 (irrigation n. 관개)
To irrigate land means to supply it with water in order to help crops grow.

oak[*]
[ouk]

n. [식물] 오크 나무
An oak or an oak tree is a large tree that often grows in woods and forests and has strong, hard wood.

shade^{복습}
[ʃeid]

vt. 그늘지게 하다; n. (pl.) 선글라스; 그늘, 음영; 색조
If you say that a place or person is shaded by objects such as trees, you mean that the place or person cannot be reached, harmed, or bothered by strong sunlight because those objects are in the way.

entire^{복습}
[intàiər]

a. 전체의; 완전한
You use entire when you want to emphasize that you are referring to the whole of something, for example, the whole of a place, time, or population.

solid**
[sálid]

a. 단단한; 견실한, 견고한; n. 고체
A substance that is solid is very hard or firm.

truck*
[trʌk]

v. 트럭[손수레 등]으로 나르다; 트럭 등에 싣다
When something or someone is trucked somewhere, they are driven there in a large vehicle.

landscape^{복습}
[lǽndskeip]

v. (나무를 심거나 지형을 바꾸어) 미화[조경]하다; n. 풍경, 경치, 조망
(landscaping n. 조경)
If an area of land is landscaped, it is changed to make it more attractive, for example by adding streams or ponds and planting trees and bushes.

air-conditioning
[έər-kəndiʃəníŋ]

n. (건물 · 자동차의) 에어컨 (장치)
Air-conditioning is a method of providing buildings and vehicles with cool dry air.

entrance**
[éntrəns]

n. 입구, 현관; 입학, 입장
The entrance to a place is the way into it, for example a door or gate.

rent**
[rent]

n. 집세, 방세; 임대료; vt. 빌려주다, 임대하다
Rent is the amount of money that you pay regularly to use a house, flat, or piece of land.

electric^{복습}
[iléktrik]

a. 전기의; 전기를 이용하는
An electric device works by means of electricity, rather than using some other source of power.

dispatcher
[dispǽtʃər]

n. (열차 · 버스 · 비행기 등이 정시 출발하도록 관리하는) 운행 관리원
A dispatcher is a person who oversees the departure of trains, airplanes or buses, as for a transportation company or railroad.

taxicab
[tǽksikæb]

n. 택시
A taxicab is the same as a taxi.

checker
[tʃékər]

n. (슈퍼마켓의) 계산대 직원; 확인[검토]하는 사람
A checker is a cashier, especially in a supermarket.

chop*
[tʃap]

vt. 잘게 썰다, 자르다; n. 잘라낸 조각; 절단, 자르기
If you chop something, you cut it into pieces with strong downward movements of a knife or an axe.

mutter*
[mʌ́tər]

v. 중얼거리다, 불평하다; n. 중얼거림, 불평
If you mutter, you speak very quietly so that you cannot easily be heard, often because you are complaining about something.

sigh*
[sai]

v. 한숨 쉬다; n. 한숨, 탄식
When you sigh, you let out a deep breath, as a way of expressing feelings such as disappointment, tiredness, or pleasure.

sweaty^{복습}
[swéti]

a. 땀이 나는, 땀투성이의
If parts of your body or your clothes are sweaty, they are soaked or covered with sweat.

go through^{복습}
idiom 겪다; 자세히 검토하다; 통과하다
If you go through an event or a period of time, you pass through it from the beginning to the end.

accuse[*]
[əkjúːz]
v. 비난하다, 고발하다
If you accuse someone of doing something wrong or dishonest, you say or tell them that you believe that they did it.

cab^{**}
[kæb]
n. 택시; (버스 · 기차 · 트럭의) 운전석
A cab is a taxi.

appreciate^{**}
[əpríːʃieit]
vt. 고맙게 생각하다; 진가를 알아보다, 인정하다
If you appreciate something that someone has done for you or is going to do for you, you are grateful for it.

attitude^{**}
[ǽtitjùːd]
n. 태도, 마음가짐; 자세
Your attitude to something is the way that you think and feel about it, especially when this shows in the way you behave.

stoned
[stound]
a. (마약 · 술에) 취한, 몽롱한
If someone is stoned, their mind is greatly affected by a drug or alcohol.

wouldn't put it past someone
idiom 누가 ~을 하고도 남으리라고 생각하다
If you say that you wouldn't put it past someone to do something bad, you mean that you would not be surprised if they did it because you think their character is bad.

admire^{복습}
[ædmáiər]
v. 감탄하다, 칭찬하다, 존경하다
If you admire someone or something, you like and respect them very much.

confidential^{복습}
[kànfədénʃəl]
a. 은밀한, 비밀의
Information that is confidential is meant to be kept secret or private.

seal[*]
[siːl]
v. 밀봉하다, 봉쇄하다; 도장을 찍다; n. 도장, 직인 (sealed a. 밀봉된)
When you seal an envelope, you close it by folding part of it over and sticking it down, so that it cannot be opened without being torn.

give up
phrasal v. 포기하다, 단념하다
If you give up, you decide that you cannot do something and stop trying to do it.

defensive[*]
[difénsiv]
a. 방어적인, 방어의, 수비의
Someone who is defensive is behaving in a way that shows they feel unsure or threatened.

march^{***}
[maːrtʃ]
① v. 당당하게 걷다, 행진하다; n. 행진, 행군 ② n. 3월
If you say that someone marches somewhere, you mean that they walk there quickly and in a determined way, for example because they are angry.

stand by
phrasal v. 수수방관하다
To stand by means to be present when something bad or unpleasant is happening, but not become involved.

ruin^{**}
[ruːin]
v. 망치다, 못쓰게 만들다; 몰락하다; n. 폐허; 파멸
To ruin something means to severely harm, damage, or spoil it.

point out^{복습}

phrasal v. ~을 지적하다
If you point out a fact or mistake, you tell someone about it or draw their attention to it.

violence**
[váiələns]

n. 폭력, 폭행
Violence is behavior which is intended to hurt, injure, or kill people.

bucket^{복습}
[bʌ́kit]

n. 버킷, 양동이
A bucket is a round metal or plastic container with a handle attached to its sides.

1분에 몇 단어를 읽는지 리딩 속도를 측정해보세요.

$$\frac{1{,}319 \text{ words}}{\text{reading time ( ) sec}} \times 60 = (\qquad) \text{ WPM}$$

Build Your Vocabulary

stick^{복습}
[stik]

① n. 막대기, 지팡이 ② v. 달라붙다, 붙이다; 내밀다; 고수하다
A stick of something is a long thin piece of it.

deodorant
[di:óudərənt]

n. 냄새[체취] 제거제, 데오도런트
Deodorant is a substance that you can use on your body to hide or prevent the smell of sweat.

armpit^{복습}
[á:rmpit]

n. 겨드랑이
Your armpits are the areas of your body under your arms where your arms join your shoulders.

splash[*]
[splæʃ]

v. (물·흙탕물 등을) 끼얹다, 튀기다; n. 첨벙 하는 소리
If you splash a liquid somewhere or if it splashes, it hits someone or something and scatters in a lot of small drops.

shave[*]
[ʃeiv]

v. 면도하다, 깎다, 밀다; n. 면도
When a man shaves, he removes the hair from his face using a razor or shaver so that his face is smooth.

lately^{**}
[léitli]

ad. 요즘에, 최근에, 근래
You use lately to describe events in the recent past, or situations that started a short time ago.

odor[*]
[óudər]

n. 냄새, 악취; 낌새, 기미
An odor is a particular and distinctive smell.

protect^{**}
[prətékt]

v. 보호하다, 막다, 지키다 (protection n. 보호)
To protect someone or something means to prevent them from being harmed or damaged.

invent^{**}
[invént]

vt. 발명하다, 고안하다; (상상력으로) 만들다
If you invent something such as a machine or process, you are the first person to think of it or make it.

stuff^{복습}
[stʌf]

n. 일[것](일반적으로 말하거나 생각하는 것); 물건, 물질; vt. 채워 넣다, 속을 채우다
You can use stuff to refer to things such as a substance, a collection of things, events, or ideas, or the contents of something in a general way without mentioning the thing itself by name.

remind^{복습}
[rimáind]

vt. 생각나게 하다, 상기시키다, 일깨우다
If someone reminds you of a fact or event that you already know about, they say something which makes you think about it.

charge^{**} [ʧɑːrdʒ]	n. 수수료, 요금; 책임, 의무; v. (지불을) 청구하다; 부담 지우다, 맡기다; 돌격하다 A charge is an amount of money that you have to pay for a service.
make sense	idiom 뜻이 통하다, 도리에 맞다 If something makes sense, it has a meaning that you can easily understand.
just in case	idiom 만일에 대비하여 Just in case means so as to be prepared for what may or may not happen.
assure^{복습} [əʃúəːr]	vt. 단언하다, 보증하다 If you assure someone that something is true or will happen, you tell them that it is definitely true or will definitely happen, often in order to make them less worried.
guarantee^{복습} [gæranti:]	vt. 보증하다, 단언하다; n. 보증 If you guarantee something, you promise that it will definitely happen, or that you will do or provide it for someone.
sticky[*] [stíki]	a. 끈적[끈끈]한, 들러붙는, 점착성의 A sticky substance is soft, or thick and liquid, and can stick to other things.
sweat^{복습} [swet]	n. 땀; v. 땀 흘리다; 습기가 차다 Sweat is the salty colorless liquid which comes through your skin when you are hot, ill, or afraid.
block^{복습} [blak]	n. (도시의) 블록, 한 구획; 덩어리; 방해물; vt. 막다, 방해하다 A block in a town is an area of land with streets on all its sides.
temperature^{**} [témpəritʃər]	n. 온도, 기온 The temperature of something is a measure of how hot or cold it is.
humid[*] [hjú:mid]	a. 습한, 눅눅한, 축축한 (humidity n. 습기, 습도) You use humid to describe an atmosphere or climate that is very damp, and usually very hot.
braid[*] [breid]	n. 땋은 머리; 끈, 노끈; vt. (머리 · 끈 등을) 꼬다, 땋다 A braid is a length of hair which has been divided into three or more lengths and then braided.
tip[*] [tip]	① n. (뾰족한) 끝 ② v. 뒤집어엎다, 기울이다 ③ n. 팁, 사례금 The tip of something long and narrow is the end of it.
goofy [gú:fi]	a. 바보 같은, 얼빠진 If you describe someone or something as goofy, you think they are rather silly or ridiculous.
casual^{**} [kǽʒuəl]	a. 태평스러운, 무심한; 우연한; 가벼운, 평상복의 If you are casual, you are, or you pretend to be, relaxed and not very concerned about what is happening or what you are doing.
abrupt[*] [əbrʌ́pt]	a. 퉁명스러운, 무뚝뚝한; 돌연한, 갑작스런 (abruptly ad. 퉁명스럽게) Someone who is abrupt speaks in a rather rude, unfriendly way.

due^{복습}
[dju:]

a. ~하기로 되어 있는; ~로 인한, ~ 때문에; n. ~에게 마땅히 주어져야 하는 것
If something is due at a particular time, it is expected to happen at that time.

extemporaneous
[ekstèmpəréiniəs]

a. 즉석의; 준비 없이 하는 (extemporaneously ad. 즉석에서)
An extemporaneous thing is something that is spoken or performed without planning or preparation.

assignment**
[əsáinmənt]

n. 숙제, 할당된 일, 임무
An assignment is a task or piece of work that you are given to do, especially as part of your job or studies.

stuffed
[stʌft]

a. 속을 채운; 배가 너무 부른 (stuffed animal n. 봉제 동물인형)
Stuffed animals are toys that are made of cloth filled with a soft material and which look like animals.

election**
[ilékʃən]

n. 선거
An election is a process in which people vote to choose a person or group of people to hold an official position.

elect***
[ilékt]

v. 선거하다, 선출하다; 결정하다
When people elect someone, they choose that person to represent them, by voting for them.

snort*
[snɔ:rt]

n. 코웃음, 콧방귀; v. 콧김을 뿜다. (경멸 등으로) 콧방귀 뀌다
A snort is a loud sound made by forcing air through the nose.

cheat**
[tʃi:t]

v. 속이다, 속임수 쓰다; 규칙을 어기다; 바람을 피우다; n. 사기, 속임수
(cheating n. 부정 행위)
To cheat means to behave in a dishonest way in order to get what you want.

shrug^{복습}
[ʃrʌg]

v. (어깨를) 으쓱하다; n. (양 손바닥을 내보이면서 어깨를) 으쓱하기
If you shrug, you raise your shoulders to show that you are not interested in something or that you do not know or care about something.

even out

phrasal v. 평등[동등]하게 되다
If something evens out, it becomes level or steady after a period when it has gone up and down or changed a lot.

economic^{복습}
[èkənámik]

a. 경제(상)의, 경제적인; 경제학의 (economics n. 경제학)
Economic means concerned with the organization of the money, industry, and trade of a country, region, or society.

bald*
[bɔ:ld]

a. (머리 등이) 벗어진, 대머리의; vi. 머리가 벗어지다
Someone who is bald has little or no hair on the top of their head.

drought
[draut]

n. 가뭄
A drought is a long period of time during which no rain falls.

bid*
[bid]

v. (경매 · 입찰에서) 값을 매기다, 입찰하다; 명령하다 (bidder n. 입찰자)
If you bid for something that is being sold, you offer to pay a particular amount of money for it.

confuse**
[kənfjú:z]

v. 어리둥절하게 하다, 혼동하다 (confused a. 당황한, 어리둥절한)
To confuse someone means to make it difficult for them to know exactly what is happening or what to do.

row^{복습}
[rou]

① n. 열, (좌석) 줄 ② vi. (노를 써서) 배를 젓다; (배가) 저어지다
A row of things or people is a number of them arranged in a line.

offer^{복습}
[ɔ́:fər]

v. 제의[제안]하다; 제공하다; n. 제공
If you offer something to someone, you ask them if they would like to have it or use it.

trade***
[treid]

v. 교환하다; 장사하다; n. 교환, 무역; 직업
If someone trades one thing for another or if two people trade things, they agree to exchange one thing for the other thing.

sapphire
[sǽfaiər]

n. 사파이어, 청옥
A sapphire is a precious stone which is blue in color.

pin**
[pin]

vt. 핀으로 꽂다, 고정하다; ~을 꼼짝 못하게 누르다; n. 핀, 장식
If you pin something on or to something, you attach it with a small thin pointed piece of metal.

lapel
[ləpél]

n. (양복 저고리 등의) 접은 옷깃
The lapels of a jacket or coat are the two top parts at the front that are folded back on each side and join on to the collar.

outfit*
[áutfit]

n. 한 벌의 옷, 복장
An outfit is a set of clothes.

figure***
[fíɡjər]

n. 수치, 숫자; 형태, 형상; 작은 조각상; v. 계산하다; 생각하다, 판단하다
A figure is a particular amount expressed as a number, especially a statistic.

agent^{복습}
[éidʒənt]

n. 대리인, 중개인; 행위자
An agent is a person who looks after someone else's business affairs or does business on their behalf.

hang***
[hæŋ]

v. (hung–hung) 매달리다; 걸다, 달아매다; 교수형에 처하다
If something hangs in a high place or position, or if you hang it there, it is attached there so it does not touch the ground.

forehead*
[fɔ́:rhèd]

n. 이마
Your forehead is the area at the front of your head between your eyebrows and your hair.

puffy
[pʌ́fi]

a. 부푼, 팽창된
If you describe something as puffy, you mean it has a round, swollen appearance.

ruin^{복습}
[rúːin]

v. 망치다, 못쓰게 만들다; 몰락하다; n. 폐허; 파멸
To ruin something means to severely harm, damage, or spoil it.

pitch*
[pitʃ]

n. (공의) 투구; 던지기; 최고도, 정점; v. 던지다; 고정시키다
In the game of baseball or rounders, when you pitch the ball, you throw it to the batter for them to hit it.

expense*
[ikspéns]

n. (pl.) 소요 경비; 비용, 지출
Expenses are amounts of money that you spend while doing something in the course of your work, which will be paid back to you afterward.

embarrass **
[imbǽrəs]

v. 부끄럽게[무안하게] 하다; 어리둥절하게 하다; 당황하다
(embarrassed a. 당혹한, 창피한)
If something or someone embarrasses you, they make you feel shy or ashamed.

salary *
[sǽləri]

n. 월급, 봉급
A salary is the money that someone is paid each month by their employer, especially when they are in a profession such as teaching, law, or medicine.

per diem
[pəːr díːəm]

n. (출장의) 일일 경비; a. 하루 단위의
A per diem is an amount of money that someone is given to cover their daily expenses while they are working.

additional *
[ədíʃənl]

a. 추가된, 첨가된
Additional things are extra things apart from the ones already present.

associate *
[əsóuʃieit]

v. 연결지어 생각하다, 연상하다; 연합시키다, 제휴하다; 교제하다; n. 동료, 한패
If you associate someone or something with another thing, the two are connected in your mind.

venue
[vénjuː]

n. (콘서트 · 스포츠 경기 · 회담 등의) 장소
The venue for an event or activity is the place where it will happen.

babysitter *
[béibisitər]

n. 아이를 봐 주는 사람
A babysitter is someone who look after children while their parents are out.

account **
[əkáunt]

n. (은행) 계좌, 예금(액); 기술, 설명; 계산; v. 설명하다; 책임지다; 생각하다
If you have an account with a bank or a similar organization, you have an arrangement to leave your money there and take some out when you need it.

get it 복습

idiom (구어) 알다, 이해하다
You can say get it when you understand or get the right answer immediately.

threat **
[θretn]

n. 위협, 협박
A threat to a person or thing is a danger that something unpleasant might happen to them.

acknowledge *
[æknálidʒ]

vt. 인정하다; 알고 있음을 알리다; 감사하다
If you acknowledge a fact or a situation, you accept or admit that it is true or that it exists.

exposure *
[ikspóuʒər]

n. (언론을 통해) 알려짐; 드러내기, 노출
Exposure is publicity that a person, company, or product receives.

patronize *
[péitrənàiz]

vt. 생색내는 듯한 태도를 취하다; 보호[수호]하다, 후원하다; 애용하다
(patronizing a. 생색내는, 거만한)
If someone patronizes you, they speak or behave toward you in a way which seems friendly, but which shows that they think they are superior to you in some way.

defensive 복습
[difénsiv]

a. 방어적인, 방어의, 수비의
Someone who is defensive is behaving in a way that shows they feel unsure or threatened.

smirk
[smə:rk]

vi. 능글맞게 웃다; n. 능글맞은 웃음

If you smirk, you smile in an unpleasant way, often because you believe that you have gained an advantage over someone else or know something that they do not know.

plant^{복습}
[plænt]

v. (나무 · 씨앗 등을) 심다; n. 식물, 초목; 공장

When you plant a seed, plant, or young tree, you put it into the ground so that it will grow there.

boast*
[boust]

v. 자랑스럽게 말하다, 뽐내다; n. 자랑(거리), 허풍

If someone boasts about something that they have done or that they own, they talk about it very proudly, in a way that other people may find irritating or offensive.

sell out

phrasal v. 다 팔리다, 매진되다

If tickets for a concert or a game sell out they are all sold and there are none left.

talent*
[tǽlənt]

n. 재능, 재주

Talent is the natural ability to do something well.

hype
[haip]

n. (대대적이고 과장된) 광고

Hype is the use of a lot of publicity and advertising to make people interested in something such as a product.

buzz^{복습}
[bʌz]

n. 소문, 수군거림; 윙윙거리는 소리; v. 윙윙거리다; 분주하게 돌아다니다

You can use buzz to refer to a word, idea, or activity which has recently become extremely popular.

scalper
[skǽlpər]

n. 암표상

A scalper is someone who sells tickets outside a sports ground or theater, usually for more than their original value.

1. What did Armpit bring with him when he waited for tickets and why?
   A. He brought his MP3 player to listen to Kaira's songs.
   B. He brought a taco to eat later in case he got hungry.
   C. He brought his economics textbook to study for the test.
   D. He brought a sketchbook to draw pictures while he waited.

2. Who were the men waiting in line behind Armpit?
   A. They were independent ticket scalpers.
   B. They were big Kaira fans.
   C. They were buying tickets for Felix and Moses.
   D. They were undercover police officers.

3. What did Felix offer Armpit and X-Ray?
   A. He offered to buy their tickets from them.
   B. He offered to sell them even better tickets.
   C. He offered them a job selling his tickets to their high school friends.
   D. He offered them a dinner in exchange for their tickets.

4. What did X-Ray need thirty dollars for after he gave Armpit a ride to school?
   A. He needed the money for gas.
   B. He needed the money for his lunch.
   C. He needed the money for posters advertising their tickets.
   D. He needed the money for an ad in the newspaper.

5. What did Armpit credit for his good score on the economics test?
   A. His economics teacher
   B. Felix's explanations using the tickets
   C. A television show Armpit watched
   D. His great handwriting

6. What common trait did Ginny's stuffed animals all seem to share?
   A. They were all birds.
   B. They were all yellow.
   C. They were all gifts from her father.
   D. They all had a disability or disease.

7. Which stuffed animal does Ginny persuade Armpit to take and why?
   A. She persuaded him to take Coo, because it was her oldest and favorite.
   B. She persuaded him to take Hooter, because he was wise.
   C. She persuaded him to take Daisy, because she could speak well.
   D. She persuaded him to take Roscoe, because he was expensive.

1분에 몇 단어를 읽는지 리딩 속도를 측정해보세요.

$$\frac{1{,}854 \text{ words}}{\text{reading time (\quad) sec}} \times 60 = (\quad) \text{ WPM}$$

Build Your Vocabulary

arena[*]
[ərí:nə]

n. 경기장, 시합장
An arena is a place where sports, entertainments, and other public events take place.

afford[**]
[əfɔ́:rd]

vt. ~해도 된다, ~할 여유가 있다
If you say that you cannot afford to do something or allow it to happen, you mean that you must not do it or must prevent it from happening because it would be harmful or embarrassing to you.

pull into

phrasal v. ~에 도착하다, 들다
If a train or a bus pulls into, it arrives somewhere and stops.

gravel[*]
[grǽvəl]

n. 자갈; vt. 자갈로 덮다, 자갈을 깔다; 어리둥절하게 하다
Gravel consists of very small stones which is often used to make paths.

pillow[복습]
[pílou]

n. 베개; 머리 받침대
A pillow is a rectangular cushion which you rest your head on when you are in bed.

smooth[**]
[smu:ð]

v. 매끄럽게 하다[되다]; a. 매끄러운; 유창한
If you smooth something out, you make something such as a piece of paper or cloth smooth and flat with your hands.

ignore[**]
[ignɔ́:r]

vt. 무시하다, 모르는 체하다
If you ignore someone or something, you pay no attention to them.

fountain[복습]
[fáuntən]

n. 분수; 샘
A fountain is an decorative feature in a pool or lake which consists of a long narrow stream of water that is forced up into the air.

youth[복습]
[ju:θ]

n. 젊음, 청춘; 청년(층), 젊은이들
Youth is the quality or state of being young.

damsel
[dǽmzəl]

n. 계집아이, 처녀
A damsel is a young, unmarried woman.

distress[*]
[distrés]

n. 고통, 곤란; 가난, 곤궁; vt. 고민하게 하다, 괴롭히다
Distress is a state of extreme sorrow, suffering, or pain.

live down

phrasal v. 잊다; (불명예를) 씻다
To live something down means to make people forget something very embarrassing or bad that you have done in the past.

ragged[*]
[rǽgid]

a. 남루한, 초라한; (옷 등이) 찢어진, 해어진
Someone who is ragged looks untidy and is wearing clothes that are old and torn.

street people
[stríːt píːpl]

n. 노숙자, 부랑자
Street people are homeless people who live outdoors in a town or city.

sanitation
[sæ̀nitéiʃən]

n. 위생 관리
Sanitation is the process of keeping places clean and healthy, especially by providing a sewage system and a clean water supply.

department[**]
[dipάːrtmənt]

n. 부분, 부, 부서
A department is one of the sections in an organization such as a government, business, or university.

interrupt[**]
[ìntərʌ́pt]

v. 중단하다, 가로막다, 저지하다
If you interrupt someone who is speaking, you say or do something that causes them to stop.

variable[*]
[vέəriəbl]

a. 변화하기 쉬운, 일정하지 않은; n. 변수
Something that is variable changes quite often, and there usually seems to be no fixed pattern to these changes.

illustrate[*]
[íləstreit]

vt. (예 · 비교 등으로) 설명하다, 명확히 하다; 삽화를 넣다
If you use an example, story, or diagram to illustrate a point, you use it show that what you are saying is true or to make your meaning clearer.

goods[**]
[gudz]

n. 상품, 제품; 재산
Goods are things that are made to be sold.

represent[**]
[rèprizént]

vt. 나타내다, 표시하다; 대표하다
If a sign or symbol represents something, it is accepted as meaning that thing.

angle[**]
[ǽŋgl]

v. (어떤 각도로) 기울이다, 굽다, 움직이다; n. 각도, 관점; 귀퉁이
If something angles, it inclines or bends from a vertical position.

might as well

idiom ～하는 것이 좋겠다
Might as well is used for saying that you will do something because it seems best in the situation that you are in, although you may not really want to do it.

point out[복습]

phrasal v. ～을 지적하다
If you point out a fact or mistake, you tell someone about it or draw their attention to it.

adjust[**]
[ədʒʌ́st]

v. 조절하다, 조정하다; (옷매무새 등을) 바로 하다; 적응하다
If you adjust something, you change it so that it is more effective or appropriate.

stick out[복습]

phrasal v. 돌출하다, 불쑥 내밀다[나오다]
If something sticks out, it is further out than something else or is partly outside something such as a container.

parallel**
[pǽrəlèl]

a. 평행인, 나란한; 일치하는, 상응하는; n. 평행(선)
If two lines, two objects, or two lines of movement are parallel, they are the same distance apart along their whole length.

grumble*
[grʌmbl]

v. 투덜거리다, 불평하다; n. 투덜댐, 불평
If someone grumbles, they complain about something in a bad-tempered way.

grubby
[grʌ́bi]

a. 더러운, 지저분한
A grubby person or object is rather dirty.

skinny 복습
[skíni]

a. 바싹 여윈, 깡마른
A skinny person is extremely thin, often in a way that you find unattractive.

dude 복습
[dju:d]

n. 사내, 녀석; (구어) 형씨, 친구
A dude is a man.

shave 복습
[ʃeiv]

v. 면도하다, 깎다, 밀다; n. 면도
When a man shaves, he removes the hair from his face using a razor or shaver so that his face is smooth.

beard*
[biərd]

n. 턱수염
A man's beard is the hair that grows on his chin and cheeks.

envelope*
[énvəlòup]

n. 봉투, 봉지
An envelope is the rectangular paper cover in which you send a letter to someone through the post.

agent 복습
[éidʒənt]

n. 대리인, 중개인; 행위자
An agent is a person who looks after someone else's business affairs or does business on their behalf.

complain 복습
[kəmpléin]

v. 불평하다, 투덜거리다
If you complain about a situation, you say that you are not satisfied with it.

apparent*
[əpǽrənt]

a. 또렷한, 명백한, 외관상의 (apparently ad. 명백하게, 보아하니)
If something is apparent to you, it is clear and obvious to you.

thermos
[θə́:rməs]

n. 보온병
A thermos is a container which is used to keep hot drinks hot or cold drinks cold.

somewhat 복습
[sʌ́mhwʌt]

ad. 어느 정도, 약간, 다소
You use somewhat to indicate that something is the case to a limited extent or degree.

offend*
[əfénd]

v. 불쾌하게 하다, 성나게 하다; 죄를 범하다 (offended a. 기분이 상한)
If you offend someone, you say or do something rude which upsets or embarrasses them.

crew*
[kru:]

n. 동료, 패거리; 승무원, 선원; 팀, 그룹
You can use crew to refer to a group of people you disapprove of.

50

independent** [indipéndənt]

a. 독자적인, 독립한. n. 독립한 사람[것]
If one thing or person is independent of another, they are separate and not connected, so the first one is not affected or influenced by the second.

scorpion 복습 [skɔ́:rpiən]

n. 전갈
A scorpion is a small creature which looks like a large insect. Scorpions have a long curved tail, and some of them are poisonous.

excruciating [ikskrú:ʃièitiŋ]

a. 극심한 고통을 주는; 맹렬한, 극심한 (excruciatingly ad. 견딜 수 없이)
If you describe something as excruciating, you are emphasizing that it is extremely painful, either physically or emotionally.

yell 복습 [jel]

v. 소리치다, 고함치다; n. 고함소리, 부르짖음
If you yell, you shout loudly, usually because you are excited, angry, or in pain.

argue*** [á:rgju:]

v. 논쟁하다; 주장하다
If one person argues with another, they speak angrily to each other about something that they disagree about.

bold* [bould]

a. (선 등이) 굵은; 대담한, 과감한; 뻔뻔스러운
Bold is print which is thicker and looks blacker than ordinary printed letters.

squat* [skwat]

n. (속어) 거의 없음, 적음; v. 웅크리고 앉(게 하)다
Squat means a minimum amount or degree.

reserve** [rizə́:rv]

vt. 남겨두다, 떼어두다; 예약하다; n. 비축, 저장; a. 예비의, 따로 둔
If you reserve something such as a table, ticket, or magazine, you arrange for it to be kept specially for you, rather than sold or given to someone else.

station 복습 [stéiʃən]

n. 방송 채널, 방송국; 역, 정류장; 지역 본부, 사업소; 부, 부서
If you talk about a particular radio or television station, you are referring to the programes broadcast by a particular radio or television company.

rip-off [ríp-ɔ̀f]

n. 속임수, 도둑질; 폭리, 바가지 (물품)
Rip-off is to steal from or cheat someone.

buck 복습 [bʌk]

① n. (속어) 달러 ② n. 수사슴, 수컷
A buck is a US or Australian dollar.

value*** [vǽlju:]

n. 값, 가치; vt. 가치를 매기다; 소중히 하다 (face value n. 액면 가격)
The value of something is how much money it is worth.

charge 복습 [ʧɑ:rdʒ]

n. 수수료, 요금; 책임, 의무; v. (지불을) 청구하다; 부담 지우다, 맡기다; 돌격하다
A charge is an amount of money that you have to pay for a service.

beat** [bi:t]

v. 능가하다, 더 낫다; 이기다, 패배시키다; 치다, 두드리다; n. 치기, 때리기; 박자
If someone beats a record or achievement, they do better than it.

risk 복습 [risk]

n. 위험; vt. 위험을 무릅쓰다
If there is a risk of something unpleasant, there is a possibility that it will happen.

demand***
[dimǽnd]

n. [경제] 수요(량), 요구; vt. 묻다, 요구하다, 청구하다
If you refer to demand, or to the demand for something, you are referring to how many people want to have it, do it, or buy it.

supply**
[səplái]

n. [경제] (수요에 대한) 공급, 보급; vt. 공급하다, 지급하다
Supply is the quantity of goods and services that can be made available for people to buy.

bust
[bʌst]

v. 부수다, 고장 내다; 파산하다; (현장을) 덮치다 (busted a. 고장난)
If you bust something, you break it or damage it so badly that it cannot be used.

cable*
[kéibl]

n. 케이블 (전선), 굵은 밧줄
A cable is a thick wire, or a group of wires inside a rubber or plastic covering, which is used to carry electricity or electronic signals.

unload*
[ʌnlóud]

v. 없애다, 처분하다; (차 · 배 등의) 짐을 내리다; (총에서) 탄알을 빼내다
If someone unloads investments, they get rid of them or sell them.

inventory
[ínvəntɔ̀:ri]

n. 재고품; 물품 목록
An inventory is a supply or stock of something.

pregnant*
[prégnənt]

a. 임신한
If a woman or female animal is pregnant, she has a baby or babies developing in her body.

political**
[pəlítikəl]

a. 정치의, 정치적인
Political means relating to the way power is achieved and used in a country or society.

protest**
[prətést]

n. 시위; 항의; v. 항의하다, 이의를 제기하다
A protest is the act of saying or showing publicly that you object to something.

ad*
[æd]

n. (= advertisement) 광고; 광고 활동
An advertisement is an announcement in a newspaper, on television, or on a poster about something such as a product, event, or job.

run***
[rʌn]

v. (광고 · 기사 등을) 싣다, 게재하다; 달리다, 뛰다; 흐르다; 경영하다
When newspapers or magazines run a particular item or story or if it runs, it is published or printed.

make sense복습

idiom 뜻이 통하다, 도리에 맞다
If something makes sense, it has a meaning that you can easily understand.

concierge
[kànsiéərʒ]

n. (호텔의) 안내원; 수위
A concierge is a person, especially in France, who looks after a block of flats and checks people entering and leaving the building.

profit복습
[práfit]

n. 이익, 수익; v. 이익을 얻다; 득이 되다
A profit is an amount of money that you gain when you are paid more for something than it cost you to make, get, or do it.

apiece
[əpí:s]

ad. 각자에게, 제각기
If people have a particular number of things apiece, they have that number each.

52

1분에 몇 단어를 읽는지 리딩 속도를 측정해보세요.

$$\frac{673 \text{ words}}{\text{reading time ( ) sec}} \times 60 = (\quad) \text{ WPM}$$

Build Your Vocabulary

big deal
[bíg díːl]
n. 대단한 것, 중대사
If you say that something is a big deal, you mean that it is important or significant in some way.

pretend***
[priténd]
v. 가장하다, ~인 체하다; a. 가짜의
If you pretend that something is the case, you act in a way that is intended to make people believe that it is the case, although in fact it is not.

menace*
[ménis]
n. 위협, 협박; 위험; v. 위협하다 (menacing a. 위협적인)
If you say that someone or something is a menace to other people or things, you mean that person or thing is likely to cause serious harm.

glare*
[glɛər]
n. 노려봄; 번쩍이는 빛; v. 노려보다; 번쩍번쩍 빛나다
A glare is an angry, hard, and unfriendly look.

ignore***
[ignɔ́ːr]
vt. 무시하다, 모르는 체하다
If you ignore someone or something, you pay no attention to them.

mood**
[muːd]
n. 기분, 심정; 분위기
Your mood is the way you are feeling at a particular time.

economic***
[èkənámik]
a. 경제(상)의, 경제적인; 경제학의 (economics n. 경제학)
Economic means concerned with the organization of the money, industry, and trade of a country, region, or society.

arena***
[əríːnə]
n. 경기장, 시합장
An arena is a place where sports, entertainments, and other public events take place.

click*
[klik]
v. (불현듯) 딱 분명해지다[이해가 되다]; 딸각 소리를 내다; n. 딸깍[찰깍]하는 소리
When you suddenly understand something, you can say that it clicks.

gasoline**
[gǽsəliːn]
n. 휘발유, 가솔린
Gasoline is a liquid which is used as a fuel for motor vehicles.

in terms of
idiom ~에 관하여, ~의 점에서 (보면)
You say in terms of to show what aspect of a subject you are talking about or how you are thinking about it.

stuffed***
[stʌft]
a. 속을 채운; 배가 너무 부른 (stuffed animal n. 봉제 동물인형)
Stuffed animals are toys that are made of cloth filled with a soft material and which look like animals.

selfish*
[sélfiʃ]

a. 이기적인, 자기 본위의
If you say that someone is selfish, you mean that he or she cares only about himself or herself, and not about other people.

definite**
[défənit]

a. 확실한, 확고한; 분명한, 뚜렷한 (definitely ad. 확실히, 명확히)
If something such as a decision or an arrangement is definite, it is firm and clear, and unlikely to be changed.

consider^{복습}
[kənsídər]

v. 고려하다, 숙고하다
If you consider something, you think about it carefully.

honor***
[ánər]

n. 명예, 영예; vt. 존경하다, 공경하다
If you describe doing or experiencing something as an honor, you mean you think it is something special and desirable.

deserve***
[dizə́:rv]

v. ~을 받을 만하다, ~할 가치가 있다
If you say that a person or thing deserves something, you mean that they should have it or receive it because of their actions or qualities.

hooter
[hú:tər]

n. [동물] 올빼미
A hooter is a bird with a flat face, large eyes, and a small sharp beak.

blind**
[blaind]

a. 눈이 먼, 장님의; 되는대로 하는, 맹목적인; vt. 눈을 멀게 하다; 가리다
Someone who is blind is unable to see because their eyes are damaged.

bump*
[bʌmp]

v. (쾅 하고) 부딪치다, 충돌하다; n. 충돌; 혹; (도로의) 튀어나온 부분
If you bump into something or someone, you accidentally hit them while you are moving.

rustle*
[rʌsl]

vi. 바스락거리다, 살랑살랑 소리 내다; n. 바스락거리는 소리
If things such as paper or leaves rustle, or if you rustle them, they move about and make a soft, dry sound.

stutter
[stʌ́tər]

vi. 말을 더듬다, 더듬거리며 말하다; n. 말더듬기
If someone stutters, they have difficulty speaking because they find it hard to say the first sound of a word.

floppy
[flápi]

a. 축 늘어진, 느슨한; 기운 없는
Something that is floppy is loose rather than stiff, and tends to hang downward.

deaf*
[def]

a. 귀가 먹은, 청각 장애가 있는
Someone who is deaf is unable to hear anything or is unable to hear very well.

keen*
[ki:n]

a. 예민한, 민감한; 날카로운, 예리한; 열정적인, 간절히 ~하고 싶은
If you have a keen eye or ear, you are able to notice things that are difficult to detect.

fuzzy
[fʌ́zi]

a. 솜털로 덮인; 흐릿한, 불분명한
If something is fuzzy, it has a covering that feels soft and like fur.

twist^{복습}
[twist]

v. 비틀다, 돌리다, 꼬다, 감기다; n. 뒤틀림; 엉킴 (twisty a. 비틀린)
If you twist something, especially a part of your body, or if it twists, it moves into an unusual, uncomfortable, or bent position, for example because of being hit or pushed, or because you are upset.

paralyze*
[pǽrəlaiz]

vt. 마비시키다; 무력[무능]하게 만들다 (paralyzed a. 마비된)
If someone is paralyzed by an accident or an illness, they have no feeling in their body, or in part of their body, and are unable to move.

horrible**
[hɔ́:rəbl]

a. 무서운, 끔찍한; 몹시 불쾌한
You can call something horrible when it causes you to feel great shock, fear, and disgust.

edge*복습
[edʒ]

n. 끝, 가장자리, 모서리
The edge of something is the place or line where it stops, or the part of it that is furthest from the middle.

bow*
[bou]

① v. 활처럼 휘(어지)다; n. 활 (bowed a. 활처럼 휜) ② v. 굽히다, 숙이다; 절하다
If a person's body is bowed, it is bent forward.

tiptoe
[típtòu]

n. 발끝; vi. 발끝으로 걷다, 발돋움하다
If you do something on tiptoe or on tiptoes, you do it standing or walking on the front part of your foot, without putting your heels on the ground.

brace*복습
[breis]

n. 버팀대; 치아 교정기; v. 버팀대로 받치다; 대비하다
A brace is a device attached to a part of a person's body, for example to a weak leg, in order to strengthen or support it.

exclaim*복습
[ikskléim]

v. 외치다, 소리치다
If you exclaim, you say or shout something suddenly because of surprise, fear and pleasure.

bunny
[bʌ́ni]

n. (구어) 토끼
A bunny is a child's word for a rabbit.

frown*
[fraun]

vi. 얼굴을 찡그리다, 눈살을 찌푸리다; n. 찌푸린 얼굴
When someone frowns, their eyebrows become drawn together, because they are annoyed or puzzled.

assure*복습
[əʃúə:r]

vt. 단언하다, 보증하다
If you assure someone that something is true or will happen, you tell them that it is definitely true or will definitely happen, often in order to make them less worried.

count on

phrasal v. 기대하다, ~을 믿다[의지하다]
If you count on something, you expect it to happen and make plans in an appropriate way.

spongy*
[spʌ́ndʒi]

a. 푹신푹신한; 흡수성의; 작은 구멍이 많은
Something that is spongy is soft and can be pressed in, like a sponge.

disability*복습
[dìsəbíləti]

n. 신체 장애; 무능력, 불능
A disability is a permanent injury, illness, or physical or mental condition that tends to restrict the way that someone can live their life.

whisper*
[hwíspə:r]

v. 속삭이다, 작은 소리로 말하다; n. 속삭임
When you whisper, you say something very quietly.

1. How did Armpit "get even" when he bought the newspaper?

    A. He decided to break the machine holding the newspapers.

    B. He ruined all of the newspapers by pouring water over them.

    C. He decided to take all of the newspapers in the machine and sell them later.

    D. He took out three copies and left two on the top of the machine.

2. Why was Armpit upset when he saw the ad in the newspaper?

    A. He thought the words were too small.

    B. He thought the ticket price was too high.

    C. He thought that they should choose a different newspaper.

    D. He thought it should have mentioned his name.

3. How did Armpit feel about his job doing yard work compared to selling tickets?

    A. He felt a sense of satisfaction doing yard work more than selling tickets.

    B. He felt that selling tickets was much easier and rewarding.

    C. He felt he could make a lot more money doing yard work.

    D. He felt that doing yard work was pointless but selling tickets helped people.

4. According to Ginny, when did she only stutter?
   A. She only stuttered when she did math.
   B. She only stuttered when she sang.
   C. She only stuttered when she talked.
   D. She only stuttered when she talked to boys.

5. Why did X-Ray want Armpit to come with him when he went to meet the ticket buyers?
   A. Armpit was good at keeping track of money.
   B. X-Ray wanted Armpit to provide backup for him.
   C. X-Ray wanted to help Armpit study for his economics test.
   D. The ticket buyers wanted to meet Armpit.

6. Why did Armpit take the speech assignment so seriously?
   A. He wanted to write his speech down so he could prepare and make Ginny proud.
   B. He knew he was great at making jokes and wanted to make the funniest speech.
   C. He just wanted to get a high score in the class and did not care about the speech.
   D. He wanted to be a professional speaker later in life and wanted to seriously practice.

7. How did Armpit react to X-Ray not selling the tickets to the men in the white Suburban?
   A. He agreed with X-Ray that the men disrespected them by being late.
   B. He was scared when he saw them approach and agreed with X-Ray not to sell the tickets.
   C. He felt that they could make more money by waiting to sell to other people.
   D. He felt angry that X-Ray refused to sell the tickets even after the men arrived.

1분에 몇 단어를 읽는지 리딩 속도를 측정해보세요.

$$\frac{1,113 \text{ words}}{\text{reading time (} \quad \text{) sec}} \times 60 = (\quad) \text{ WPM}$$

Build Your Vocabulary

ad^{복습}
[æd]

n. (= advertisement) 광고; 광고 활동
An advertisement is an announcement in a newspaper, on television, or on a poster about something such as a product, event, or job.

might as well^{복습}

idiom ~하는 것이 좋겠다
Might as well is used for saying that you will do something because it seems best in the situation that you are in, although you may not really want to do it.

vending machine
[véndiŋ məʃíːn]

n. 자동 판매기
A vending machine is a machine from which you can get things such as chocolate or coffee by putting in money and pressing a button.

slam^{복습}
[slæm]

v. 세게 치다; (문 따위를) 탕 닫다; 털썩 내려놓다; n. 쾅 (하는 소리)
If one thing slams into or against another, it crashes into it with great force.

remind^{복습}
[rimáind]

vt. 생각나게 하다, 상기시키다, 일깨우다
If someone reminds you of a fact or event that you already know about, they say something which makes you think about it.

worth^{복습}
[wəːrθ]

a. 가치가 있는; n. 가치, 값어치
If you say that something is worth having, you mean that it is pleasant or useful, and therefore a good thing to have.

clerk**
[kləːrk]

n. (가게의) 점원, 판매원; (회사의) 사무원
A clerk is someone who works in a store.

get even

idiom (~에게 해를 입은 만큼) 되갚아 주다
If you get even with someone, you cause them the same amount of trouble or harm as they have caused you.

spread***
[spred]

v. 펴다, 펼치다; 뿌리다; n. 퍼짐, 폭, 넓이
If you spread something out, you open it that is folded and put it down on a flat surface

classify*
[klǽsəfài]

vt. 분류하다, 등급을 나누다 (classified ad n. 안내 광고)
To classify things means to divide them into groups or types so that things with similar characteristics are in the same group.

range**
[reindʒ]

v. (양 · 크기 등의 범위가) ~에서 ~사이이다; n. 다양성; (변화 · 차이의) 범위
If things range between two points or range from one point to another, they vary within these points on a scale of measurement or quality.

insane[*]
[inséin]

a. 미친, 정신 이상의
Someone who is insane has a mind that does not work in a normal way, with the result that their behavior is very strange.

install[복습]
[instɔ́:l]

vt. 설치하다, 장치하다
If you install a piece of equipment, you fit it or put it somewhere so that it is ready to be used.

sprinkler
[spríŋklə:r]

n. 스프링클러(물을 뿌리는 장치)
A sprinkler is a device used to spray water to plants or grass, or to put out fires in buildings.

reimburse
[rì:imbə́:rs]

vt. 배상하다, 변상하다
If you reimburse someone for something, you pay them back the money that they have spent or lost because of it.

buck[복습]
[bʌk]

① n. (속어) 달러 ② n. 수사슴, 수컷
A buck is a US or Australian dollar.

accidental[복습]
[æksədéntl]

a. 우연한; 부수적인 (accidentally ad. 우연히)
An accidental event happens by chance or as the result of an accident, and is not deliberately intended.

row[복습]
[rou]

① n. 열, (좌석) 줄 ② vi. (노를 써서) 배를 젓다; (배가) 저어지다
A row of things or people is a number of them arranged in a line.

profit[복습]
[práfit]

n. 이익, 수익; v. 이익을 얻다; 득이 되다
A profit is an amount of money that you gain when you are paid more for something than it cost you to make, get, or do it.

hold out for

idiom (보다 좋은 것을 얻으려고) 버티다, 견디다
If you hold out for something, you wait patiently or uncompromisingly for it.

get rid of

idiom 제거하다, 없애다
If you get rid of something, you make yourself free of it that is annoying you or that you do not want.

offer[복습]
[ɔ́:fər]

v. 제의[제안]하다; 제공하다; n. 제공
If you offer something to someone, you ask them if they would like to have it or use it.

on the line

idiom 위태로운
If something is on the line, it is at risk.

heave[*]
[hi:v]

v. (한숨을) 쉬다; (무거운 것을) 들어올리다, 내던지다; n. 들어올림, 내던짐
If you heave a sigh, you give a big sigh.

sigh[복습]
[sai]

n. 한숨, 탄식; v. 한숨 쉬다
When you sigh, you let out a deep breath, as a way of expressing feelings such as disappointment, tiredness, or pleasure.

get off

phrasal v. 일을 마치다; 쉬다
If you get off work, you leave the work with permission.

tip[복습]
[tip]

① n. (뾰족한) 끝 ② v. 뒤집어엎다, 기울이다 ③ n. 팁, 사례금
The tip of something long and narrow is the end of it.

enormous*
[inɔ́:rməs]

a. 엄청난, 거대한, 막대한
You can use enormous to emphasize the great degree or extent of something.

bush**
[buʃ]

n. 덤불, 관목숲; v. 무성해지다
A bush is a large plant which is smaller than a tree and has a lot of branches.

octopus
[áktəpəs]

n. 문어
An octopus is a soft sea creature with eight long arms called tentacles which it uses to catch food.

tentacle
[téntəkl]

n. [동물] 촉수, 더듬이
The tentacles of an animal such as an octopus are the long thin parts that are used for feeling and holding things, for getting food, and for moving.

axe*
[æks]

n. (= ax) 도끼; vt. 도끼로 자르다
An axe is a tool used for cutting wood which consists of a heavy metal blade.

hack
[hæk]

v. 마구 자르다, 난도질하다; 파다, 갈다, 깎다
If you hack something or hack at it, you cut it with strong, rough strokes using a sharp tool such as an axe or knife.

offshoot
[ɔ́fʃùːt]

n. 나뭇가지
Offshoots are branches or lateral new parts growing from a main stem, as of a plant.

to no avail

idiom 도움되지 않고, 헛되이
If you do something to no avail, what you do fails to achieve what you want.

attach복습
[ətǽtʃ]

vt. 붙이다, 달다
If you attach something to an object, you connect it or fasten it to the object.

pickup truck
[píkʌp trʌ̀k]

n. 소형 오픈 트럭
A pickup truck is a light motor vehicle with an open-top rear cargo area.

cab복습
[kæb]

n. (버스·기차·트럭의) 운전석; 택시
The cab of a truck or train is the front part in which the driver sits.

shift복습
[ʃift]

v. (차의 기어를) 바꾸어 넣다; 옮기다, 이동하다; n. 변속 장치; 변화, 변경; 교대 근무
If you shift gears in a car, you put the car into a different gear.

uncertainty*
[ʌnsə́:rtnti]

n. 불확실, 반신반의
Uncertainty is a state of doubt about the future or about what is the right thing to do.

destroy***
[distrɔ́i]

vt. 파괴하다, 엉망으로 만들다
To destroy something means to cause so much damage to it that it is completely ruined or does not exist any more.

pop out

phrasal v. 튀어나오다, 갑자기 뛰어나가다; 갑자기 꺼지다, 급사하다
If something pops out, it suddenly comes out from a place.

60

sore**
[sɔːr]

a. 아픈, 쓰린
If part of your body is sore, it causes you pain and discomfort.

sweat^{복습}
[swet]

n. 땀; v. 땀 흘리다; 습기가 차다
Sweat is the salty colorless liquid which comes through your skin when you are hot, ill, or afraid.

satisfaction**
[sætisfǽkʃən]

n. 만족(감), 만족을 주는 것
Satisfaction is the pleasure that you feel when you do something or get something that you wanted or needed to do or get.

scalp
[skælp]

v. 암표를 팔다; n. 두피, 머리 가죽
If someone scalps tickets, they sell them outside a sports ground or theater, usually for more than their original value.

compare**
[kəmpέər]

v. ~와 비교하다, 견주다; 비유하다 (in comparison idiom ~와 비교하여)
When you compare things, you consider them and discover the differences or similarities between them.

1분에 몇 단어를 읽는지 리딩 속도를 측정해보세요.

$$\frac{1,369 \text{ words}}{\text{reading time ( ) sec}} \times 60 = (\quad) \text{ WPM}$$

Build Your Vocabulary

widen*
[waidn]

v. 넓어지다; 넓히다
If you widen something or if it widens, it becomes greater in measurement from one side or edge to the other.

split복습
[split]

v. 분배하다; 쪼개다, 찢다, 째다; n. 쪼개기, 분열
If something splits or if you split it, it is divided into two or more parts.

stutter복습
[stʌ́tər]

v. 말을 더듬다, 더듬거리며 말하다; n. 말더듬기
If someone stutters, they have difficulty speaking because they find it hard to say the first sound of a word.

point out복습
phrasal v. ~을 지적하다
If you point out a fact or mistake, you tell someone about it or draw their attention to it.

suspicious*
[səspíʃəs]

a. 수상쩍은, 의심하는
If you are suspicious of someone or something, you do not trust them, and are careful when dealing with them.

turn out
phrasal v. 결국은 ~이 되다, 결국은 ~임이 밝혀지다
To turn out means to happen in a particular way or to have a particular result.

abduct
[æbdʌ́kt]

vt. 유괴하다, 납치하다
If someone is abducted by another person, he or she is taken away illegally, usually using force.

bother*
[bɑ́ðər]

vt. 귀찮게 하다, 괴롭히다, 폐 끼치다
If something bothers you, or if you bother about it, it worries, annoys, or upsets you.

passenger복습
[pǽsəndʒər]

n. 승객, 여객 (passenger side n. 조수석)
A passenger in a vehicle such as a bus, boat, or plane is a person who is traveling in it, but who is not driving it or working on it.

bull*
[bul]

n. 허풍, 거짓말; 황소; 수컷; v. 밀고 나아가다; 허풍 떨다
(no bull idiom 허풍이 아니고)
If you say that something is bull or a load of bull, you mean that it is complete nonsense or absolutely untrue.

respect복습
[rispékt]

n. 존중, 주의, 관심; v. 존경하다, 소중히 여기다
If you have respect for someone, you have a good opinion of them.

affection[*]
[əfékʃən]

n. 애정, 애착, 보살핌, 호의
Your affections are your feelings of love or fondness for someone.

gash
[gæʃ]

n. 깊은 상처, 갈라진 금[틈]; vt. 상처를 입히다, 깊이 베다
A gash is a long, deep cut in your skin or in the surface of something.

dinosaur
[dáinəsɔ̀ːr]

n. 공룡
Dinosaurs were large reptiles which lived in prehistoric times.

dude[복습]
[djuːd]

n. 사내, 녀석; (구어) 형씨, 친구
A dude is a man.

stand for

phrasal v. ~을 나타내다, 상징하다
To stand for something means to represent or mean it.

grocery[*]
[gróusəri]

n. (pl.) 식료 잡화류; 식료 잡화점
Groceries are foods you buy at a grocer's or at a supermarket such as flour, sugar, and tinned foods.

crack up

phrasal v. 크게 웃다
If you crack up, you suddenly laugh a lot.

glare[복습]
[glɛər]

v. 노려보다; 번쩍번쩍 빛나다; n. 노려봄; 번쩍이는 빛
If you glare at someone, you look at them with an angry expression on your face.

let down

phrasal v. ~을 실망시키다, 기대를 저버리다
If you let someone down, you fail to help or support them in the way that they hoped or expected.

maniac
[méiniæk]

n. 미치광이, 광적인 열중가; a. 광적인, 광란의
A maniac is a mad person who is violent and dangerous.

obese
[oubíːs]

a. 비만인
If someone is obese, they are extremely fat.

pull up

phrasal v. (차 등이) 서다, 차를 세우다
When a vehicle or driver pulls up, the vehicle slows down and stops.

license[복습]
[láisəns]

n. 면허(증), 허가(증); v. 면허를 주다 (license plate n. (자동차의) 번호판)
A license plate is a sign on the front and back of a vehicle that shows its license number.

check[**]
[tʃek]

n. 수표; 확인, 검사; v. 살피다, 점검하다
A check is a printed form on which you write an amount of money and who it is to be paid to. Your bank then pays the money to that person from your account.

riff
[rif]

n. 대화 주제에서 벗어나는 말을 하는 것
A riff is a short piece of speech or writing that develops a particular theme or idea.

backup
[bækʌp]

n. 지원, 뒷받침; 예비, 대체(물); a. 지원의; 예비의
Backup consists of extra equipment, resources, or people that you can get help or support from if necessary.

outline[*]
[áutlàin]

n. 개요, 요점; 윤곽; 약도; vt. 윤곽을 그리다
An outline is a general explanation or description of something.

come up with^{복습}	idiom ~을 생각하다, 제안하다 If you come up with a plan or idea, you think of it and suggest it.
comfort** [kʌ́mfərt]	n. 위로, 위안; 마음이 편안함, 안락; vt. 위로[위안]하다 Comfort is what you feel when worries or unhappiness stop.
confidence** [kɑ́nfədəns]	n. 자신(감), 확신; 신용, 신뢰 If you have confidence, you feel sure about your abilities, qualities, or ideas.
assignment^{복습} [əsáinmənt]	n. 숙제, 할당된 일, 임무 An assignment is a task or piece of work that you are given to do, especially as part of your job or studies.
election^{복습} [ilékʃən]	n. 선거 An election is a process in which people vote to choose a person or group of people to hold an official position.
urge* [əːrdʒ]	v. 강력히 주장하다, 설득하다; 몰아대다, 재촉하다; n. (강한) 충동 If you urge someone to do something, you try hard to persuade them to do it.
vote** [vout]	v. 투표하다; n. 투표, 투표권 When you vote, you indicate your choice officially at a meeting or in an election.
plant^{복습} [plænt]	v. (나무 · 씨앗 등을) 심다; n. 식물, 초목; 공장 When you plant a seed, plant, or young tree, you put it into the ground so that it will grow there.
destruction** [distrʌ́kʃən]	n. 파괴, 멸망, 파멸 Destruction is the act of destroying something, or the state of being destroyed.
rain forest [rein fɔ́ːrist]	n. 열대 우림 A rain forest is a thick forest of tall trees which is found in tropical areas where there is a lot of rain.
prevent** [privént]	vt. 예방[방지]하다; 막다, 방해하다 To prevent something means to ensure that it does not happen.
global warming [glóubəl wɔ́ːrmiŋ]	n. 지구 온난화 Global warming is the gradual rise in the earth's temperature caused by high levels of carbon dioxide and other gases in the atmosphere.
bring about	phrasal v. 야기하다, 초래하다 If you bring something about, you make it happen.
babble [bǽbəl]	v. 중얼중얼 말하다, 불명료한 소리를 내다; 쓸데없는 말을 하다; n. 재잘거림 If someone babbles, they talk in a confused or excited way.
for one's sake	idiom ~ 때문에, ~를 위해서 When you do something for someone's sake, you do it in order to help them or make them happy.
be off	phrasal v. 떠나다, 출발하다 If you be off, you leave or go especially in a hurry.

64

submit*
[səbmít]

v. 제출하다; 복종시키다, 굴복하다, 따르다
If you submit a proposal, report, or request to someone, you formally send it to them so that they can consider it or decide about it.

shift복습
[ʃift]

n. 교대 근무; 교체, 순환; v. 옮기다, 이동하다 (night shift n. 야간 근무)
If a group of factory workers, nurses, or other people work shifts, they work for a set period before being replaced by another group, so that there is always a group working.

jerk around

idiom 괴롭히다, 당황하게 만들다
If you jerk someone around, you treat them badly and cause them problems, espicially by not telling the truth.

joker
[dʒóukər]

n. 멍청한[골치 아픈] 사람; 우스갯소리를 잘하는 사람; 조커
You can call someone a joker if you think they are behaving in a stupid or dangerous way.

complain복습
[kəmpléin]

v. 불평하다, 투덜거리다
If you complain about a situation, you say that you are not satisfied with it.

disrespect
[disrispékt]

n. 무례, 결례; vt. ~에 결례되는 짓을 하다
If someone shows disrespect, they speak or behave in a way that shows lack of respect for a person, law, or custom.

claustrophobic
[klɔ̀ːstrəfóubik]

a. 밀실 공포증을 앓는[느끼게 하는]
You describe a place or situation as claustrophobic when it makes you feel uncomfortable and unhappy because you are enclosed or restricted.

stretch복습
[stretʃ]

v. 쭉 펴다, 뻗다, 늘이다; n. (특히 길게 뻗은) 길, 구간; 뻗침
When you stretch, you put your arms or legs out straight and tighten your muscles.

aisle*
[ail]

n. 통로, 측면의 복도
An aisle is a long narrow gap that people can walk along between rows of seats in a public building.

spot**
[spat]

n. 장소, 지점; 반점, 얼룩; vt. 발견하다, 분별하다
You can refer to a particular place as a spot.

announce**
[ənáuns]

vt. 알리다, 공고하다, 전하다
If you announce a piece of news or an intention, especially something that people may not like, you say it loudly and clearly, so that everyone you are with can hear it.

pull into복습

phrasal v. ~에 도착하다, 들다
If a train or a bus pulls into, it arrives somewhere and stops.

bounce복습
[bauns]

v. 튀다, 튀게 하다; 급히 움직이다, 뛰어다니다; n. 튐, 바운드
If something bounces off a surface or is bounced off it, it reaches the surface and is reflected back.

bump복습
[bʌmp]

n. (도로의) 튀어나온 부분; 충돌, 혹; v. (쾅 하고) 부딪치다, 충돌하다
(speed bump n. 과속방지턱)
A bump on a road is a raised, uneven part.

horn[*]
[hɔːrn]

n. (자동차 등의) 경적; 뿔
On a vehicle such as a car, the horn is the device that makes a loud noise as a signal or warning.

yell[복습]
[jel]

v. 소리치다, 고함치다; n. 고함소리, 부르짖음
If you yell, you shout loudly, usually because you are excited, angry, or in pain.

obscenity
[əbsénəti]

n. 욕설, 음란한 말; 외설
An obscenity is a very offensive word or expression.

lurch
[ləːrtʃ]

v. 휘청하다, 비틀거리다; n. 갑작스런 요동, 기울어짐
To lurch means to make a sudden movement, especially forward, in an uncontrolled way.

traffic[복습]
[trǽfik]

n. 교통(량), 통행, 왕래; 거래, 무역; v. 매매하다, 거래하다
Traffic refers to all the vehicles that are moving along the roads in a particular area.

nuts
[nʌts]

a. 미친, 제정신이 아닌
Nuts is a slang word for insane.

1. What happened to Armpit on the way to school?
   A. Armpit was offered a ride by some older students but refused it.
   B. Armpit was offered a ride to school and accepted it.
   C. Armpit lost Coo after some older students stole it.
   D. Armpit was offered a new job and accepted it.

2. Why did Armpit's classmates laugh at his speech?
   A. They thought that leukemia was a funny topic.
   B. They expected a funny speech and Armpit looked funny with Coo.
   C. They thought that Armpit had a funny voice.
   D. They thought that Armpit had a lot of well prepared jokes in his speech.

3. How did X-Ray sell the first four tickets?
   A. The men in the white Suburban came back to X-Ray.
   B. A woman bought them for her child's birthday.
   C. The people who offered Armpit a ride bought them.
   D. Felix and Moses bought them.

4. Why was Kaira riding the bus with the band members?
   A. Her bus was being renovated.
   B. She needed more practice time.
   C. She wanted to work on new songs.
   D. She was sick of being alone.

5. Which musician did the band members play for Kaira?
   A. Bob Dylan
   B. Miles Davis
   C. Janis Joplin
   D. The Beatles

6. What did the band members suggest about Aileen?
   A. She might be ready to retire from work soon.
   B. She might be stealing money from the tour.
   C. She might be dating one of the other band members.
   D. She might be having an affair with El Genius.

7. What kind of names did Aileen use to register for Kaira at hotels?
   A. Comic book superheroes
   B. Famous past musicians
   C. Old television show characters
   D. Famous politicians

1분에 몇 단어를 읽는지 리딩 속도를 측정해보세요.

$$\frac{1,344 \text{ words}}{\text{reading time ( ) sec}} \times 60 = (\quad) \text{ WPM}$$

Build Your Vocabulary

glance^{복습}
[glæns]

v. 흘끗 보다, 잠깐 보다; n. 흘끗 봄
If you glance at something or someone, you look at them very quickly and then look away again immediately.

recognize**
[rékəgnaiz]

vt. 인지하다, 알아보다
If you recognize someone or something, you know who that person is or what that thing is.

hop in

phrasal v. (자동차에) 뛰어 올라타다
If you hop in to a vehicle, you jump into it.

trick**
[trik]

n. 비결, 요령; 책략, 속임수; 장난; v. 속이다; 장난치다
A trick is a clever way of doing something.

offend^{복습}
[əfénd]

v. 불쾌하게 하다, 성나게 하다; 죄를 범하다
If you offend someone, you say or do something rude which upsets or embarrasses them.

high***
[hai]

a. (술·마약에) 취한; 높은
If someone is high on drink or drugs, they are affected by the alcoholic drink or drugs they have taken.

lap*
[læp]

① n. 무릎; (트랙의) 한 바퀴 ② v. (파도가) 찰싹거리다; (할짝할짝) 핥다
If you have something on your lap, it is on top of your legs and near to your body.

alongside*
[əlɔ́:ŋsáid]

prep. ~의 옆에, ~와 나란히; ad. 옆에
If one thing is alongside another thing, the first thing is next to the second.

through with

idiom 끝내다, 절교하다
If you are through with someone or something, you have finished a relationship with them or have finished using or doing it.

swerve
[swəːrv]

v. 휙 방향을 틀다, 벗어나다, 빗나가다; n. 벗어남, 빗나감
If a vehicle or other moving thing swerves or if you swerve it, it suddenly changes direction, often in order to avoid hitting something.

block^{복습}
[blak]

vt. 막다, 방해하다; n. (도시의) 블록, 한 구획; 덩어리; 방해물
If you block someone's way, you prevent them from going somewhere or entering a place by standing in front of them.

offer^{복습}
[ɔ́:fər]

v. 제공하다, 제의[제안]하다; n. 제공
If you offer something to someone, you ask them if they would like to have it or use it.

70

disrespect[복습]
[dìsrispékt]

n. 무례, 결례; vt. ~에 결례되는 짓을 하다
If someone shows disrespect, they speak or behave in a way that shows lack of respect for a person, law, or custom.

casual[복습]
[kǽʒuəl]

a. 태평스러운, 무심한; 우연한; 가벼운, 평상복의
If you are casual, you are, or you pretend to be, relaxed and not very concerned about what is happening or what you are doing.

bunny[복습]
[bʌ́ni]

n. (구어) 토끼
A bunny is a child's word for a rabbit.

tighten[*]
[taitn]

v. 단단히 죄다; 단단해지다, 팽팽해지다
If you tighten your grip on something, or if your grip tightens, you hold the thing more firmly or securely.

grip[복습]
[grip]

n. 꽉 붙잡음, 움켜짐; 손잡이; v. 꽉 잡다, 움켜잡다
A grip is a firm, strong hold on something.

give up[복습]

phrasal v. 포기하다, 단념하다
If you give up, you decide that you cannot do something and stop trying to do it.

retard[복습]
[rítaːrd]

n. 모자라는 사람, 저능아; 지연, 지체; v. 더디게 하다
If you describe someone as a retard, you mean that they have not developed normally, either mentally or socially.

tactic[*]
[tǽktik]

n. 작전, 전술
Tactics are the methods that you choose to use in order to achieve what you want in a particular situation.

bleed[복습]
[bliːd]

v. 피가 나다, 출혈하다 (bleeding n. 출혈)
When you bleed, you lose blood from your body as a result of injury or illness.

cruel[복습]
[krúːəl]

a. 잔인한, 잔혹한, 끔찍한
Someone who is cruel deliberately causes pain or distress to people or animals.

humorous[*]
[hjúːmərəs]

a. 유머러스한, 익살스러운
If someone or something is humorous, they are amusing, especially in a clever or witty way.

sink in

phrasal v. 서서히 이해되다
When a statement or fact sinks in, you finally understand or realize it fully.

sweat[복습]
[swet]

n. 땀; v. 땀 흘리다; 습기가 차다
Sweat is the salty colorless liquid which comes through your skin when you are hot, ill, or afraid.

drip[*]
[drip]

v. 방울방울[뚝뚝] 떨어지다; 가득[넘칠 듯이] 지니고 있다
When something drips, drops of liquid fall from it.

elect[복습]
[ilékt]

v. 선출하다, 선거하다; 결정하다
When people elect someone, they choose that person to represent them, by voting for them.

comfort[복습]
[kʌ́mfərt]

n. 위로, 위안; 마음이 편안함, 안락; vt. 위로[위안]하다
Comfort is what you feel when worries or unhappiness stop.

confidence[복습]
[kʌ́nfədəns]

n. 자신(감), 확신; 신용, 신뢰
If you have confidence, you feel sure about your abilities, qualities, or ideas.

fumble[복습]
[fʌ́mbl]

vi. 만지작거리다, 손으로 더듬어 찾다; (말을) 더듬거리다
If you fumble for something or fumble with something, you try and reach for it or hold it in a clumsy way.

wing it

idiom 즉흥적으로 하다, 즉석에서 말하다
If you wing it, you do something without planning or preparing it first.

process[복습]
[práses]

v. (정보 · 데이터를) 처리하다; (식품을) 가공하다; n. 과정, 진행
When people process information, they put it through a system or into a computer in order to deal with it.

decode
[di:kóud]

v. 해독하다, 이해하다
If you decode a message that has been written or spoken in a code, you change it into ordinary language.

pressure[**]
[préʃər]

vt. 강요하다, 압력을 가하다; n. 압력, 압박
If you pressure someone to do something, you try forcefully to persuade them to do it.

spastic
[spǽstik]

a. 경련성의, 뇌성마비의; n. 경련 환자
Someone who is spastic is born with a disability which makes it difficult for them to control their muscles, especially in their arms and legs.

seizure
[síːʒər]

n. (병의) 발작; 잡기; 체포; 압수
If someone has a seizure, they have a sudden violent attack of an illness, especially one that affects their heart or brain.

vote[복습]
[vout]

v. 투표하다; n. 투표, 투표권
When you vote, you indicate your choice officially at a meeting or in an election.

stuffed[복습]
[stʌft]

a. 속을 채운; 배가 너무 부른 (stuffed animal n. 봉제 동물인형)
Stuffed animals are toys that are made of cloth filled with a soft material and which look like animals.

assignment[복습]
[əsáinmənt]

n. 숙제, 할당된 일, 임무
An assignment is a task or piece of work that you are given to do, especially as part of your job or studies.

erupt
[irʌ́pt]

v. 폭발하다, 분출하다
You say that someone erupts when they suddenly have a change in mood, usually becoming quite noisy.

press on

phrasal v. 밀고 나아가다, 자꾸 추진하다
To press on means to continue to do a task in a determined way.

weigh[**]
[wei]

v. 무게가 ~이다, 무게를 달다; 심사숙고하다, 고찰하다
If someone or something weighs a particular amount, this amount is how heavy they are.

72

make sense^{복습}

idiom 뜻이 통하다, 도리에 맞다
If something makes sense, it has a meaning that you can easily understand.

crooked
[krúkid]

a. 비뚤어진, 구부러진; 부정직한
If you describe something as crooked, especially something that is usually straight, you mean that it is bent or twisted.

correct^{복습}
[kərékt]

v. 정정하다, 고치다; 나무라다, 벌주다; a. 옳은
If you correct someone, you say something which you think is more accurate or appropriate than what they have just said.

breeze[*]
[bri:z]

v. 거침없이[경쾌하게] 걷다; n. 산들바람, 미풍
If you breeze into a place or a position, you enter it in a very casual or relaxed manner.

wad
[wad]

n. 뭉치, 다발; 다수, 많음
A wad of something such as paper or cloth is a tight bundle or ball of it.

practically[*]
[prǽktikəli]

ad. 거의, ~이나 마찬가지; 실지로, 실질상
Practically means almost, but not completely or exactly.

clown[*]
[klaun]

n. 쓸모없는 사람; 어릿광대, 익살꾼; v. 익살부리다, 어릿광대짓을 하다
If you describe someone as a clown, you disapprove of them and have no respect for them.

joker^{복습}
[dʒóukər]

n. 멍청한[골치 아픈] 사람; 우스갯소리를 잘하는 사람; 조커
You can call someone a joker if you think they are behaving in a stupid or dangerous way.

string along

phrasal v. (~을) 속이다
To string someone along means to allow them to believe something that is not true for a long time, especially when you encourage them to have false hopes.

1분에 몇 단어를 읽는지 리딩 속도를 측정해보세요.

$$\frac{1{,}500 \text{ words}}{\text{reading time } (\quad) \text{ sec}} \times 60 = (\quad) \text{ WPM}$$

Build Your Vocabulary

journey**
[dʒə́:rni]

n. 여정, 여행
When you make a journey, you travel from one place to another.

equip*
[ikwíp]

vt. 갖추다, 장비하다
If you equip a person or thing with something, you give them the tools or equipment that are needed.

refrigerator*
[rifrídʒərèitə:r]

n. 냉장고
A refrigerator is a large container which is kept cool inside, usually by electricity, so that the food and drink in it stays fresh.

microwave
[máikrouwèiv]

n. 전자레인지; v. 전자레인지로 조리하다
A microwave or a microwave oven is an oven which cooks food very quickly by electromagnetic radiation rather than by heat.

makeup*
[méikʌp]

n. 화장, 분장; 조립, 구성
Makeup consists of things such as lipstick, eye shadow, and powder which some women put on their faces to make themselves look more attractive or which actors use to change or improve their appearance.

freak^{복습}
[fri:k]

v. 기겁하(게 하)다; n. 열광자, 괴짜; 희한한 것
If someone freaks out or if something freaks them out, they react very strongly to something that shocks, angers, excites or frightens them.

goings-on
[góuiŋz-án]

n. (비난받을 만한) 행위, 일, 짓
If you describe events or activities as goings-on, you mean that they are strange, interesting, amusing, or dishonest.

sip*
[sip]

n. 한 모금; vt. (음료를) 홀짝거리다, 조금씩 마시다
A sip is a small amount of drink that you take into your mouth.

bald^{복습}
[bɔ:ld]

a. (머리 등이) 벗어진, 대머리의; vi. 머리가 벗어지다
Someone who is bald has little or no hair on the top of their head.

goatee
[goutí:]

n. (사람의 턱에 난) 염소 수염
A goatee is a very short pointed beard that covers a man's chin but not his cheeks.

bass*
[beis]

n. 베이스, 저음; a. 베이스의
In popular music, a bass is a bass guitar or a double bass.

shave^{복습}
[ʃeiv]

v. 면도하다, 깎다, 밀다; n. 면도
When a man shaves, he removes the hair from his face using a razor or shaver so that his face is smooth.

bunch *
[bʌntʃ]

n. 떼, 한패; 다발, 송이; 다량
A bunch of people is a group of people who share one or more characteristics or who are doing something together.

monotonous *
[mənátənəs]

a. 단조로운, 지루한
Sommething that is monotonous is very boring because it has a regular, repeated pattern which never changes.

dare *
[dɛər]

v. 감히 ~하다, 무릅쓰다, 도전하다
If you dare to do something, you do something which requires a lot of courage.

sacrilege
[sǽkrəlidʒ]

n. 모독 (행위); 신성 모독
You can use sacrilege to refer to disrespect that is shown for someone who is widely admired or for a belief that is widely accepted.

pretend 복습
[priténd]

v. 가장하다, ~인 체하다; a. 가짜의
If you pretend that something is the case, you act in a way that is intended to make people believe that it is the case, although in fact it is not.

cigarette *
[sìɡərét]

n. 담배
Cigarettes are small tubes of paper containing tobacco which people smoke.

smoke **
[smouk]

n. 연기, 매연; 흡연; vi. 연기를 내뿜다; 담배를 피우다
Smoke consists of gas and small bits of solid material that are sent into the air when something burns.

bother 복습
[báðər]

vt. 귀찮게 하다, 괴롭히다, 폐 끼치다
If something bothers you, or if you bother about it, it worries, annoys, or upsets you.

spoil **
[spɔil]

v. 버릇없이 만들다, 응석을 받아주다; 망치다 (spoiled a. 버릇없이 자란)
If you spoil children, you give them everything they want or ask for.

mention ***
[ménʃən]

vt. 말하다, 언급하다; n. 언급, 진술
If you mention something, you say something about it, usually briefly.

giggle 복습
[gigl]

vi. 낄낄 웃다; n. 낄낄 웃음
If someone giggles, they laugh in a childlike way, because they are amused, nervous, or embarrassed.

stick 복습
[stik]

① v. (stuck–stuck) 달라붙다, 붙이다; 내밀다; 고수하다 ② n. 막대기, 지팡이
If one thing sticks to another, it becomes attached to it and is difficult to remove.

couch 복습
[kautʃ]

n. 소파, 긴 의자
A couch is a long, comfortable seat for two or three people.

angle 복습
[ǽŋgl]

n. 각도, 관점; 귀퉁이; vt. (어떤 각도로) 기울이다, 굽다, 움직이다
(at an angle idiom 어떤 각도로, 비스듬이)
If something is at an angle, it is leaning in a particular direction so that it is not straight, horizontal, or vertical.

stumble *
[stʌmbl]

vi. 비틀거리며 걷다, 발부리가 걸리다; n. 비틀거림
If you stumble, you put your foot down awkwardly while you are walking or running and nearly fall over.

get to one's feet

idiom 벌떡 일어서다
If you get or rise to your feet, you stand up.

rack* [ræk]

n. 선반, 걸이; vt. 괴롭히다
A rack is a frame or shelf, usually with bars or hooks, that is used for holding things or for hanging things on.

hesitate* [hézətèit]

v. 주저하다, 머뭇거리다, 망설이다
If you hesitate, you do not speak or act for a short time, usually because you are uncertain, embarrassed, or worried about what you are going to say or do.

rock* [rak]

① v. 음악을 멋지게 연주하다, 로큰롤로 노래하다; 흔들(리)다, 진동하다; 동요하다
② n. 바위, 암석
If you say someone rocks, you mean they are very good, impressive, or effective.

fumble복습 [fʌmbl]

vi. 손으로 더듬어 찾다, 만지작거리다; (말을) 더듬거리다
If you fumble for something or fumble with something, you try and reach for it or hold it in a clumsy way.

raw* [rɔː]

a. 가공하지 않은, 원재료의; 날것의
Raw materials or substances are in their natural state before being processed or used in manufacturing.

drink to

idiom ~을 위해 건배하다
If you drink to something, you wish it good luck, success or happiness, by raising your glass and then drinking.

clink [kliŋk]

v. 쨍그랑[짤랑] 하는 소리를 내다; n. (유리 등의) 땡그랑 소리
If objects made of glass, pottery, or metal clink or if you clink them, they touch each other and make a short, light sound.

blank* [blæŋk]

a. 공백의, 공허한; 멍한, 얼빠진; n. 공백 (blank space n. 여백)
Something that is blank has nothing on it.

take up

phrasal v. (시간 · 공간을) 차지하다
To take up space or time means to occupy or fill it.

worth복습 [wɔːrθ]

a. 가치가 있는; n. 가치, 값어치
If you say that something is worth having, you mean that it is pleasant or useful, and therefore a good thing to have.

right off

idiom 곧, 즉각
If something occurs right off, it happens immediately or right away.

raspy [ráspi]

a. 거친, 목이 쉰 듯한, 쇳소리의
If someone has a raspy voice, they make rough sounds as if they have a sore throat or have difficulty in breathing.

drip복습 [drip]

v. 가득[넘칠 듯이] 지니고 있다; 방울방울[뚝뚝] 떨어지다
If you say that something is dripping with a particular thing, you mean that it contains a lot of that thing.

polish* [páliʃ]

v. 다듬다, 세련되게 하다; 닦다, 윤내다; n. 광택; 세련 (polished a. (기교 등이) 세련된)
If you polish your technique, performance, or skill at doing something, you work on improving it.

note ^{복습}
[nout]

n. (악기의) 음; (짧은) 기록; 짧은 편지; v. 주목하다, 알아채다; 메모하다
In music, a note is the sound of a particular pitch, or a written symbol representing this sound.

orchestrate
[ɔ́:rkəstrèit]

v. 조정하다, 편성하다; 관현악용으로 편곡하다
If you say that someone orchestrates an event or situation, you mean that they carefully organize it in a way that will produce the result that they want.

allow^{***}
[əláu]

v. 허락하다, ~하게 두다; 인정하다
If someone is allowed to do something, it is all right for them to do it and they will not get into trouble.

protect ^{복습}
[prətékt]

v. 보호하다, 막다, 지키다
To protect someone or something means to prevent them from being harmed or damaged.

be better off ^{복습}

idiom (~하는 것이) 더 낫다
Be better off is used to say that someone would be happier or more satisfied if they were in a particular position or did a particular thing.

watchful
[wɑ́ʧfəl]

a. (위험·사고 등이 생기지 않도록) 지켜보는[신경 쓰는]
Someone who is watchful notices everything that is happening.

might as well ^{복습}

idiom ~하는 것이 좋겠다
Might as well is used for saying that you will do something because it seems best in the situation that you are in, although you may not really want to do it.

charge ^{복습}
[ʧa:rdʒ]

n. 책임, 의무; 수수료, 요금; v. (지불을) 청구하다; 부담 지우다, 맡기다; 돌격하다
(in charge of idiom ~을 관리하는, 담당하는)
A charge is an amount of money that you have to pay for a service.

coordinate[*]
[kouɔ́:rdənət]

v. 조정하다, 조직하다; 대등하게 하다; a. 동등한
If you coordinate something, you organize or integrate it in a harmonious operation.

arrange^{**}
[əréindʒ]

v. 준비하다, 계획을 짜다; 가지런히 하다, 배열하다 (arrangement n. 준비, 계획)
If you arrange an event or meeting, you make plans for it to happen.

pillow ^{복습}
[pílou]

n. 베개; 머리 받침대
A pillow is a rectangular cushion which you rest your head on when you are in bed.

personal ^{복습}
[pə́rsənl]

a. 자신이 직접 하는; 개인의, 사사로운 (personally ad. 몸소, 개인적으로)
If you give something your personal care or attention, you deal with it yourself rather than letting someone else deal with it.

laundry ^{복습}
[lɔ́:ndri]

n. 세탁물; 세탁소
Laundry is used to refer to clothes, sheets, and towels that are about to be washed, are being washed, or have just been washed.

have one's act together

idiom 일을 척척 해내다, 정신 차리다
If you have your act together, you manage to organize or control something better than you have done before.

betray[*]
[bitréi]

vt. 배반하다; 누설하다, 드러내다
If you betray someone who loves or trusts you, your actions hurt and disappoint them.

gross[*]
[grous]

a. 역겨운, 기분 나쁜; 큰, 비대한; 전체의
If you describe something as gross, you think it is very unpleasant.

spree
[spri:]

vi. 흥청대다; n. 흥청망청 떠들고 놀기 (shopping spree n. 물건을 마구 사들이기)
If you spend a period of time doing something in an excessive way, you can say that you are going on a particular kind of spree.

gaudy
[gɔ́:di]

a. 화려한, 지나치게 장식한
If something is gaudy, it is very brightly-colored and showy.

ridiculous^{**}
[ridíkjuləs]

a. 웃기는, 우스꽝스러운; 터무니없는
If you say that something or someone is ridiculous, you mean that they are very foolish.

taste^{***}
[teist]

n. 취향, 기호; 맛, 미각; v. 맛보다, 맛이 나다
A person's taste is their choice in the things that they like or buy, for example their clothes, possessions, or music.

cheat^{복습}
[tʃi:t]

v. 바람을 피우다; 속이다, 속임수 쓰다; 규칙을 어기다; n. 사기, 부정 행위
If you cheat on someone, you secretly have a relationship with him or her who is not your regular partner.

divorce[*]
[divɔ́:rs]

v. 이혼하다; n. 이혼, 별거
If a man and woman divorce or if one of them divorces the other, their marriage is legally ended.

blues
[blu:z]

n. [음악] 블루스; 우울, 울적
The blues is a type of folk song devised by African Americans.

suffer^{***}
[sʌ́fər]

v. 괴로워하다, 고통 받다; 겪다, 당하다 (suffering n. 괴로움)
If you suffer, you are badly affected by an event or situation.

tender[*]
[téndər]

a. 부드러운, 상냥한, 다정한 (tenderness n. 부드러움)
Someone or something that is tender expresses gentle and caring feelings.

overdose
[óuvərdòus]

n. 과다 복용[투여]; vt. 너무 많이 투여하다
If someone takes an overdose of a drug, they take more of it than is safe.

kid^{**}
[kid]

v. 놀리다, 장난치다; 속이다; n. 어린이
If you are kidding, you are saying something that is not really true, as a joke.

shrug^{복습}
[ʃrʌg]

v. (어깨를) 으쓱하다; n. (양 손바닥을 내보이면서 어깨를) 으쓱하기
If you shrug, you raise your shoulders to show that you are not interested in something or that you do not know or care about something.

luggage^{**}
[lʌ́gidʒ]

n. 여행 가방, (여행자의) 수하물
Luggage is the suitcases and bags that you take with you when travel.

betrayal
[bitréiəl]

n. 배신; 밀고, 내통
A betrayal is an action which hurts and disappoints someone.

efficient*
[ifíʃənt]

a. 유능한, 실력 있는; 능률적인, 효과가 있는
If something or someone is efficient, they are able to do tasks successfully, without wasting time or energy.

compact*
[kəmpǽk]

a. (체격이) 옹골찬; 소형의; 빽빽한, 꽉 찬; v. 압축하다, 꽉 채우다
A compact person is small but strong.

register*
[rédʒistər]

vt. 기재하다, 등록하다; n. 기록, 등록(부)
If you register to do something, you put your name on an official list, in order to be able to do that thing or to receive a service.

assume**
[əsjúːm]

vt. 가장하다, 꾸미다; 추정하다, 가정하다; (역할 · 임무 등을) 맡다
(assumed name n. 가명)
If you assume something, you pretend it.

hassle
[hǽsl]

v. 괴롭히다, 들볶다; 말다툼하다; n. 소란, 소동; 말다툼
If someone hassles you, they cause problems for you, often by repeatedly telling you or asking you to do something, in an annoying way.

stump*
[stʌmp]

v. (너무 어려운 질문으로) 당황하게 하다; 쿵쿵거리며 걷다; n. (나무의) 그루터기
If you are stumped by a question or problem, you cannot think of any solution or answer to it.

1. What sounded suspicious to Armpit about Murdock?
   A. His name
   B. His working hours
   C. His job site
   D. His interest in Kaira

2. Why did Murdock want to buy the tickets?
   A. He wanted to buy them for his daughter.
   B. He wanted to buy them for his wife.
   C. He wanted to buy them for himself and his friend.
   D. He wanted to buy them for a loyal customer.

3. What did Murdock offer the boys after he paid?
   A. He offered them food and drinks.
   B. He offered them a job doing delivery for him.
   C. He offered X-Ray a date with his daughter.
   D. He offered them a free meal if they would advertise for him.

4. Who won the ruler-of-the-world speech and why?
   A. Coo won because everyone sympathized with it.
   B. Joe the Armadillo won because people remembered the last speech.
   C. Dumbo won because everyone loved the movie.
   D. Nobody one because nobody cared.

5. What did Armpit ask Tatiana?

   A. He asked her if she wanted a ride home.

   B. He asked her to help him make his next speech better.

   C. He asked her to come with him to the Kaira concert.

   D. He asked her if she could get her friends to vote again for Coo.

6. Why did Armpit rush to call X-Ray after class?

   A. He wanted X-Ray to raise the price of the tickets.

   B. He needed to get an urgent ride to work.

   C. He needed the Kaira concert tickets and was afraid they were already sold.

   D. He wanted to warn X-Ray about the police investigating ticket sellers.

7. How much did X-Ray charge Armpit for the tickets?

   A. He charged him fifteen hundred.

   B. He didn't charge Armpit at all.

   C. He charged him a hundred and thirty-five.

   D. He charged him two hundred and seventy.

1분에 몇 단어를 읽는지 리딩 속도를 측정해보세요.

$$\frac{1,154 \text{ words}}{\text{reading time (} \quad \text{) sec}} \times 60 = (\quad) \text{ WPM}$$

Build Your Vocabulary

congress*
[káŋgres]

n. 국회, 의회; 회의, 학회; vi. 모이다, 회합하다
Congress is the elected group of politicians that is responsible for making the law in the United States.

in search of

idiom ~을 찾아서; ~을 추구하여
If you go in search of something or someone, you try to find them.

joint**
[dʒɔint]

n. (값싼) 음식점; 관절; a. 공동의, 합동의
You can refer to a cheap place where people go for some form of entertainment as a joint.

territory*
[térətɔːri]

n. 영토, 영지, 영역
Territory is land which is controlled by a particular country or ruler.

suspicious*복습
[səspíʃəs]

a. 수상쩍은, 의심하는
If you are suspicious of someone or something, you do not trust them, and are careful when dealing with them.

remind*복습
[rimáind]

vt. 생각나게 하다, 상기시키다, 일깨우다
If someone reminds you of a fact or event that you already know about, they say something which makes you think about it.

assure*복습
[əʃúəːr]

vt. 단언하다, 보증하다
If you assure someone that something is true or will happen, you tell them that it is definitely true or will definitely happen, often in order to make them less worried.

majestic
[mədʒéstik]

a. 위엄 있는, 장엄한
If you describe something or someone as majestic, you think they are very beautiful, dignified, and impressive.

dome*
[doum]

n. 돔, (반구 모양의) 둥근 지붕[천장]
A dome is a round roof.

column*
[káləm]

n. (연기 등의) 기둥; (신문의) 기고란
A column is something that has a tall narrow shape.

financial**
[fainǽnʃəl]

a. 금융의, 재정(상)의, 재무의
Financial means relating to or involving money.

district**
[dístrikt]

n. 구역, 지역
A district is a particular area of a town or country.

colony* [kάləni]	n. (동일 지역에 서식하는 동 · 식물의) 군집; 식민지 A colony of birds, insects, or animals is a group of them that live together.
crack^{복습} [kræk]	n. 갈라진 틈[금]; 갑작스런 날카로운 소리; v. 금이 가다, 깨다, 부수다 A crack is a very narrow gap between two things, or between two parts of a thing.
crevice [krévis]	n. 갈라진 틈, 균열 A crevice is a narrow crack or gap, especially in a rock.
fancy** [fǽnsi]	a. 화려한, 고급스러운; v. 공상하다; 좋아하다; n. 공상; 기호, 선호 If you describe something as fancy, you mean that it is very expensive or of very high quality.
bank** [bæŋk]	① n. 둑, 제방; v. 둑으로 둘러싸다 ② n. 은행; v. 은행에 예금하나 The banks of a river, canal, or lake are the raised areas of ground along its edge.
sundown [sΛndàun]	n. 일몰, 해질 때 Sundown is the time when the sun sets.
swarm* [swɔːrm]	v. 떼 지어 움직이다[날다]; 가득 차다; n. 무리, 떼 When bees or other insects swarm, they move or fly in a large group.
mosquito^{복습} [məskíːtou]	n. 모기 Mosquitos are small flying insects which bite people and animals in order to suck their blood.
population** [pàpjuléiʃən]	n. 인구; 무리, 집단; 주민 If you refer to a particular type of population in a country or area, you are referring to all the people or animals of that type there.
keep under control	idiom ~을 계속 제어하다 If you keep something under control, you succeed in dealing with it so that it does not cause any harm.
resemble* [rizémbl]	vt. ~을 닮다, ~와 공통점이 있다 If one thing or person resembles another, they are similar to each other.
board*** [bɔːrd]	v. 판자로 둘러막다; (배 · 비행기 등에) 타다; n. 판자, 널빤지; 게시판, 칠판 To board something up means to cover a window or a door with boards.
liquor* [líkər]	n. (모든 종류의) 술; 독한 술 Strong alcoholic drinks such as whisky, vodka, and gin can be referred to as liquor.
tattoo [tætúː]	n. 문신; v. 문신을 새기다 A tattoo is a design that is drawn on someone's skin using needles to make little holes and filling them with colored dye.
parlor* [pάːrlər]	n. 가게, 영업실; 거실, 응접실 Parlor is used in the names of some types of shops which provide a service, rather than selling things.

glare^{복습}
[glɛər]

n. 번쩍이는 빛; 노려봄; v. 번쩍번쩍 빛나다; 노려보다
Glare is very bright light that is difficult to look at.

entire^{복습}
[intàiər]

a. 전체의; 완전한
You use entire when you want to emphasize that you are referring to the whole of something, for example, the whole of a place, time, or population.

suffer^{복습}
[sʌ́fər]

v. 괴로워하다, 고통 받다; 겪다, 당하다
If you suffer from an illness or from some other bad condition, you are badly affected by it.

hangover
[hǽŋóuvər]

n. 숙취
If someone wakes up with a hangover, they feel sick and have a headache because they have drunk a lot of alcohol the night before.

smoke^{복습}
[smouk]

n. 연기, 매연; 흡연; vi. 연기를 내뿜다; 담배를 피우다 (smoky a. 연기 나는)
Smoke consists of gas and small bits of solid material that are sent into the air when something burns.

storefront
[stɔ́:rfrʌnt]

n. 가게[점포] 앞에 딸린 공간(이 있는 가게)
A storefront is a small shop or office that opens onto the street and is part of a row of shops or offices.

locate*
[lóukeit]

v. ~에 위치하다, 놓다, 두다; ~의 위치를 결정하다
If you locate something in a particular place, you put it there or build it there.

emporium
[impɔ́:riəm]

n. 큰 상점, 대형 슈퍼마켓
An emporium is a store or large shop.

chop^{복습}
[tʃɑp]

vt. 잘게 썰다, 자르다; n. 잘라낸 조각; 절단, 자르기
If you chop something, you cut it into pieces with strong downward movements of a knife or an axe.

jangle
[dʒǽŋgl]

v. 쨍그렁[땡그랑]거리다
When objects strike against each other and make an unpleasant ringing noise, you can say that they jangle or are jangled.

occupy^{복습}
[ɑ́kjupài]

vt. 차지하다, 점령하다, 거주하다; 주의를 끌다
If a room or something such as a seat is occupied, someone is using it, so that it is not available for anyone else.

various*
[vέəriəs]

a. 여러 가지의, 다양한; 많은
If you say that there are various things, you mean there are several different things of the type mentioned.

display*
[displéi]

n. 진열(품), 전시; 표시; v. 보이다, 나타내다, 진열(전시)하다
(be on disply idiom 진열되어 있다)
A display is an arrangement of things that have been put in a particular place, so that people can see them easily.

beard^{복습}
[biərd]

n. 턱수염
A man's beard is the hair that grows on his chin and cheeks.

apron[*]
[éiprən]

n. 앞치마
An apron is a piece of clothing that you put on over the front of your normal clothes and tie round your waist, especially when you are cooking.

splatter
[splǽtə:r]

v. 튀다, 튀기다; **n.** 튀기기; 철벅철벅 소리
If a thick wet substance splatters on something or is splattered on it, it drops or is thrown over it.

grease[*]
[gri:s]

n. 기름, 지방분; **vt.** ~에 기름을 바르다[치다]
Grease is animal fat that is produced by cooking meat.

dude[복습]
[dju:d]

n. 사내, 녀석; (구어) 형씨, 친구
A dude is a man.

instrument[**]
[ínstrəmənt]

n. 악기; 기구, 도구
A musical instrument is an object such as a piano, guitar, or flute, which you play in order to produce music.

scorpion[복습]
[skɔ́:rpiən]

n. 전갈
A scorpion is a small creature which looks like a large insect. Scorpions have a long curved tail, and some of them are poisonous.

row[복습]
[rou]

① **n.** 열, (좌석) 줄 ② **vi.** (노를 써서) 배를 젓다; (배가) 저어지다
A row of things or people is a number of them arranged in a line.

bargain[**]
[bá:rgən]

n. 싼 물건, 특가품, 특매품; 매매 계약, 거래; **v.** 흥정하다, 거래하다
Something that is a bargain is good value for money, usually because it has been sold at a lower price than normal.

make the most of

idiom ~을 최대한 활용하다, ~에서 최선의 것을 얻다
If you make the most of something, you get as much good as you can out of it.

knock one's socks off

idiom (구어) ~에게 큰 영향을 미치다, 타격을 주다
If you knock someone's socks off, you impress or amaze them greatly.

appreciate[복습]
[əprí:ʃieit]

vt. 고맙게 생각하다; 진가를 알아보다, 인정하다
If you appreciate something that someone has done for you or is going to do for you, you are grateful for it.

you name it

idiom 그 밖에 뭐든지, 전부
You say you name it, usually after or before a list, to indicate that you are talking about a very wide range of things.

fumble[복습]
[fʌmbl]

vi. 만지작거리다, 손으로 더듬어 찾다; (말을) 더듬거리다
If you fumble for something or fumble with something, you try and reach for it or hold it in a clumsy way.

on the house

idiom (술집이나 식당에서) 무료로 제공되는
Something is on the house, like alcoholic drinks, is a thing which is given to a customer free by the hotel, restaurant, or bar.

mild[*]
[maild]

a. (정도가) 심하지 않은; 유순한, 부드러운; 온화한
You describe food as mild when it does not taste or smell strong, sharp, or bitter, especially when you like it because of this.

apt[*]
[æpt]

a. ~하기 쉬운, ~하는 경향이 있는
If someone is apt to do something, they often do it and so it is likely that they will do it again.

settle down

phrasal v. 정착하다, 자리잡다; 진정하다
If you settle down, you start to have a calmer or quieter way of life, without many changes, especially living in one place.

get around

phrasal v. (여기저기 · 이 사람 저 사람에게로) 돌아다니다
If you get around, you move from place to place or to go to lots of different places.

register[복습]
[rédʒistər]

n. 기록, 등록(부); vt. 기재하다, 등록하다 (cash register n. 금전 등록기)
A cash register is a machine in a shop, pub, or restaurant that is used to add up and record how much money people pay, and in which the money is kept.

bucket[복습]
[bʌ́kit]

n. 버킷, 양동이
A bucket is a round metal or plastic container with a handle attached to its sides.

shrug[복습]
[ʃrʌg]

v. (어깨를) 으쓱하다; n. (양 손바닥을 내보이면서 어깨를) 으쓱하기
If you shrug, you raise your shoulders to show that you are not interested in something or that you do not know or care about something.

sheepish
[ʃíːpiʃ]

a. 매우 수줍어하는, 부끄러워하는 (sheepishly ad. 소심하게)
If you look sheepish, you look slightly embarrassed because you feel foolish or you have done something silly.

have something to do with[복습]

idiom ~와 관계가 있다
To have something to do with another thing means to be connected or concerned with it.

86

1분에 몇 단어를 읽는지 리딩 속도를 측정해보세요.

$$\frac{830 \text{ words}}{\text{reading time ( ) sec}} \times 60 = (\quad) \text{ WPM}$$

Build Your Vocabulary

make fun of

idiom ~을 놀리다, 웃음거리로 만들다
If you make fun of someone, you make unkind remarks or jokes about them.

end up

phrasal v. 마침내는 (~으로) 되다; 끝나다
If you end up doing something or end up in a particular state, you do that thing or get into that state even though you did not originally intend to.

feather*
[féðər]

n. 깃털, 깃
A bird's feathers are the soft covering on its body.

whisper복습
[hwíspə:r]

v. 속삭이다, 작은 소리로 말하다; n. 속삭임
When you whisper, you say something very quietly.

vote복습
[vout]

v. 투표하다; n. 투표, 투표권
When you vote, you indicate your choice officially at a meeting or in an election.

obvious**
[ábviəs]

a. 명백한, 분명한 (obviously ad. 명백히)
If something is obvious, it is easy to see or understand.

shell**
[ʃel]

n. 껍데기; 조가비; v. 껍데기를 벗기다
The shell of an animal such as a tortoise, snail, or crab is the hard protective covering that it has around its body or on its back.

elect복습
[ilékt]

v. 선거하다, 선출하다; 결정하다
When people elect someone, they choose that person to represent them, by voting for them.

vice
[vais]

a. 부(副)의, 차석의
Vice is used before a rank or title to indicate that someone is next in importance to the person who holds the rank or title mentioned.

fulfill*
[fulfíl]

vt. (의무 · 명령을) 이행하다, 다하다; 이루다, 달성하다
To fulfill a task, role, or requirement means to do or be what is required, necessary, or expected.

obligation*
[àbləgéiʃən]

n. 의무, 책무; 은혜, 의리
If you have an obligation to do something, it is your duty to do that thing.

take over

phrasal v. (~로부터) (~을) 인계받다, (기업 등을) 인수하다
If you take over something from someone, you do it instead of them.

assignment^{복습}
[əsáinmənt]

n. 숙제, 할당된 일, 임무
An assignment is a task or piece of work that you are given to do, especially as part of your job or studies.

biggie
[bígi]

n. 중요한 것[사람 · 행사]
People sometimes refer to something or someone successful, well-known, or big as a biggie.

perfume[*]
[pə́:rfju:m]

n. 향수, 향기
Perfume is a pleasant-smelling liquid which women put on their skin to make themselves smell nice.

squeeze[*]
[skwi:z]

vt. 꽉 쥐다[죄다]; 짜다, 압착하다; 밀어 넣다, 쑤셔 넣다; n. 압착, 짜냄
If you squeeze something, you press it firmly, usually with your hands.

alert^{복습}
[ələ́:rt]

n. 경보, 경계; a. 방심하지 않는; v. 경고하다
An alert is a situation in which people prepare themselves for something dangerous that might happen soon.

economic^{복습}
[èkənámik]

a. 경제(상)의, 경제적인; 경제학의 (economics n. 경제학)
Economic means concerned with the organization of the money, industry, and trade of a country, region, or society.

convince[*]
[kənvíns]

vt. 확신시키다, 납득시키다; 설득하다
If someone or something convinces you of something, they make you believe that it is true or that it exists.

scalper^{복습}
[skǽlpər]

n. 암표상
A scalper is someone who sells tickets outside a sports ground or theater, usually for more than their original value.

bolt[*]
[boult]

v. 뛰어 나가다; 빗장을 걸다; n. 급히 뛰쳐 나가기; 볼트, 나사못
If a person or animal bolts, they suddenly start to run very fast, often because something has frightened them.

secretary[*]
[sékrətèri]

n. 비서, 서기; 사무관, 서기관
A secretary is a person who is employed to do office work, such as typing letters, answering phone calls, and arranging meetings.

sympathetic[*]
[simpəθétik]

a. 동정심 있는; 공감하는
If you are sympathetic to someone who is in a bad situation, you are kind to them and show that you understand their feelings.

policy[*]
[páləsi]

n. 정책, 방침
A policy is a set of ideas or plans that is used as a basis for making decisions, especially in politics, economics, or business.

apparent^{복습}
[əpǽrənt]

a. 또렷한, 명백한, 외관상의 (apparently ad. 명백하게, 보아하니)
If something is apparent to you, it is clear and obvious to you.

principal[*]
[prínsəpəl]

n. 교장, 장(長); a. 주요한, 주된
The principal of a school, or the principal of a college, is the person in charge of the school or college.

superintendent
[sù:pərinténdənt]

n. 경찰서장; 감독자, 관리자
A superintendent is the head of a police department.

88

spot ^{복습}
[spat]

vt. 발견하다, 분별하다; n. 장소, 지점; 반점, 얼룩
If you spot something or someone, you notice them.

skinny ^{복습}
[skíni]

a. 바싹 여윈, 깡마른
A skinny person is extremely thin, often in a way that you find unattractive.

charge ^{복습}
[ʧɑːrdʒ]

v. 돌격하다; (지불을) 청구하다; 부담 지우다, 맡기다; n. 수수료, 요금; 책임, 의무
If you charge toward someone or something, you move quickly and aggressively toward them.

desperate**
[désparat]

a. 필사적인; 자포자기의, 절망적인
If you are desperate for something or desperate to do something, you want or need it very much indeed.

locker
[lάkər]

n. 자물쇠 있는 사물함
A locker is a small metal or wooden cupboard with a lock, where you can put your personal possessions, for example in a school, place of work, or sports club.

sidestep
[sάidstep]

vi. 옆으로 한 발짝 비키다
If you sidestep, you step sideway in order to avoid something or someone that is coming toward you or going to hit you.

soothe*
[suːð]

vt. 진정시키다, 달래다, 누그러뜨리다 (soothing a. 달래는, 위로하는)
If you soothe someone who is angry or upset, you make them feel calmer.

goofy ^{복습}
[gúːfi]

a. 바보 같은, 얼빠진
If you describe someone or something as goofy, you think they are rather silly or ridiculous.

share**
[ʃɛ̀ər]

n. 몫, 분담; vt. 분배하다, 공유하다
If you have or do your share of something, you have or do an amount that seems reasonable to you, or to other people.

bargain ^{복습}
[bάːrgən]

n. 싼 물건, 특가품, 특매품; 매매 계약, 거래; v. 흥정하다, 거래하다
Something that is a bargain is good value for money, usually because it has been sold at a lower price than normal.

relieve*
[rilíːv]

vt. (걱정·고통 등을) 덜다, 안도하게 하다, 완화하다 (relieved a. 안도하는)
If you are relieved, you feel happy because something unpleasant has not happened or is no longer happening.

get to someone

idiom ~에게 감명을 주다, 감동시키다
If you get to someone, you affect them, even though they try not to let it.

1. How did Ginny react to Armpit asking Tatiana to the concert?

   A. She was jealous that he didn't ask her instead.

   B. She thought that Tatiana was a perfect match for Armpit.

   C. She thought it was cute and teased Armpit about it.

   D. She thought that he actually liked Kaira more than Tatiana.

2. How did Tatiana's friends feel about Armpit?

   A. They admired and respected him.

   B. They were happy for Tatiana going on a date.

   C. They thought that he was a sweet guy.

   D. They thought that he was dangerous and had almost killed people.

3. Why was Ginny upset on the day of the concert?

   A. Ginny's father came back to visit her and said some mean things.

   B. Ginny's mother mentioned that Ginny's father left because of her disability.

   C. Ginny wanted to go to the Kaira concert but couldn't buy a ticket.

   D. Ginny had caught a cold and couldn't go to the concert.

4. Why did Tatiana say she could not go with Armpit to the concert?

   A. She had a family event.

   B. She had a dentist appointment.

   C. She thought she had caught the flu.

   D. She didn't want to spend time with Armpit.

5. What did Armpit do with the tickets after Tatiana could not go?

   A. He sold them back to X-Ray.

   B. He sold them to his parents.

   C. He offered to take Ginny to the concert.

   D. He offered to take X-Ray to the concert.

6. How did X-Ray react to Armpit wanting to take Ginny to the concert?

   A. He thought that is was a very kind and sweet thing to do.

   B. He thought that they should sell the tickets instead.

   C. He thought that Ginny might be hurt at a concert.

   D. He thought that Ginny had a crush on Armpit.

7. How did Armpit and Ginny go to the concert?

   A. Armpit borrowed Ginny's mother's car.

   B. Armpit borrowed X-Ray's car.

   C. X-Ray gave them a ride.

   D. They both took the city bus.

1분에 몇 단어를 읽는지 리딩 속도를 측정해보세요.

$$\frac{1,427 \text{ words}}{\text{reading time (} \quad \text{) sec}} \times 60 = (\quad \text{) WPM}$$

Build Your Vocabulary

block^{복습}
[blak]

n. (도시의) 블록, 한 구획; 덩어리; 방해물; vt. 막다, 방해하다
A block in a town is an area of land with streets on all its sides.

candidate[*]
[kǽndidèit]

n. 지원자, 후보자
A candidate is someone who is being considered for a position, for example someone who is running in an election or applying for a job.

ballot[*]
[bǽlət]

n. 투표용지, 투표; v. 투표하다
A ballot is a piece of paper on which you indicate your choice or opinion in a secret vote.

twitch
[twitʃ]

v. (손가락·근육 따위가) 씰룩거리다; 홱 잡아당기다, 잡아채다; n. 씰룩거림, 경련
If something, especially a part of your body, twitches or if you twitch it, it makes a little jumping movement.

due^{복습}
[dju:]

a. ~로 인한, ~ 때문에; ~하기로 되어 있는; n. ~에게 마땅히 주어져야 하는 것
If an event is due to something, it happens or exists as a direct result of that thing.

disability^{복습}
[dìsəbíləti]

n. 신체 장애; 무능력, 불능
A disability is a permanent injury, illness, or physical or mental condition that tends to restrict the way that someone can live their life.

stutter^{복습}
[stʌ́tər]

v. 말을 더듬다, 더듬거리며 말하다; n. 말더듬기
If someone stutters, they have difficulty speaking because they find it hard to say the first sound of a word.

creative[*]
[kriéitiv]

a. 창의적인, 독창적인 (creativity n. 창의성)
If you use something in a creative way, you use it in a new way that produces interesting and unusual results.

soul^{**}
[soul]

n. (음악·예술 등의) 혼, 기백; 영혼; 정신, 마음
Your soul is the part of you that consists of your mind, character, thoughts, and feelings.

seizure^{복습}
[síːʒər]

n. (병의) 발작; 잡기, 체포; 압수
If someone has a seizure, they have a sudden violent attack of an illness, especially one that affects their heart or brain.

bet^{**}
[bet]

v. 틀림없이 ~이다, 확신하다; (돈을) 걸다, 내기를 하다; n. 내기, 건 돈
You use expressions such as 'I bet' to indicate that you are sure something is true.

thoughtful*
[θɔ́:tfəl]

a. 사려 깊은, 친절한; 생각에 잠긴
If you describe someone as thoughtful, you approve of them because they remember what other people want, need, or feel, and try not to upset them.

caring
[kέəriŋ]

a. 배려하는, 보살피는
If someone is caring, they are affectionate, helpful, and sympathetic.

gape
[geip]

vi. (놀람·감탄으로) 입을 딱 벌리다; 크게 갈라지다; n. 갈라진 틈
If you gape, you look at someone or something in surprise, usually with an open mouth.

giggle^{복습}
[gigl]

vi. 낄낄 웃다; n. 낄낄 웃음
If someone giggles, they laugh in a childlike way, because they are amused, nervous, or embarrassed.

dreamy
[drí:mi]

a. 꿈꾸는 듯한, 꿈 많은
If you say that someone has a dreamy expression, you mean that they are not paying attention to things around them and look as if they are thinking about something pleasant.

tease*
[ti:z]

v. 놀리다, 괴롭히다; 졸라대다; n. 굶리기
To tease someone means to laugh at them or make jokes about them in order to embarrass, annoy, or upset them.

normal**
[nɔ́:rməl]

a. 보통의, 정상적인; n. 보통; 표준, 기준
Something that is normal is usual and ordinary, and is what people expect.

imperfection
[impərfékʃən]

n. 불완전, 결함, 결점
An imperfection in someone or something is a fault, weakness, or undesirable feature that they have.

reflect**
[riflékt]

v. 심사숙고하다, 깊이 생각하다; 반영하다, 나타내다; 비추다, 반사하다
(reflection n. (거울 등에 비친) 모습)
When you reflect on something, you think deeply about it.

quality**
[kwálɔti]

n. 특성, 특질; 품질, 질; a. 양질의, 고급의
Someone's qualities are the good characteristics that they have which are part of their nature.

perfume^{복습}
[pɔ́:rfju:m]

n. 향수, 향기
Perfume is a pleasant-smelling liquid which women put on their skin to make themselves smell nice.

soda*
[sóudə]

n. 탄산 음료, 소다수
Soda is a sweet drink that contain small bubbles of carbon dioxide.

knowing
[nóuiŋ]

a. 아는 체하는; 지식이 있는, 박식한 (knowingly ad. 다 알고 있다는 듯이)
A knowing gesture or remark is one that shows that you understand something, for example the way that someone is feeling or what they really mean, even though it has not been mentioned directly.

remind^{복습}
[rimáind]

vt. 생각나게 하다, 상기시키다, 일깨우다
If someone reminds you of a fact or event that you already know about, they say something which makes you think about it.

nasty* [nǽsti]
a. 추잡한, 더러운; 못된, 고약한
Something that is nasty is very unpleasant to see, experience, or feel.

sweaty^{복습} [swéti]
a. 땀이 나는, 땀투성이의
If parts of your body or your clothes are sweaty, they are soaked or covered with sweat.

stink [stiŋk]
vi. 악취가 나다, 냄새가 코를 찌르다; n. 냄새, 악취
To stink means to smell extremely unpleasant.

arena^{복습} [ərí:nə]
n. 경기장, 시합장
An arena is a place where sports, entertainments, and other public events take place.

jam** [dʒæm]
v. 밀어붙이다, 가득 차다; 쑤셔 넣다, 채워 넣다; n. 혼잡; 고장 (jammed a. 빽빽히 찬)
If a lot of people jam a place, or jam into a place, they are pressed tightly together so that they can hardly move.

in person
idiom 몸소, 직접
If you do something in person, you do it yourself rather than letting someone else do it.

splash^{복습} [splæʃ]
v. (물 · 흙탕물 등을) 끼얹다, 튀기다; n. 첨벙 하는 소리
If you splash a liquid somewhere or if it splashes, it hits someone or something and scatters in a lot of small drops.

catch up
idiom (움직이는 사람 · 물건을) 따라잡다, 접근하다; 뒤처진 것을 만회하다
If you catch up with someone, you reach them ahead of you by going faster than them.

maneuver* [mənú:vəːr]
v. 교묘히 이동하다[다루다]; n. 교묘한 조종; 책략, 술책
If you manoeuver something into or out of an awkward position, you skillfully move it there.

physical** [fízikəl]
a. 신체의, 육체의; 물리적인, 물질의
Physical qualities, actions, or things are connected with a person's body, rather than with their mind.

labor** [léibər]
n. 노동, 노력; v. 일하다, 노동하다
Labor is very hard work, usually physical work.

dump* [dʌmp]
vt. 아무렇게나 내려놓다; (쓰레기를) 버리다; n. 쓰레기 더미
If you dump something somewhere, you put it or unload it there quickly and carelessly.

truckload [trʌ́klòud]
n. 트럭 한 대분의 짐
A truckload of goods or people is the amount of them that a truck can carry.

dirt^{복습} [dəːrt]
n. 흙, 진흙, 먼지; 가십, 스캔들
You can refer to the earth on the ground as dirt, especially when it is dusty.

frazzle [fræzl]
vt. 지치게 하다; 닳아 떨어지게 하다 (frazzled a. 지친)
If something frazzles you, it make you exhausted or weary.

exclaim^{복습} [ikskléim]
v. 외치다, 소리치다
If you exclaim, you say or shout something suddenly because of surprise, fear and pleasure.

94

disable
[diséibl]

vt. 불구로 만들다, 무력하게 하다 (disabled a. 신체 장애가 있는)
Someone who is disabled has an illness, injury, or condition that tends to restrict the way that they can live their life, especially by making it difficult for them to move about.

be worse off

idiom 지내기가 어렵다, 형편이 나쁘다
If someone is worse off, they are poorer or unhappier than before or than someone else.

shrug^{복습}
[ʃrʌg]

v. (어깨를) 으쓱하다; n. (양 손바닥을 내보이면서 어깨를) 으쓱하기
If you shrug, you raise your shoulders to show that you are not interested in something or that you do not know or care about something.

therapy^{복습}
[θérəpi]

n. 치료, 요법
Therapy is the treatment of someone with mental or physical illness without the use of drugs or operations.

lean^{**}
[liːn]

① v. 상체를 굽히다, 기울다; 기대다, 의지하다 ② a. 야윈, 마른
When you lean in a particular direction, you bend your body in that direction.

mouthpiece
[máuθpiːs]

n. (전화기의) 송화구; (악기 등의) 입을 대는 부분
The mouthpiece of a telephone is the part that you speak into.

hang out

phrasal v. (~에서) 많은 시간을 보내다
If you hang out, you spend a lot of time in a place or with a person or a group of people.

privacy^{복습}
[práivəsi]

n. 사생활; 비밀, 은밀
If you have privacy, you are in a place or situation which allows you to do things without other people seeing you or disturbing you.

hang up

phrasal v. 전화를 끊다
To hang up means to end a telephone conversation, often very suddenly, by putting down the part of the telephone that you speak into or switching the telephone off.

dial^{복습}
[dáiəl]

v. 전화를 걸다, 다이얼을 돌리다; n. 다이얼
If you dial or if you dial a number, you turn the dial or press the buttons on a telephone in order to phone someone.

offer^{복습}
[ɔ́ːfər]

v. 제의[제안]하다; 제공하다; n. 제공
If you offer something to someone, you ask them if they would like to have it or use it.

widen^{복습}
[waidn]

v. 넓어지다; 넓히다
If you widen something or if it widens, it becomes greater in measurement from one side or edge to the other.

nod^{**}
[nad]

v. 끄덕이다, 끄덕여 표시하다; n. (동의 · 인사 · 신호 · 명령의) 끄덕임
If you nod, you move your head downward and upward to show agreement, understanding, or approval.

approval^{**}
[əprúːvəl]

n. 찬성, 동의; 승인
If you win someone's approval for something that you ask for or suggest, they agree to it.

Check Your Reading Speed

1분에 몇 단어를 읽는지 리딩 속도를 측정해보세요.

$$\frac{677 \text{ words}}{\text{reading time ( ) sec}} \times 60 = (\qquad) \text{ WPM}$$

Build Your Vocabulary

pierce**
[piərs]

v. 뚫다. 찌르다; 꿰뚫다. 통찰하다 (pierced a. 구멍을 뚫은)
If a sharp object pierces something, or if you pierce something with a sharp object, the object goes into it and makes a hole in it.

argue^{복습}
[áːrgjuː]

v. 논쟁하다; 주장하다
If one person argues with another, they speak angrily to each other about something that they disagree about.

tattoo^{복습}
[tætúː]

n. 문신; v. 문신을 새기다
A tattoo is a design that is drawn on someone's skin using needles to make little holes and filling them with colored dye.

tongue**
[tʌŋ]

n. 혀; 말, 이야기; 언어
Your tongue is the soft movable part inside your mouth which you use for tasting, eating, and speaking.

responsible**
[rispánsəbl]

a. 책임 있는, 책임을 져야 할
If you are responsible for something, it is your job or duty to deal with it and make decisions relating to it.

scene**
[siːn]

n. 장소, 현장; 장면, 무대; 경치
The scene of an event is the place where it happened.

intend***
[inténd]

v. ~할 작정이다; 의도하다, 꾀하다 (intention n. 의지, 의도)
If you intend to do something, you have decided or planned to do it.

protect^{복습}
[prətékt]

v. 보호하다, 막다, 지키다
To protect someone or something means to prevent them from being harmed or damaged.

line***
[lain]

n. (연결되어 있는 상태의) 전화; 선, 금; 열, 줄 (on the line idiom 전화선에)
A line is a connection which makes it possible for two people to speak to each other on the telephone.

out of one's gourd

idiom 머리가 돌아서, 미쳐서
Out of one's gourd means lose one's mind.

beat^{복습}
[biːt]

v. 능가하다, 더 낫다; 이기다, 패배시키다; 치다, 두드리다; n. 치기, 때리기; 박자
If someone beats a record or achievement, they do better than it.

sigh^{복습}
[sai]

v. 한숨 쉬다; n. 한숨, 탄식
When you sigh, you let out a deep breath, as a way of expressing feelings such as disappointment, tiredness, or pleasure.

96

cradle[*]
[kreidl]

n. (전화의) 수화기대; 요람, 유아용 침대; v. 떠받치다, 살짝 안다
The cradle is the part of a telephone on which the receiver rests while it is not being used.

handle[**]
[hændl]

v. 다루다, 처리하다; n. 손잡이, 핸들
If you say that someone can handle a problem or situation, you mean that they have the ability to deal with it successfully.

porch[복습]
[pɔːrtʃ]

n. (본 건물 입구에 달린 지붕이 있는) 현관, 포치
A porch is a sheltered area at the entrance to a building, which has a roof and sometimes has walls.

insist[**]
[insíst]

v. 우기다, 주장하다; 강요하다
If you insist that something is the case, you say so very firmly and refuse to say otherwise, even though other people do not believe you.

run out of

idiom ~을 다 써버리다, 동나다
If you runs out of something, you finish it or use it all up.

undoubted
[ʌndáutid]

a. 의심할 여지가 없는, 진정한 (undoubtedly ad. 의심할 여지 없이)
You can use undoubted to emphasize that something exists or is true.

reliable[*]
[riláiəbl]

a. 의지할 수 있는, 신뢰할 수 있는
People or things that are reliable can be trusted to work well or to behave in the way that you want them to.

catch off guard

idiom 허를 찌르다, 방심하게 하다
If someone is caught off guard, they are not expecting a surprise or danger that suddenly occurs.

passenger[복습]
[pǽsəndʒər]

n. 승객, 여객 (passenger side n. 조수석)
A passenger in a vehicle such as a bus, boat, or plane is a person who is traveling in it, but who is not driving it or working on it.

ignore[복습]
[ignɔ́ːr]

vt. 무시하다, 모르는 체하다
If you ignore someone or something, you pay no attention to them.

envelope[복습]
[énvəlòup]

n. 봉투, 봉지
An envelope is the rectangular paper cover in which you send a letter to someone through the post.

flexible[**]
[fléksəbl]

a. 융통성 있는, 유연한; 구부리기 쉬운
Something or someone that is flexible is able to change easily and adapt to different conditions and circumstances as they occur.

nonsense[**]
[nánsens]

n. 허튼소리, 무의미한 말; 터무니없는 것
If you say that something spoken or written is nonsense, you mean that you consider it to be untrue or silly.

dashboard
[dǽʃbɔːrd]

n. (자동차 등의) 계기판
The dashboard in a car is the panel facing the driver's seat where most of the instruments and switches are.

1. What did Armpit notice about Ginny when she sang?
   A. She blinked.
   B. She didn't breathe.
   C. She danced.
   D. She didn't stutter.

2. Why did the police officers push Armpit to the floor and handcuff him?
   A. They thought he was being forceful when they accused him of having counterfeit tickets.
   B. They wanted to protect him from the angry crowd around them.
   C. They thought that he had kidnapped Ginny and was a dangerous criminal.
   D. They thought that he was somebody else and made a mistake.

3. What did the police think of Ginny's seizure?
   A. They thought that she was just pretending to get attention.
   B. They had experience with seizures and knew how to handle it.
   C. They thought that she would hurt other people around her.
   D. They thought she was on drugs given to her by Armpit.

4. How did the mayor help Armpit and Ginny?

   A. She told the officers that Armpit worked for her and she would punish him herself.

   B. She called Ginny's mother to come take Ginny home.

   C. She made the police remove Armpit's handcuffs and let him go.

   D. She asked Kaira to let them stay at the concert.

5. How did El Genius react to the incident involving Armpit and Ginny?

   A. He thought it was tragic that Ginny might have been hurt.

   B. He thought it was distracting from the concert.

   C. He thought it was funny seeing Ginny having a seizure.

   D. He thought it was wrong seeing the police hurt Armpit.

6. What did Kaira do when she heard about the incident involving Armpit and Ginny?

   A. She wanted them immediately removed from her concert.

   B. She personally went to them and invited them backstage.

   C. She angrily told them not to buy counterfeit tickets.

   D. She told El Genius to give them souvenir shirts.

7. Which of the following did Kaira NOT do during the concert?

   A. She invited Armpit and Ginny out on the stage.

   B. She said a line that was unscripted.

   C. She sang one of Janis Joplin's songs.

   D. She refused to do an encore for the audience.

1분에 몇 단어를 읽는지 리딩 속도를 측정해보세요.

$$\frac{2{,}613 \text{ words}}{\text{reading time ( ) sec}} \times 60 = (\quad\quad) \text{ WPM}$$

Build Your Vocabulary

arena 복습
[ərí:nə]

n. 경기장, 시합장
An arena is a place where sports, entertainments, and other public events take place.

stutter 복습
[stʌ́tər]

v. 말을 더듬다, 더듬거리며 말하다; n. 말더듬기
If someone stutters, they have difficulty speaking because they find it hard to say the first sound of a word.

point out 복습

phrasal v. ~을 지적하다
If you point out a fact or mistake, you tell someone about it or draw their attention to it.

pull into 복습

phrasal v. ~에 도착하다, 들다
If a train or a bus pulls into, it arrives somewhere and stops.

cram
[kræm]

vt. 가득 채우다, 쑤셔 넣다, 밀어 넣다
If a place is crammed with things or people, it is full of them, so that there is hardly room for anything or anyone else.

resemble 복습
[rizémbl]

vt. ~을 닮다, ~와 공통점이 있다
If one thing or person resembles another, they are similar to each other.

handicapped
[hǽndikæpt]

a. (신체적 · 정신적) 장애가 있는; n. (pl.) 장애인들
Someone who is handicapped has a physical or mental disability that prevents them living a totally normal life.

placard
[plǽkɑːrd]

n. 플래카드, 현수막
A placard is a large notice that is carried in a march or displayed in a public place.

nod 복습
[nad]

v. 끄덕이다, 끄덕여 표시하다; n. (동의 · 인사 · 신호 · 명령의) 끄덕임
If you nod, you move your head downward and upward to show agreement, understanding, or approval.

hang 복습
[hæŋ]

v. (hung–hung) 걸다, 달아매다; 매달리다; 교수형에 처하다
If something hangs in a high place or position, or if you hang it there, it is attached there so it does not touch the ground.

rearview mirror
[ríərvjuː mírər]

n. (자동차의) 백미러
Inside a car, the rearview mirror is the mirror that enables you to see the traffic behind when you are driving.

100

remind^{복습}
[rimáind]
vt. 생각나게 하다, 상기시키다, 일깨우다
If someone reminds you of a fact or event that you already know about, they say something which makes you think about it.

maneuver^{복습}
[mənúːvəːr]
v. 교묘히 이동하다[다루다]; n. 교묘한 조종; 책략, 술책
If you manoeuver something into or out of an awkward position, you skillfully move it there.

throng[*]
[θrɔːŋ]
n. 군중, 인파; v. 떼지어 모이다
A throng is a large crowd of people.

concession[*]
[kənséʃən]
n. (공원 · 극장 안의) 매점, 매장; 양보; 면허, 특허
A concession is an arrangement where someone is given the right to sell a product or to run a business, especially in a building belonging to another business.

official[*]
[əfíʃəl]
a. 공식의, 공인된; n. 공무원, 관리, 임원
Official activities are carried out by a person in authority as part of their job.

tax^{복습}
[tæks]
n. 세금; 부담, 과중한 요구; vt. 세금을 부과하다
Tax is an amount of money that you have to pay to the government so that it can pay for public services.

souvenir[*]
[sùːvəníər]
n. 기념품
A souvenir is something which you buy or keep to remind you of a holiday, place, or event.

bucket^{복습}
[bʌ́kit]
n. 버킷, 양동이
A bucket is a round metal or plastic container with a handle attached to its sides.

section^{**}
[sékʃən]
n. 조각, 잘라낸 부분; 구역, 지역; (신문 등의) 난; vt. 구분하다, 구획하다
A section of something is one of the parts into which it is divided or from which it is formed.

row^{복습}
[rou]
① n. 열, (좌석) 줄 ② vi. (노를 써서) 배를 젓다; (배가) 저어지다
A row of things or people is a number of them arranged in a line.

incident^{**}
[ínsədənt]
n. (우발) 사건, 일
An incident is something that happens, often something that is unpleasant.

jut
[dʒʌt]
v. 돌출하다, 튀어나오다; 돌출시키다, 내밀다
If something juts out, it sticks out above or beyond a surface.

tier
[tiər]
n. (극장 등의 관람석) 줄, 층; vi. 층층으로 늘어 세우다
A tier is a row or layer of something that has other layers above or below it.

bleacher
[blíːtʃər]
n. (pl.) (지붕 없는) 야외 관람석
The bleachers are a part of an outdoor sports stadium, or the seats in that area, which are usually uncovered and are the least expensive place where people can sit.

glance^{복습}
[glæns]
v. 흘끗 보다, 잠깐 보다; n. 흘끗 봄
If you glance at something or someone, you look at them very quickly and then look away again immediately.

worth [복습]
[wəːrθ]

n. 가치, 값어치; a. 가치가 있는
When you talk about a particular amount of money's worth of something, you mean the quantity of it that you can buy for that amount of money.

chew *
[ʧuː]

v. 씹다, 씹어서 으깨다
If you chew gum, you keep biting it and moving it around your mouth to taste the flavor of it.

flavor *
[fléivər]

n. 맛, 풍미; 정취, 멋
The flavor of a food or drink is its taste.

recognize [복습]
[rékəgnaiz]

vt. 인지하다, 알아보다
If you recognize someone or something, you know who that person is or what that thing is.

executive *
[igzékjətiv]

n. 경영진, 간부; a. 경영의; 행정의
An executive is someone who is employed by a business at a senior level.

security [복습]
[sikjúərəti]

n. 안전, 보호; 보안, 경비
A feeling of security is a feeling of being safe and free from worry.

personnel *
[pə̀ːrsənél]

n. 인원, 직원들
The personnel of an organization are the people who work for it.

slip *
[slip]

vi. 살짝 들어가[게 하]다; 미끄러지다, 미끄러지듯이 움직이다
If you slip somewhere, you go there quickly and quietly.

autograph *
[ɔ́ːtəgræf]

n. 서명, 사인; 자필; vt. 서명하다, 자필로 쓰다
An autograph is the signature of someone famous which is specially written for a fan to keep.

outfit [복습]
[áutfit]

n. 한 벌의 옷, 복장
An outfit is a set of clothes.

sparkle *
[spáːrkl]

v. 반짝거리다, 빛나[게 하]다; n. 불꽃, 섬광 (sparkling a. 반짝이는)
If something sparkles, it is clear and bright and shines with a lot of very small points of light.

fringe *
[frindʒ]

n. (숄·테이블 가장자리의) 술 (장식); 가장자리, 주변; v. 술을 달다, 테를 두르다
A fringe is a decoration attached to clothes, or other objects such as curtains, consisting of a row of hanging strips or threads.

embarrass [복습]
[imbǽrəs]

v. 부끄럽게[무안하게] 하다; 어리둥절하게 하다; 당황하다
(embarrassing a. 난처하게 하는)
If something or someone embarrasses you, they make you feel shy or ashamed.

on time

idiom 정각에, 제 시간에
On time means at the correct time, neither early nor late.

frenzy
[frénzi]

n. 열광, 광란; 격분, 격앙; vt. 격분[광란]하게 하다
Frenzy or a frenzy is great excitement or wild behavior that often results from losing control of your feelings.

pity [복습]
[píti]

v. 동정하다, 불쌍히 여기다; n. 동정, 연민
If you feel pity for someone, you feel very sorry for them.

horrible^{복습}
[hɔ́:rəbl]

a. 무서운, 끔찍한; 몹시 불쾌한
You can call something horrible when it causes you to feel great shock, fear, and disgust.

lately^{복습}
[léitli]

ad. 요즘에, 최근에, 근래
You use lately to describe events in the recent past, or situations that started a short time ago.

stand^{복습}
[stænd]

v. 참다, 견디다; 키[높이]가 ～이다; 서다, 일어서다; n. 가판대, 좌판; 관람석
If you cannot stand something, you cannot bear it or tolerate it.

arrange^{복습}
[əréindʒ]

v. 준비하다, 계획을 짜다; 가지런히 하다, 배열하다 (arrangement n. 준비, 계획)
If you arrange an event or meeting, you make plans for it to happen.

suspect^{복습}
[səspékt]

v. 짐작하다, 의심하다, 혐의를 두다; n. 용의자
If you suspect that something dishonest or unpleasant has been done, you believe that it has probably been done.

onstage
[ɔ̀nsteidʒ]

ad. 무대 위에서
When someone such as an actor or musician goes onstage, they go onto the stage in a theater to give a performance.

fire up

phrasal v. ～에게 흥미를 불어넣다
To fire someone up means to make them become excited or enthusiastic about something.

at the top of one's lungs

idiom (목청이 터지도록) 큰 소리로
If you scream at the top of your lungs, you scream as loud as you possible.

very***
[véri]

a. 바로, 딱; 정말의, 순전한; ad. 정말로; 매우
You use very with nouns to emphasize that something is exactly the right one or exactly the same one.

spot^{복습}
[spat]

n. 장소, 지점; 반점, 얼룩; vt. 발견하다, 분별하다
You can refer to a particular place as a spot.

cheer**
[tʃiər]

v. 환호하다, 기운나게 하다; n. 환호, 갈채; 건배
When people cheer, they shout loudly to show their approval or to encourage someone who is doing something such as taking part in a game.

aware^{복습}
[əwéər]

a. 알고 있는, 의식하고 있는, 알아차린
If you are aware of something, you know about it.

tap*
[tæp]

① v. 가볍게 두드리다; n. 가볍게 두드리기 ② n. 주둥이, (수도 등의) 꼭지
If you tap something, you hit it with a quick light blow or a series of quick light blows.

apparent^{복습}
[əpǽrənt]

a. 또렷한, 명백한, 외관상의 (apparently ad. 명백하게, 보아하니)
If something is apparent to you, it is clear and obvious to you.

soda^{복습}
[sóudə]

n. 탄산 음료, 소다수
Soda is a sweet drink that contain small bubbles of carbon dioxide.

accuse^{복습}
[əkjú:z]

v. 비난하다, 고발하다
If you accuse someone of doing something wrong or dishonest, you say or tell them that you believe that they did it.

instinctive*
[instíŋktiv]

a. 본능적인, 직관적인; 무의식적인 (instinctively ad. 본능적으로)
An instinctive feeling, idea, or action is one that you have or do without thinking or reasoning.

frustrate*
[frʌ́streit]

v. 좌절시키다, 불만스럽게 만들다; 방해하다 (frustration n. 낙담, 좌절)
If something frustrates you, it upsets or angers you because you are unable to do anything about the problems it creates.

stomp^{복습}
[stamp]

v. 발을 구르다, 쿵쿵거리며 걷다; 짓밟다
If you stomp somewhere, you walk there with very heavy steps, often because you are angry.

impatient*
[impéiʃənt]

a. 참을 수 없는, 성급한; 초조하게 기다리는 (impatience n. 성급함, 안달)
If you are impatient, you are annoyed because you have to wait too long for something.

correct^{복습}
[kərékt]

a. 옳은; v. 정정하다, 고치다; 나무라다, 벌주다
If something is correct, it is in accordance with the facts and has no mistakes.

exclaim^{복습}
[ikskléim]

v. 외치다, 소리치다
If you exclaim, you say or shout something suddenly because of surprise, fear and pleasure.

stub*
[stʌb]

n. (표 · 입장권의) 반쪽, 보관용 부분; 토막, 그루터기
A ticket stub is the part that you keep when you go in to watch a performance.

aisle^{복습}
[ail]

n. 통로, 측면의 복도
An aisle is a long narrow gap that people can walk along between rows of seats in a public building.

counterfeit
[káuntərfit]

a. 가짜의, 모조의; v. (화폐 · 지폐 · 문서 등을) 위조하다
Counterfeit money, goods, or documents are not genuine, but have been made to look exactly like genuine ones in order to deceive people.

refuse***
[rifjúːz]

vt. 거절하다, 거부하다
If you refuse to do something, you deliberately do not do it, or you say firmly that you will not do it.

grab*
[græb]

v. 부여잡다, 움켜쥐다; n. 부여잡기
If you grab something, you take it or pick it up suddenly and roughly.

twist^{복습}
[twist]

v. 비틀다, 돌리다, 꼬다, 감기다; n. 뒤틀림, 엉킴
If you twist something, especially a part of your body, or if it twists, it moves into an unusual, uncomfortable, or bent position, for example because of being hit or pushed, or because you are upset.

spin**
[spin]

v. 돌(리)다, 맴돌리다; 오래[질질] 끌다; n. 회전
If something spins or if you spin it, it turns quickly around a central point.

jerk*
[dʒəːrk]

① v. 갑자기 움직이다; n. 갑자기 움직임; 반사 운동; ② n. 바보, 멍청이
If you jerk something or someone in a particular direction, or they jerk in a particular direction, they move a short distance very suddenly and quickly.

rip*
[rip]

v. 잡아채다; 찢다, 벗겨내다; 돌진하다; n. 찢어진 틈, 잡아 찢음
When something rips or when you rip it, you tear it forcefully with your hands or with a tool such as a knife.

socket
[sάkit]

n. 꽂는[끼우는] 구멍; vt. 소켓에 끼우다
You can refer to any hollow part or opening in a structure which another part fits into as a socket.

handcuff
[hǽndkʌf]

vt. 수갑을 채우다; n. 수갑
If you handcuff someone, you put two metal rings around their wrists.

wince
[wins]

vi. (아픔·무서움 때문에) 얼굴을 찡그리다; 움찔하다, 주춤하다; n. 위축
If you wince, you suddenly look as if you are suffering because you feel pain.

pump one's stomach

idiom 위세척을 하다
To pump someone's stomach means to remove the contents of the stomach using a pump, because they have swallowed something harmful.

abrupt^복습
[əbrʌ́pt]

a. 돌연한, 갑작스런; 퉁명스러운, 무뚝뚝한 (abruptly ad. 갑작스럽게)
An abrupt change or action is very sudden, often in a way which is unpleasant.

bang*
[bæŋ]

v. 부딪치다, 탕 치다, 쾅 닫(히)다; n. 쾅 하는 소리
If you bang on something or if you bang it, you hit it hard, making a loud noise.

glimpse*
[glimps]

n. 흘끗 봄[보임]; v. 흘끗 보다
If you get a glimpse of someone or something, you see them very briefly and not very well.

lurch^복습
[ləːrtʃ]

v. 휘청하다, 비틀거리다; n. 갑작스런 요동, 기울어짐
To lurch means to make a sudden movement, especially forward, in an uncontrolled way.

tackle*
[tǽkl]

v. 때려눕히다, 잡다; 태클하다; n. 연장, 도구
If you tackle someone, you attack them and fight them.

billy club
[bíli klʌ́b]

n. 곤봉, 경찰봉
A billy or billy club is a short heavy stick which is sometimes used as a weapon by the police.

slam^복습
[slæm]

v. 세게 치다; (문 따위를) 탕 닫다; 털썩 내려놓다; n. 쾅 (하는 소리)
If one thing slams into or against another, it crashes into it with great force.

mayor^복습
[méiər]

n. 시장(市長); (지방 자치단체의) 행정장관
The mayor of a town or city is the person who has been elected to represent it for a fixed period of time or, in some places, to run its government.

whack
[wæk]

v. 후려치다, 세게 때리다; n. 구타, 강타
If you whack someone or something, you hit them hard.

gasp*
[gæsp]

v. (놀람 따위로) 헐떡거리다, 숨이 막히다; n. 헐떡거림
When you gasp, you take a short quick breath through your mouth, especially when you are surprised, shocked, or in pain.

trench [복습]
[trentʃ]

n. 깊은 도랑; 방어 전선; v. 도랑을 파다, (홈 따위를) 새기다
A trench is a long narrow channel that is cut into the ground, for example in order to lay pipes or get rid of water.

admire [복습]
[ædmáiər]

v. 감탄하다, 칭찬하다, 존경하다
If you admire someone or something, you like and respect them very much.

lean [복습]
[li:n]

① v. 상체를 굽히다, 기울다; 기대다, 의지하다 ② a. 야윈, 마른
When you lean in a particular direction, you bend your body in that direction.

swear**
[swɛər]

v. 맹세하다, 증언하다
If you say that you swear that something is true or that you can swear to it, you are saying very firmly that it is true.

seizure [복습]
[síːʒər]

n. (병의) 발작; 잡기, 체포; 압수
If someone has a seizure, they have a sudden violent attack of an illness, especially one that affects their heart or brain.

plead*
[pli:d]

v. 탄원하다, 간청하다; 주장하다
If you plead with someone to do something, you ask them in an intense, emotional way to do it.

baton
[bætán]

n. 경찰봉, 지휘봉
A baton is a short heavy stick which is sometimes used as a weapon by the police.

drool
[dru:l]

n. 군침; v. 군침을 흘리다, 침이 나오다
If a person or animal drools, saliva drops slowly from their mouth.

drip [복습]
[drip]

v. 방울방울[뚝뚝] 떨어지다; 가득[넘칠 듯이] 지니고 있다
When something drips, drops of liquid fall from it.

writhe
[raið]

v. (고통으로) 몸부림치다, 몸을 뒤틀다
If you writhe, your body twists and turns violently backward and forward, usually because you are in great pain or discomfort.

twitch [복습]
[twitʃ]

v. (손가락 · 근육 따위가) 씰룩거리다; 확 잡아당기다, 잡아채다; n. 씰룩거림, 경련
If something, especially a part of your body, twitches or if you twitch it, it makes a little jumping movement.

sticky [복습]
[stíki]

a. 끈적[끈끈]한, 들러붙는, 점착성의
A sticky substance is soft, or thick and liquid, and can stick to other things.

spill [복습]
[spil]

v. 엎지르다, 흘리다; n. 엎지름, 유출
If a liquid spills or if you spill it, it accidentally flows over the edge of a container.

adjust [복습]
[ədʒʌ́st]

v. (옷매무새 등을) 바로 하다; 적응하다; 조절하다, 조정하다
If you adjust something such as your clothing or a machine, you correct or alter its position or setting.

whisper [복습]
[hwíspə:r]

v. 속삭이다, 작은 소리로 말하다; n. 속삭임
When you whisper, you say something very quietly.

106

tremble[*]
[trémbl]

v. 떨다; 떨리다 (trembling a. 떨리는, 진동하는)
If something trembles, it shakes slightly.

disturbance[*]
[distə́:rbəns]

n. 소란, 소동; 불안, 동요; 방해, 장애(물)
A disturbance is an incident in which people behave violently in public.

wriggle
[rigl]

v. 몸부림치다; 꿈틀거리다; n. 몸부림침, 꿈틀거림
If you wriggle or wriggle part of your body, you twist and turn with quick movements.

flop
[flap]

v. 퍼덕거리다, 털썩 쓰러지다
If you flop into a chair, for example, you sit down suddenly and heavily because you are so tired.

spastic[복습]
[spǽstik]

a. 경련성의, 뇌성마비의; n. 경련 환자
Someone who is spastic is born with a disability which makes it difficult for them to control their muscles, especially in their arms and legs.

awful[**]
[ɔ́:fəl]

a. 몹시 나쁜, 무서운, 지독한
If you say that something is awful, you mean that it is extremely unpleasant, shocking, or bad.

dude[복습]
[dju:d]

n. 사내, 녀석; (구어) 형씨, 친구
A dude is a man.

cop[*]
[kap]

n. (구어) 경찰관, 순경
A cop is a policeman or policewoman.

crap
[kræp]

n. 허튼소리, 헛소리; 쓰레기 같은 것
If you describe something as crap, you mean it is nonsense.

spaz
[spæz]

n. 발작
A spaz attack is a sudden burst of excitement or nervousness.

unusual[복습]
[ʌnjú:ʒuəl]

a. 보통이 아닌, 드문
If you describe someone as unusual, you think that they are interesting and different from other people.

scalper[복습]
[skǽlpər]

n. 암표상
A scalper is someone who sells tickets outside a sports ground or theater, usually for more than their original value.

touch-up
[tʌ́tʃ-ʌp]

n. 재빠른 손질[수정]
Touch-up is an act or instance of touching up.

cot
[kat]

n. 접이 침대, 간이[야영용] 침대; 소아용 침대
A cot is a narrow bed, usually made of canvas fitted over a frame which can be folded up.

surround[**]
[səráund]

vt. 둘러싸다, 에워싸다; n. 둘러싸는 것; 환경, 주위
If a person or thing is surrounded by something, that thing is situated all around them.

subside
[səbsáid]

vi. 가라앉다, 진정되다
If a feeling or noise subsides, it becomes less strong or loud.

hiccup
[híkʌp]

n. 딸꾹질; vi. 딸꾹질을 하다
When you have hiccups, you make repeated sharp sounds in your throat, often because you have been eating or drinking too quickly.

handle^{복습}
[hǽndl]

v. 다루다, 처리하다; n. 손잡이, 핸들
If you say that someone can handle a problem or situation, you mean that they have the ability to deal with it successfully.

overdose^{복습}
[óuvərdòus]

n. 과다 복용[투여]; vt. 너무 많이 투여하다
If someone takes an overdose of a drug, they take more of it than is safe.

minor^{**}
[máinər]

a. 작은 쪽의, 중요치 않은
A minor illness or operation is not likely to be dangerous to someone's life or health.

wrist[*]
[rist]

n. 손목
Your wrist is the part of your body between your hand and your arm which bends when you move your hand.

pulse[*]
[pʌls]

n. 맥박, 고동; 파동; v. 고동치다, 맥이 뛰다
Your pulse is the regular beating of blood through your body, which you can feel when you touch particular parts of your body, especially your wrist.

vibrate[*]
[váibreit]

v. 진동하다, 떨리다 (vibration n. 진동, 떨림)
If something vibrates or if you vibrate it, it shakes with repeated small, quick movements.

charge^{복습}
[ʧa:rdʒ]

n. 책임, 의무; 수수료, 요금; v. (지불을) 청구하다; 부담 지우다, 맡기다; 돌격하다
(in charge idiom ~을 관리하는, 담당하는)
If you are in charge in a particular situation, you are the most senior person and have control over something or someone.

outburst
[áutbə:rst]

n. 폭발, 돌발; 급격한 증가
An outburst of an emotion, especially anger, is a sudden strong expression of that emotion.

threaten^{복습}
[θretn]

v. 위협하다, 협박하다; 조짐을 보이다
If something or someone threatens a person or thing, they are likely to harm that person or thing.

resist^{**}
[rizíst]

v. 저항하다, 반대하다, 방해하다
If you resist doing something, or resist the temptation to do it, you stop yourself from doing it although you would like to do it.

arrest^{복습}
[ərést]

n. 체포, 검거, 구속; vt. 체포하다, 저지하다; (주의·이목·흥미 등을) 끌다
If the police arrest you, they take charge of you and take you to a police station, because they believe you may have committed a crime.

justify[*]
[dʒʌ́stəfài]

v. 정당화하다, 변명하다
To justify a decision, action, or idea means to show or prove that it is reasonable or necessary.

blame^{**}
[bleim]

vt. ~의 탓으로 돌리다; 비난하다, 나무라다
If you blame a person or thing for something bad, you believe or say that they are responsible for it or that they caused it.

108

victim[*]
[víktim]

n. 피해자, 희생(자)
A victim is someone who has suffered as a result of someone else's actions or beliefs, or as a result of unpleasant circumstances.

firm^{복습}
[fə:rm]

① a. 굳은, 단단한; 견고한 (firmly ad. 단호하게) ② n. 회사
If you describe someone as firm, you mean they behave in a way that shows that they are not going to change their mind, or that they are the person who is in control.

**have to
hand it to**

idiom ~는 칭찬[인정]해 줘야 한다
You say things such as 'You have to hand it to her' or 'You've got to hand it to them' when you admire someone for their skills or achievements and you think they deserve a lot of praise.

persecute[*]
[pə́:rsikjù:t]

vt. 압박하다, 박해하다; 귀찮게 하다, 괴롭히다
If someone is persecuted, they are treated cruelly and unfairly, often because of their race or beliefs.

sob[*]
[sab]

n. 흐느낌, 오열; v. 흐느껴 울다
A sob is one of the noises that you make when you are crying.

cease[*]
[si:s]

v. 그만두다, 중지하다
If you cease something, you stop it happening or working.

enthusiastic[*]
[inθù:ziǽstik]

a. 열렬한, 열광적인
If you are enthusiastic about something, you show how much you like or enjoy it by the way that you behave and talk.

madhouse
[mǽdhaus]

n. (혼란스럽고 시끄러워) 정신없는 곳
If you describe a place or situation as a madhouse, you mean that it is full of confusion and noise.

alert^{복습}
[ələ́:rt]

n. 경보, 경계; a. 방심하지 않는; v. 경고하다
An alert is a situation in which people prepare themselves for something dangerous that might happen soon.

1분에 몇 단어를 읽는지 리딩 속도를 측정해보세요.

$$\frac{2{,}565 \text{ words}}{\text{reading time (}\quad\text{) sec}} \times 60 = (\quad\quad) \text{ WPM}$$

Build Your Vocabulary

arena ^{복습}
[ərí:nə]

n. 경기장, 시합장
An arena is a place where sports, entertainments, and other public events take place.

stomp ^{복습}
[stamp]

v. 짓밟다; 발을 구르다, 쿵쿵거리며 걷다
If you stomp somewhere, you walk there with very heavy steps, often because you are angry.

clap[*]
[klæp]

v. 박수를 치다, 손뼉을 치다; n. 박수[손뼉] (소리)
When you clap, you hit your hands together to show appreciation or attract attention.

assume ^{복습}
[əsjú:m]

vt. 추정하다, 가정하다; 가장하다, 꾸미다; (역할·임무 등을) 맡다
If you assume that something is true, you imagine that it is true, sometimes wrongly.

racism
[réisizm]

n. 인종차별(주의)
Racism is the belief that people of some races are inferior to others, and the behavior which is the result of this belief.

protect ^{복습}
[prətékt]

v. 보호하다, 막다, 지키다
To protect someone or something means to prevent them from being harmed or damaged.

handle ^{복습}
[hǽndl]

v. 다루다, 처리하다; n. 손잡이, 핸들
If you say that someone can handle a problem or situation, you mean that they have the ability to deal with it successfully.

awful ^{복습}
[ɔ́:fəl]

a. 몹시 나쁜, 무서운, 지독한 (awfully ad. 아주, 몹시)
If you say that something is awful, you mean that it is extremely unpleasant, shocking, or bad.

flight^{**}
[flait]

n. 계단, 층계; 날기, 비행
A flight of steps or stairs is a set of steps or stairs that lead from one level to another without changing direction.

extend ^{복습}
[iksténd]

v. (손·발 등을) 뻗다, 늘이다; 넓히다, 확장하다
If someone extends their hand, they stretch out their arm and hand to shake hands with someone.

on the other hand

idiom 다른 한편으로는, 반면에
You use on the one hand to introduce the first of two contrasting points, facts, or ways of looking at something.

beard ^{복습}
[biərd]

n. 턱수염
A man's beard is the hair that grows on his chin and cheeks.

various ^{복습}
[véəriəs]

a. 여러 가지의, 다양한; 많은
If you say that there are various things, you mean there are several different things of the type mentioned.

attach ^{복습}
[ətǽtʃ]

vt. 붙이다, 달다
If you attach something to an object, you connect it or fasten it to the object.

makeup ^{복습}
[méikʌp]

n. 화장, 분장; 조립, 구성
Makeup consists of things such as lipstick, eye shadow, and powder which some women put on their faces to make themselves look more attractive or which actors use to change or improve their appearance.

smoke ^{복습}
[smouk]

vi. 담배를 피우다; 연기를 내뿜다; n. 연기, 매연; 흡연
When someone smokes a cigarette, cigar, or pipe, they suck the smoke from it into their mouth and blow it out again.

souvenir ^{복습}
[sùːvəníər]

n. 기념품
A souvenir is something which you buy or keep to remind you of a holiday, place, or event.

mess *
[mes]

n. 엉망진창, 난잡함; v. 망쳐놓다, 방해하다
If you say that something is a mess or in a mess, you think that it is in an untidy state.

grab ^{복습}
[græb]

v. 부여잡다, 움켜쥐다; n. 부여잡기
If you grab something, you take it or pick it up suddenly and roughly.

note ^{복습}
[nout]

n. (악기의) 음; (짧은) 기록; 짧은 편지; v. 주목하다, 알아채다; 메모하다
In music, a note is the sound of a particular pitch, or a written symbol representing this sound.

yell ^{복습}
[jel]

v. 소리치다, 고함치다; n. 고함소리, 부르짖음
If you yell, you shout loudly, usually because you are excited, angry, or in pain.

impatient ^{복습}
[impéiʃənt]

a. 참을 수 없는, 성급한; 초조하게 기다리는 (impatiently ad. 성급하게)
If you are impatient, you are annoyed because you have to wait too long for something.

applaud *
[əplɔ́ːd]

v. 박수를 보내다, 성원하다
When a group of people applaud, they clap their hands in order to show approval, for example when they have enjoyed a play or concert.

squeeze ^{복습}
[skwiːz]

vt. 꽉 쥐다[죄다]; 짜다, 압착하다; 밀어 넣다, 쑤셔 넣다; n. 압착, 짜냄
If you squeeze something, you press it firmly, usually with your hands.

equip ^{복습}
[ikwíp]

vt. 갖추다, 장비하다 (equipment n. 장치, 장비)
If you equip a person or thing with something, you give them the tools or equipment that are needed.

visible ^{복습}
[vízəbl]

a. 알아볼 수 있는, 뚜렷한; 눈에 보이는 (invisible a. 눈에 띄지 않는)
If something is visible, it can be seen.

blast[*]
[blæst]

v. 쾅쾅 울리다; 폭파하다; n. 폭발, 폭파; 폭풍, 돌풍
If you blast something such as a car horn, or if it blasts, it makes a sudden, loud sound. If something blasts music, or music blasts, the music is very loud.

operate[**]
[ápərèit]

v. (기계 · 장치 등을) 움직이다, 작동하다; 사업하다, 경영하다; 수술하다
(operator n. (기계 등의) 조작자)
When you operate a machine or device, or when it operates, you make it work.

consist[**]
[kənsíst]

vi. ~으로 이루어지다, 구성되다
Something that consists of particular things or people is formed from them.

panel[*]
[pǽnl]

n. (자동차 · 비행기 등의) 계기판; (넓은 직사각형의) 합판, 벽판
A control panel or instrument panel is a board or surface which contains switches and controls to operate a machine or piece of equipment.

dial[복습]
[dáiəl]

n. 다이얼; v. 전화를 걸다, 다이얼을 돌리다
A dial is a control on a device or piece of equipment which you can move in order to adjust the setting.

soda[복습]
[sóudə]

n. 탄산 음료, 소다수
Soda is a sweet drink that contain small bubbles of carbon dioxide.

pitch dark
[pitʃ dá:rk]

a. 칠흑같이 어두운
If a place or the night is pitch dark, it is completely dark.

spotlight
[spátlàit]

n. 스포트라이트, 집중 광선; vt. 스포트라이트를 비추다, 두드러져 보이게 하다
A spotlight is a powerful light, for example in a theater, which can be directed so that it lights up a small area.

naughty[*]
[nɔ́:ti]

a. 장난꾸러기인, 말을 안 듣는
If you say that a child is naughty, you mean that they behave badly or do not do what they are told.

innocent[*]
[ínəsənt]

a. 순진한, 천진난만한; 결백한, 무고한
If someone is innocent, they have no experience or knowledge of the more complex or unpleasant aspects of life.

chew[복습]
[tʃu:]

v. 씹다, 씹어서 으깨다
If you chew gum, you keep biting it and moving it around your mouth to taste the flavor of it.

dazzle[*]
[dǽzl]

v. 눈부시(게 하)다; 감탄하(게 하)다; n. 눈부심 (dazzlingly ad. 눈부시게)
If someone or something dazzles you, you are extremely impressed by their skill, qualities, or beauty.

nightmare[*]
[náitmɛər]

n. 악몽
A nightmare is a very frightening dream.

delight[*]
[diláit]

n. 기쁨, 즐거움; v. 즐겁게 하다, 매우 기쁘게 하다
Delight is a feeling of very great pleasure.

bounce[복습]
[bauns]

v. 튀다, 튀게 하다; 급히 움직이다, 뛰어다니다; n. 팀, 바운드
If something bounces off a surface or is bounced off it, it reaches the surface and is reflected back.

112

beat [bi:t]

n. 박자; 치기, 때리기; v. 능가하다, 더 낫다; 이기다, 패배시키다; 치다, 두드리다
The beat of a piece of music is the main rhythm that it has.

bass [beis]

n. 베이스, 저음; a. 베이스의
In popular music, a bass is a bass guitar or a double bass.

vibrate [váibreit]

v. 진동하다, 떨리다
If something vibrates or if you vibrate it, it shakes with repeated small, quick movements.

mesmerize [mézməràiz]

vt. 매혹시키다, 감화시키다; ~에게 최면술을 걸다
If you are mesmerized by something, you are so interested in it or so attracted to it that you cannot think about anything else.

fringe [frindʒ]

v. 술을 달다, 테를 두르다; n. (숄·테이블 가장자리의) 술 (장식); 가장자리, 주변 (fringed a. 술 장식이 달린)
Fringed clothes, curtains, or lampshades are decorated with fringes.

outfit [áutfit]

n. 한 벌의 옷, 복장
An outfit is a set of clothes.

shimmer [ʃímər]

vi. 희미하게 빛나다, 어른거리다; n. 미광
If something shimmers, it shines with a faint, unsteady light or has an unclear, unsteady appearance.

charm [ʧa:rm]

n. 매력, 마력; 마술; v. 매력이 있다; 황홀하게 하다
Charm is the quality of being pleasant or attractive.

hesitate [hézətèit]

v. 주저하다, 머뭇거리다, 망설이다
If you hesitate, you do not speak or act for a short time, usually because you are uncertain, embarrassed, or worried about what you are going to say or do.

funky [fʌ́ŋki]

a. 비트가 강한, 펑키한; 파격적인, 멋진; 지독한 악취가 나는
Funky jazz, blues, or pop music has a very strong, repeated bass part.

sincere^{**} [sinsíə:r]

a. 진지한, 진심 어린
If you say that someone is sincere, you approve of them because they really mean the things they say.

maintain^{**} [meintéin]

vt. 유지하다, 계속하다; 주장하다, 우기다
If you maintain something, you continue to have it, and do not let it stop or grow weaker.

normal [nɔ́:rməl]

a. 보통의, 정상적인; n. 보통; 표준, 기준 (normally ad. 보통은, 일반적으로)
Something that is normal is usual and ordinary, and is what people expect.

feed off

phrasal v. (정보·동력 등을) ~에서 얻다; ~을 먹다
If you feed off something, you get strength from it.

hatred^{**} [héitrid]

n. 증오, 미움, 원한
Hatred is an extremely strong feeling of dislike for someone or something.

cruel [krú:əl]

a. 잔인한, 잔혹한, 끔찍한
Someone who is cruel deliberately causes pain or distress to people or animals.

pound[*] [paund]	① v. 마구 치다, 세게 두드리다; 쿵쿵 울리다; 고동치다; n. 타격 ② n. 파운드 (무게의 단위) ③ n. 울타리, 우리 If you pound something or pound on it, you hit it with great force, usually loudly and repeatedly.
rip into	phrasal v. ~속으로 거칠게 들어가다 If you rip into something, you go very quickly or violently into or through it.
punctuate [pʌ́ŋktʃueit]	vt. 간간이 끼어들다; ~에 구두점을 찍다 If an activity or situation is punctuated by particular things, it is interrupted by them at intervals.
drive home	idiom 충분히 이해시키다, 납득시키다 If you drive something home to someone, you make sure that they understand it completely, for example by repeating it often.
spew [spjuː]	v. (노여움 · 비난 등을) 분출하다, 쏟아내다; 토하다, 게우다 When something spews out a substance or when a substance spews from something, the substance flows out quickly in large quantities.
twist[복습] [twist]	v. 꼬다, 비틀다, 돌리다, 감기다; n. 뒤틀림, 엉킴 (twisted a. 뒤틀린) If you say that someone has twisted something that you have said, you disapprove of them because they have repeated it in a way that changes its meaning, in order to harm you or benefit themselves.
hateful[*] [héitfəl]	a. 혐오스러운 Someone or something that is hateful is extremely bad or unpleasant.
fire[복습] [faiər]	n. 정열, 흥분; 불; v. 해고하다; 발사하다; 불을 지르다 You can use fire to refer in an approving way to someone's energy and enthusiasm.
release[복습] [rilíːs]	vt. 해방하다, 석방하다, 놓아주다; n. 석방 If someone or something releases you from a duty, task, or feeling, they free you from it.
rage[*] [reidʒ]	n. 격노, 격분; 격심함, 격렬; vi. 몹시 화내다 Rage is strong anger that is difficult to control.
cage[*] [keidʒ]	n. 새장, 우리; vt. ~을 새장[우리]에 가두다 A cage is a structure of wire or metal bars in which birds or animals are kept.
imperfection[복습] [impərfékʃən]	n. 불완전, 결함, 결점 An imperfection in someone or something is a fault, weakness, or undesirable feature that they have.
end up[복습]	phrasal v. 마침내는 (~으로) 되다; 끝나다 If you end up doing something or end up in a particular state, you do that thing or get into that state even though you did not originally intend to.

onstage^{복습}
[ɔ́nsteidʒ]

ad. 무대 위에서
When someone such as an actor or musician goes onstage, they go onto the stage in a theater to give a performance.

damsel^{복습}
[dǽmzəl]

n. 계집아이, 처녀
A damsel is a young, unmarried woman.

distress^{복습}
[distrés]

n. 고통, 곤란; 가난, 곤궁; vt. 고민하게 하다, 괴롭히다
Distress is a state of extreme sorrow, suffering, or pain.

hush[*]
[hʌʃ]

v. 조용하게 하다, 조용해지다; int. 쉿, 조용히
If you hush someone or if they hush, they stop speaking or making a noise.

vulnerable[*]
[vʌ́lnərəbl]

a. 상처받기 쉬운; 공격 당하기 쉬운
Someone who is vulnerable is weak and without protection, with the result that they are easily hurt physically or emotionally.

pace[*]
[peis]

n. 속도; 걸음걸이, 보폭; v. 왔다 갔다 하다, 보조를 맞추어 걷다
The pace of something is the speed at which it happens or is done.

bullet^{**}
[búlit]

n. 총알, 탄환; 총알 모양의 것, 작은 공
A bullet is a small piece of metal with a pointed or rounded end, which is fired out of a gun.

inquire[*]
[inkwáiər]

v. 묻다, 알아보다
If you inquire about something, you ask for information about it.

desire^{***}
[dizáiər]

n. 욕망, 욕구; vt. 바라다, 원하다
A desire is a strong wish to do or have something.

subscription
[səbskrípʃən]

n. 예약 구독; 지불, 기부(금)
A subscription is an amount of money that you pay regularly in order to receive copies of a magazine or newspaper.

verse[*]
[vəːrs]

n. (노래의) 절; (시의) 절; (성서 · 기도서의) 절
A verse is one of the parts into which a poem, a song is divided.

hoot
[huːt]

n. 외침, 고함소리; v. 야유하다, 고함치다; 경적을 울리다
If you hoot, you make a loud high-pitched noise when you are laughing or showing disapproval.

virgin[*]
[və́ːrdʒin]

n. 숫처녀[총각]; a. 성경험이 없는; 원래 그대로의, 깨끗한
A virgin is someone who has never had sex.

pop[*]
[pap]

v. 뻥 하고 소리를 내다, 터뜨리다; 불쑥 움직이다; n. 뻥[탁] 하는 소리; 발포
If something pops, it makes a short sharp sound.

string^{복습}
[striŋ]

n. (악기의) 현[줄]; 끈, 실; 일련, 한 줄; v. 묶다, 매달다
The strings on a musical instrument such as a violin or guitar are the thin pieces of wire or nylon stretched across it that make sounds when the instrument is played.

script[*]
[skript]

v. 대본을 쓰다; n. 대본
The person who scripts a film or a radio or television play writes it.

stun[*]
[stʌn]

vt. 놀라게 하다; 기절시키다 (stunned a. 어리벙벙하게 하는)
If you are stunned by something, you are extremely shocked or surprised by it and are therefore unable to speak or do anything.

launch[*]
[lɔ:ntʃ]

v. 내보내다; 시작하다, 착수하다; 발사하다, 던지다; n. 개시; 발포
To launch a large and important activity, for example a military attack, means to start it.

rise to one's feet^{복습}

idiom 벌떡 일어서다
If you get or rise to your feet, you stand up.

twirl
[twə:rl]

v. 빙빙 돌(리)다, 휘두르다; n. 빨리 돌리기
If you twirl something or if it twirls, it turns around and around with a smooth, fairly fast movement.

accuse^{복습}
[əkjú:z]

v. 비난하다, 고발하다
If you accuse someone of doing something wrong or dishonest, you say or tell them that you believe that they did it.

rearview mirror^{복습}
[ríərvju: mírər]

n. (자동차의) 백미러
Inside a car, the rearview mirror is the mirror that enables you to see the traffic behind when you are driving.

announce^{복습}
[ənáuns]

vt. 알리다, 공고하다, 전하다
If you announce a piece of news or an intention, especially something that people may not like, you say it loudly and clearly, so that everyone you are with can hear it.

horror[*]
[hɔ́:rər]

n. 공포, 무서움; 반감, 증오 (to one's horror idiom 무섭게도)
Horror is a feeling of great shock, fear, and worry caused by something extremely unpleasant.

wiggle^{복습}
[wigl]

v. (좌우로) 움직이다, (몸을) 뒤흔들다; n. 뒤흔듦
If you wiggle something or if it wiggles, it moves up and down or from side to side in small quick movements.

glue[*]
[glu:]

vt. ~에 꼭 붙여서 떨어지지 않게 하다; 접착제를 바르다; n. 접착제
If you say that someone is glued to something, you mean that they are giving it all their attention.

low-life
[lóu-laif]

n. 비열한 사람, 범죄자; 하층민
People sometimes use low-life to refer in a disapproving way to people who are involved in criminal, dishonest, or immoral activities, or to these activities.

scalper^{복습}
[skǽlpər]

n. 암표상
A scalper is someone who sells tickets outside a sports ground or theater, usually for more than their original value.

counterfeit^{복습}
[káuntərfit]

a. 가짜의, 모조의; v. (화폐·지폐·문서 등을) 위조하다
Counterfeit money, goods, or documents are not genuine, but have been made to look exactly like genuine ones in order to deceive people.

boo
[bu:]

v. 야유하다, 놀라게 하다; n. 야유하는 소리
If you boo a speaker or performer, you shout 'boo' or make other loud sounds to indicate that you do not like them, their opinions, or their performance.

116

flinch
[flintʃ]

v. (고통 · 공포로) 주춤하다, 위축되다
If you flinch, you make a small sudden movement, especially when something surprises you or hurts you.

startle*
[staːrtl]

v. 깜짝 놀라(게 하)다, 움찔하다
If something sudden and unexpected startles you, it surprises and frightens you slightly.

amplify
[ǽmpləfài]

v. 증폭시키다, 확대하다
If you amplify a sound, you make it louder, usually by using electronic equipment.

cheer^{복습}
[tʃiər]

n. 환호, 갈채; 건배; v. 환호하다, 기운나게 하다
When people cheer, they shout loudly to show their approval or to encourage someone who is doing something such as taking part in a game.

echo*
[ékou]

v. (남의 말 · 의견을) 그대로 되풀이하다; 울려 퍼지다, 메아리치다; n. 메아리
If you echo someone's words, you repeat them or express agreement with their attitude or opinion.

rat-a-tat
[ræt-ə-tǽt]

v. 둥둥[쾅쾅]거리다; n. 둥둥, 쾅쾅
You use rat-a-tat to represent a series of sharp, repeated sounds, for example the sound of someone knocking at a door.

whine
[hwain]

v. 윙윙 소리내다; 우는 소리를 하다, 칭얼거리다, 푸념하다
If something or someone whines, they make a long, high-pitched noise, especially one which sounds sad or unpleasant.

siren^{복습}
[sáiərən]

n. (신호 · 경보 따위를 나타내는) 사이렌
A siren is a warning device which makes a long, loud noise.

rock^{복습}
[rak]

① v. 흔들(리)다, 진동하다; 음악을 멋지게 연주하다, 로큰롤로 노래하다
② n. 바위, 암석
When something rocks or when you rock it, it moves slowly and regularly backward and forward or from side to side.

threaten^{복습}
[θretn]

v. 위협하다, 협박하다; 조짐을 보이다
If something or someone threatens a person or thing, they are likely to harm that person or thing.

thump*
[θʌmp]

v. 쿵쿵[쿵쾅]거리다; 탁치다, 부딪치다; n. 탁[쿵] 하는 소리; 세게 쥐어박음
When your heart thumps, it beats strongly and quickly, usually because you are afraid or excited.

nerve**
[nəːrv]

n. 신경; (어려움에 맞서는) 대담성, 용기
Nerves are long thin fibers that transmit messages between your brain and other parts of your body.

ease^{복습}
[iːz]

v. 살짝 움직이다[옮기다]; (고통 · 고민 등을) 진정[완화]시키다; n. 편함, 안정
If you ease your way somewhere or ease somewhere, you move there slowly, carefully, and gently.

shut down^{복습}

phrasal v. (기계가) 멈추다, 정지하다
If a machine shuts down, or someone shuts it down, it stops working.

house lights
[háus làits]

n. 극장 객석의 조명
In a theater or cinema, when the house lights dim or go down, the lights where the audience sits are switched off.

encore
[ά:ŋkɔ:r]

n. 앙코르
An encore is a short extra performance at the end of a longer one, which an entertainer gives because the audience asks for it.

raucous
[rɔ́:kəs]

a. 요란하고 거친, 시끌벅적한
A raucous sound is loud, harsh, and rather unpleasant.

performance**
[pərfɔ́:rməns]

n. 공연, 연주; 실행, 수행, 성과
A performance involves entertaining an audience by doing something such as singing, dancing, or acting.

skip*
[skip]

v. 거르다, 건너뛰다, 빼먹다; 깡총 뛰다, 가볍게 뛰다
If you skip or skip over a part of something you are reading or a story you are telling, you miss it out or pass over it quickly and move on to something else.

struggle**
[strʌgl]

v. 분투하다, 열심히 하다; 버둥거리다, 허덕이다; n. 노력, 분투
If you struggle to do something, you try hard to do it, even though other people or things may be making it difficult for you to succeed.

keep up

idiom 뒤떨어지지 않도록 따라가다
If you keep up with something, you continue to pay or do something regularly.

at the top of one's lungs**폐
[]

idiom (목청이 터지도록) 큰 소리로
If you scream at the top of your lungs, you scream as loud as you possible.

improvise
[ímprəvàiz]

v. 즉석에서 하다, 즉흥 연주[작곡, 노래]를 하다
If you improvise, you make or do something using whatever you have or without having planned it in advance.

fizzle
[fizl]

vi. 약하게 쉿 소리 나다; 실패하다
If something fizzles, it ends in a weak or disappointing way after starting off strongly.

amid
[əmíd]

pre. ~의 한 복판에, 한창 ~할 때에
If something happens amid noises or events of some kind, it happens while the other things are happening.

for good

idiom 이것을 최후로, 영원히
If you say that something will happen or continue for good, you mean that it will always happen or continue forever.

118

1. Why was Kaira's manager upset with the performance?
   A. He didn't want Kaira having fun.
   B. He was worried about what the critics would say.
   C. He thought that she shouldn't have invited out Armpit and Ginny.
   D. He thought that she should have done another encore.

2. What flavor of ice cream did Armpit and Ginny eat with Kaira?
   A. Vanilla
   B. Chocolate
   C. Chocolate chip
   D. Cookies and cream

3. What happened to Cotton, the band's drummer?
   A. He broke his arm playing too quickly.
   B. He had to pay a fine for copyright infringement.
   C. He was fired by El Genius for playing that last song.
   D. He was given a promotion for his great skill.

4. What kind of hint did Ginny give Kaira about Armpit's nickname?

   A. She said that it was smelly.

   B. She said that it was dirty.

   C. She said that it included the word 'arm.'

   D. She said that it was a body part.

5. How did Ginny's mother feel about Armpit bring Ginny back late?

   A. She was delighted that Ginny had fun.

   B. She was upset with Armpit for being irresponsible.

   C. She regretted letting Ginny go to the concert.

   D. She almost called the police.

6. Why did X-Ray make copies of the tickets?

   A. He had made copies of tickets before at Copy King.

   B. He wanted to see how copies would look.

   C. He wanted to make copies to keep as records.

   D. He thought that he might lose the real tickets.

7. Why did Kaira call Armpit after the concert?

   A. Armpit had left his shirt at the concert.

   B. She wanted to offer Armpit a job with her crew.

   C. She wanted to meet Armpit for breakfast.

   D. She wanted to give Armpit a refund for his ticket.

Check Your Reading Speed

1분에 몇 단어를 읽는지 리딩 속도를 측정해보세요.

$$\frac{1,626 \text{ words}}{\text{reading time ( ) sec}} \times 60 = (\quad) \text{ WPM}$$

Build Your Vocabulary

army**
[áːrmi]

n. 다수; 집단, 떼; 군대
An army of people, animals, or things is a large number of them, especially when they are regarded as a force of some kind.

unhook
[ʌnhúk]

v. (갈고리 등에 걸린 것을) 떼어 내다, (의복 등의) 훅을 끄르다
If you unhook something that is held in place by hooks, you open it or remove it by undoing the hooks.

cord*
[kɔːrd]

n. (전기) 코드, 끈, 줄; 굴레, 속박; vt. 끈으로 묶다
Cord is wire covered in rubber or plastic which connects electrical equipment to an electricity supply.

instrument**
[ínstrəmənt]

n. 악기; 기구, 도구
A musical instrument is an object such as a piano, guitar, or flute, which you play in order to produce music.

equip**
[ikwíp]

vt. 갖추다, 장비하다 (equipment n. 장치, 장비)
If you equip a person or thing with something, you give them the tools or equipment that are needed.

constant*
[kánstənt]

a. 끊임없이 계속되는; 변함없는, 불변의
You use constant to describe something that happens all the time or is always there.

motion*
[móuʃən]

n. 움직임, 운동; 몸짓, 신호; vt. 몸짓으로 신호하다
Motion is the activity or process of continually changing position or moving from one place to another.

wheel**
[hwiːl]

vt. ~을 나르다; (차를) 움직이다, 운전하다; 돌리다, 회전시키다; n. 바퀴
If you wheel an object that has wheels somewhere, you push it along.

loading dock
n. (건물의) 짐 싣는 곳
A loading dock is a platform for loading vehicles or trains.

beard**
[biərd]

n. 턱수염 (bearded a. 수염이 있는)
A man's beard is the hair that grows on his chin and cheeks.

passageway
[pǽsidʒwèi]

n. 복도, 통로
A passageway is a long narrow space with walls or fences on both sides, which connects one place or room with another.

argue**
[áːrgjuː]

v. 논쟁하다; 주장하다
If one person argues with another, they speak angrily to each other about something that they disagree about.

122

athletic[*]
[æθlétik]

a. 강건한, 운동선수다운
An athletic person is fit, and able to perform energetic movements easily.

performance[복습]
[pərfɔ́:rməns]

n. 공연, 연주; 실행, 수행, 성과
A performance involves entertaining an audience by doing something such as singing, dancing, or acting.

critic[복습]
[krítik]

n. 비평가, 평론가
A critic is a person who writes about and expresses opinions about things such as books, films, music, or art.

butcher[*]
[bútʃər]

vt. ~을 엉망진창으로 만들다; 도살하다, 학살하다; n. 고깃간 주인, 도살업자
If you butcher something, you do it clumsily and awkwardly.

spontaneous[*]
[spɑntéiniəs]

a. 자연히 일어나는, 자연적인
Spontaneous acts are not planned or arranged, but are done because someone suddenly wants to do them.

glance[복습]
[glæns]

v. 흘끗 보다, 잠깐 보다; n. 흘끗 봄
If you glance at something or someone, you look at them very quickly and then look away again immediately.

off limits
[ɔ́:f límits]

a. 출입 금지(구역)의
If a place is off limits to someone, they are not allowed to go there.

scowl[복습]
[skaul]

vi. 얼굴을 찌푸리다, 싫은 기색을 하다; n. 찌푸린 얼굴
When someone scowls, an angry or hostile expression appears on their face.

flavor[복습]
[fléivər]

n. 맛, 풍미; 정취, 멋
The flavor of a food or drink is its taste.

utility[*]
[ju:tíləti]

n. 실용, 유용; (pl.) 공공시설; a. 실용적인; 공공사업의
The utility of something is its usefulness.

closet[*]
[klɑ́zit]

n. 벽장; 작은 방
A closet is a very small room for storing things, especially one without windows.

couch[복습]
[kautʃ]

n. 소파, 긴 의자
A couch is a long, comfortable seat for two or three people.

squeeze[복습]
[skwi:z]

vt. 밀어 넣다, 쑤셔 넣다; 꽉 쥐다[죄다]; 짜다, 압착하다; n. 압착, 짜냄
If you squeeze a person or thing somewhere or if they squeeze there, they manage to get through or into a small space.

miniature
[míniətʃər]

a. 소형의, 작은; n. 축소모형
Miniature is used to describe something which is very small, especially a smaller version of something which is normally much bigger.

freezer[*]
[frí:zər]

n. 냉동고
A freezer is a large container like a fridge in which the temperature is kept below freezing point so that you can store food inside it for long periods.

compartment*
[kəmpáːrtmənt]

n. 구획, 칸막이
A compartment is one of the separate parts of an object that is used for keeping things in.

scoop
[skuːp]

vt. 퍼내다, 푸다; (양손·양팔로) 단번에 그러모으다; n. 국자, 주걱
If you scoop something from a container, you remove it with something such as a spoon.

carton*
[káːrtn]

n. 종이[플라스틱] 용기; 한 상자분의 용량
A carton is a plastic or cardboard container in which food or drink is sold.

drench^{복습}
[drentʃ]

vt. 흠뻑 젖게 하다; 담그다
To drench something or someone means to make them completely wet.

sweat^{복습}
[swet]

n. 땀; v. 땀 흘리다; 습기가 차다
Sweat is the salty colorless liquid which comes through your skin when you are hot, ill, or afraid.

gross^{복습}
[grous]

a. 역겨운, 기분 나쁜; 큰, 비대한; 전체의
If you describe something as gross, you think it is very unpleasant.

sweaty^{복습}
[swéti]

a. 땀이 나는, 땀투성이의
If parts of your body or your clothes are sweaty, they are soaked or covered with sweat.

dare^{복습}
[dɛər]

v. 감히 ~하다, 무릅쓰다, 도전하다
If you dare to do something, you do something which requires a lot of courage.

piss off

phrasal v. 화나게 하다, 애먹이다; 나가다, 떠나다
If someone piss you off, they make you annoyed or irritated.

admit***
[ædmít]

v. 인정하다, 시인하다; 들이다, 허락하다
If you admit that something bad, unpleasant, or embarrassing is true, you agree, often unwillingly, that it is true.

gasp^{복습}
[gæsp]

v. (놀람 따위로) 숨이 막히다, 헐떡거리다; n. 헐떡거림
When you gasp, you take a short quick breath through your mouth, especially when you are surprised, shocked, or in pain.

senior^{복습}
[síːnjər]

n. 선배, 연장자; a. 최고 학년의, 상위의; 손위의
Seniors are students in a high school, university, or college who are the oldest and who have reached an advanced level in their studies.

juvenile^{복습}
[dʒúːvənl]

n. 청소년; a. 유치한, 미숙한; 젊은, 나이 어린
A juvenile is a child or young person who is not yet old enough to be regarded as an adult.

correct^{복습}
[kərékt]

v. 나무라다, 벌주다; 정정하다, 고치다; a. 옳은 (correctional a. 처벌의)
If you correct someone, you scold or punish them in order to improve.

facility^{복습}
[fəsíləti]

n. 기관, 시설; 편의, 쉬움
A facility isa building or place that provides a particular service or is used for a particular industry.

pronounce**
[prənáuns]

v. 발음하다; 선언하다
To pronounce a word means to say it using particular sounds.

out of hand

idiom 감당할 수 없이, 주체하지 못하게
If something get out of hand, it becomes difficult or impossible to control.

catch up^{복습}

idiom 뒤처진 것을 만회하다; (움직이는 사람 · 물건을) 따라잡다, 접근하다
To catch up means to spend extra time doing all the work or tasks that you should have done earlier.

coax
[kouks]

vt. 유도해내다, 구슬리다, 달래다
If you coax someone into doing something, you gently try to persuade them to do it.

whisper^{복습}
[hwíspə:r]

v. 속삭이다, 작은 소리로 말하다; n. 속삭임
When you whisper, you say something very quietly.

conspiratorial
[kənspìrətɔ́:riəl]

a. 공모의, 음모의 (conspiratorially ad. 공모하여)
If someone does something such as speak or smile in a conspiratorial way, they do it in a way that suggests they are sharing a secret with someone.

bald^{복습}
[bɔ:ld]

a. (머리 등이) 벗어진, 대머리의; vi. 머리가 벗어지다
Someone who is bald has little or no hair on the top of their head.

apologetic
[əpὰlədʒétik]

a. 사과하는, 미안해 하는 (apologetically ad. 사과하듯)
If you are apologetic, you show or say that you are sorry for causing trouble for someone, for hurting them, or for disappointing them.

suck**
[sʌk]

v. 형편없다; 빨다, 삼키다; 흡수하다, 얻다
If someone says that something sucks, they are indicating that they think it is very bad.

swear^{복습}
[swɛər]

v. 맹세하다, 증언하다
If you say that you swear that something is true or that you can swear to it, you are saying very firmly that it is true.

neat**
[ni:t]

a. 말끔한, 정돈된, 깨끗한 (neatly ad. 깔끔하게)
A neat place, thing, or person is tidy and smart, and has everything in the correct place.

shrug^{복습}
[ʃrʌg]

v. (어깨를) 으쓱하다; n. (양 손바닥을 내보이면서 어깨를) 으쓱하기
If you shrug, you raise your shoulders to show that you are not interested in something or that you do not know or care about something.

1분에 몇 단어를 읽는지 리딩 속도를 측정해보세요.

$$\frac{1,231 \text{ words}}{\text{reading time ( ) sec}} \times 60 = (\quad) \text{ WPM}$$

Build Your Vocabulary

responsible^{복습}
[rispánsəbl]

a. 책임 있는, 책임을 져야 할 (responsibility n. 책임)
If you are responsible for something, it is your job or duty to deal with it and make decisions relating to it.

delight^{복습}
[diláit]

v. 즐겁게 하다, 매우 기쁘게 하다; n. 기쁨, 즐거움
If you delight in something, you get a lot of pleasure from it.

counterfeit^{복습}
[káuntərfit]

a. 가짜의, 모조의; v. (화폐 · 지폐 · 문서 등을) 위조하다
Counterfeit money, goods, or documents are not genuine, but have been made to look exactly like genuine ones in order to deceive people.

suffer^{복습}
[sʌ́fər]

v. 괴로워하다, 고통 받다; 겪다, 당하다
If you suffer from an illness or from some other bad condition, you are badly affected by it.

mild^{복습}
[maild]

a. (정도가) 심하지 않은; 유순한, 부드러운; 온화한
Mild is used to describe something such as a feeling, attitude, or illness that is not very strong or severe.

seizure^{복습}
[síːʒər]

n. (병의) 발작; 잡기, 체포; 압수
If someone has a seizure, they have a sudden violent attack of an illness, especially one that affects their heart or brain.

station^{복습}
[stéiʃən]

n. 부, 부서; 방송 채널, 방송국; 역, 정류장; 지역 본부, 사업소
A station is a facility equipped with special equipment and personnel for a particular purpose.

shield[*]
[ʃiːld]

v. 보호하다, 숨겨서 지키다; 방패가 되다; n. 방패, 보호[물]
If you shield your eyes, you put your hand above your eyes to protect them from direct sunlight.

hoarse
[hɔːrs]

a. 목소리가 쉰, 허스키한
If your voice is hoarse or if you are hoarse, your voice sounds rough and unclear, for example because your throat is sore.

serve right

idiom 인과응보다; 당연한 보복이 되다
If you say it serves someone right when something unpleasant happens to them, you mean that it is their own fault and you have no sympathy for them.

force^{***}
[fɔːrs]

v. 강요하다, 억지로 시키다; (힘 · 목소리를) 무리하게 내다, 짜내다; n. 힘; 영향력
If someone forces you to do something, they make you do it even though you do not want to, for example by threatening you.

release^{복습}
[rilíːs]

vt. 해방하다, 석방하다, 놓아주다; n. 석방
If a person or animal is released from somewhere where they have been looked after, they are set free or allowed to go.

internal[*]
[intə́ːrnl]

a. 체내의, 내부의; 내면의, 정신의
Internal is used to describe things that exist or happen inside a particular person, object, or place.

permanent^{**}
[pə́ːrmənənt]

a. 영구적인, 불변의 (permanently ad. 영구히)
Something that is permanent lasts forever.

out of whack

idiom 고장난
Something is out of whack is not working as it should.

foul[*]
[faul]

n. 반칙; 싫은 것, 더러운 것; a. 규칙 위반인, 반칙인; 더러운, 악취 나는
A foul is an act in a game or sport that is not allowed according to the rules.

cool one's jets

idiom 진정시키다
If something cools your jets, it makes you become less excited, intense, or active.

wad^{복습}
[wad]

n. 뭉치, 다발; 다수, 많음
A wad of something such as paper or cloth is a tight bundle or ball of it.

grab^{복습}
[græb]

v. 부여잡다, 움켜쥐다; n. 부여잡기
If you grab something, you take it or pick it up suddenly and roughly.

collar^{**}
[kɑ́lər]

n. 칼라, 깃; vt. 목덜미를 잡다, 체포하다; 깃을[목걸이를] 달다
The collar of a shirt or coat is the part which fits round the neck and is usually folded over.

dude^{복습}
[djuːd]

n. 사내, 녀석; (구어) 형씨, 친구
A dude is a man.

disrespect^{복습}
[dìsrispékt]

vt. ~에 결례되는 짓을 하다; n. 무례, 결례
If someone disrespects, they speak or behave in a way that shows lack of respect for a person, law, or custom.

compare^{복습}
[kəmpéər]

v. ~와 비교하다, 견주다; 비유하다
When you compare things, you consider them and discover the differences or similarities between them.

desperate^{복습}
[déspərət]

a. 필사적인; 자포자기의, 절망적인
If you are desperate for something or desperate to do something, you want or need it very much indeed.

offer^{복습}
[ɔ́ːfər]

v. 제의[제안]하다; 제공하다; n. 제공
If you offer something to someone, you ask them if they would like to have it or use it.

apiece^{복습}
[əpíːs]

ad. 제각기, 각자에게
If people have a particular number of things apiece, they have that number each.

glare^{복습}
[glɛər]

v. 노려보다; 번쩍번쩍 빛나다; n. 노려봄; 번쩍이는 빛
If you glare at someone, you look at them with an angry expression on your face.

figure out^{복습}

phrasal v. ~을 생각해내다, 발견하다
If you figure out a solution to a problem or the reason for something, you succeed in solving it or understanding it.

flexible^{복습}
[fléksəbl]

a. 융통성 있는, 유연한; 구부리기 쉬운
Something or someone that is flexible is able to change easily and adapt to different conditions and circumstances as they occur.

stretch^{복습}
[stretʃ]

v. 쭉 펴다, 뻗다, 늘이다; n. (특히 길게 뻗은) 길, 구간; 뻗침
When you stretch, you put your arms or legs out straight and tighten your muscles.

blow^{**}
[blou]

v. 누설하다, 고자질하다; 불다; 폭파하다; n. 강타, 급습
If you blow something like a rumor, you spread or make it widely known.

guilty^{**}
[gílti]

a. 죄의식이 있는, 유죄의, 범죄적인
If you feel guilty, you feel unhappy because you think that you have done something wrong or have failed to do something which you should have done.

waltz
[wɔːlts]

v. 당당하게 걷다; 왈츠를 추다; n. 왈츠(두 사람이 추는 3박자의 춤)
If you say that someone waltzes somewhere, you mean that they do something in a relaxed and confident way.

witch[*]
[witʃ]

n. 마녀, 여자 마법사; vt. 마법을 걸다, 황홀하게 하다
In fairy stories, a witch is a woman, usually an old woman, who has evil magic powers.

fake[*]
[feik]

a. 가짜의, 위조의; v. 가장하다, 꾸며내다, 위조하다
A fake fur or a fake painting, for example, is a fur or painting that has been made to look valuable or genuine, usually in order to deceive people.

hang up^{복습}

phrasal v. 전화를 끊다
To hang up means to end a telephone conversation, often very suddenly, by putting down the part of the telephone that you speak into or switching the telephone off.

scoop^{복습}
[skuːp]

vt. (양손 · 양팔로) 단번에 그러모으다; 퍼내다, 푸다; n. 국자, 주걱
If you scoop something up, you move of lift it using a quick continuous movement.

figure^{복습}
[fíɡjər]

v. 계산하다; 생각하다, 판단하다; n. 수치, 숫자; 형태, 형상; 작은 조각상
If you figure something out, you calculate the total amount of something.

split^{복습}
[split]

v. 분배하다; 쪼개다, 찢다, 째다; n. 쪼개기, 분열
If something splits or if you split it, it is divided into two or more parts.

toss[*]
[tɔːs]

v. 던지다; 흔들(리)다; n. 던지기
If you toss something somewhere, you throw it there lightly, often in a rather careless way.

128

buck^{복습}
[bʌk]

① n. (속어) 달러 ② n. 수사슴, 수컷
A buck is a US or Australian dollar.

1. What did Armpit do in order to contact Kaira at the Four Seasons hotel?
   A. He asked a family about a character in Bewitched in order to remember the name Kaira used.
   B. He called Kaira on her cell phone to tell her that he was there.
   C. He sent her a text message on her phone telling her to meet him in the lobby.
   D. He had X-Ray honk his car horn loud to get Kaira's attention.

2. What name did Kaira use when she registered at the Four Seasons hotel?
   A. Mindy Tyler
   B. Elizabeth Montgomery
   C. Samantha Stevens
   D. Kaira DeLeon

3. Armpit was told to take small steps. Why was Kaira told to take big steps?
   A. Kaira had to do well quickly before she lost her popularity.
   B. Kaira had to earn money quickly in order to save her friend from a disease.
   C. Kaira had to marry a famous and wealthy prince later in life.
   D. Kaira wanted to impress her mother with her success.

4. What deal did Armpit make with Kaira regarding his nickname?

   A. He would tell her if she closed her eyes.

   B. He would give her three guesses and he would tell her if she was right.

   C. He would tell her if she agreed to touch the named body part.

   D. He would let Ginny tell her his nickname if Kaira called her.

5. Why did NOT Armpit kiss Kaira?

   A. He was afraid that he had bad breath.

   B. He thought it was too early in their relationship.

   C. He didn't know how to kiss.

   D. He couldn't in front of her bodyguard.

6. Who was the woman who came to Armpit's house and why did she come?

   A. Kaira DeLeon's mother came to check out Armpit.

   B. Detective Debbie Newberg came to talk with him about the concert tickets.

   C. Ginny's mother came to get help from Armpit.

   D. A police officer came to apologize to Armpit for what happened at the concert.

7. Which of the following did NOT describe how Armpit felt after meeting the woman?

   A. He thought she was nice and had a sweet smile.

   B. He felt bad for lying to her.

   C. He worried that she might get hurt.

   D. He hoped that she would arrest X-Ray.

1분에 몇 단어를 읽는지 리딩 속도를 측정해보세요.

$$\frac{2{,}423 \text{ words}}{\text{reading time (\quad) sec}} \times 60 = (\qquad) \text{ WPM}$$

Build Your Vocabulary

payback
[péibæk]
n. 보복, 앙갚음; 환불, 원금 회수
Payback refers to the act of harming someone in revenge for something harmful that they have done.

phony
[fóuni]
a. 가짜의, 엉터리의; n. 가짜, 위조품, 사기꾼
If you describe something as phony, you disapprove of it because it is false rather than genuine.

clue*
[klu:]
n. 실마리, 단서; vt. 암시를 주다, 귀띔하다
A clue to a problem or mystery is something that helps you to find the answer to it.

ordinary**
[ɔ́:rdənèri]
n. 보통의 상태[정도]; a. 보통의, 평범한
(out of ordinary idiom 보통 이상의, 비정상의)
Something that is out of the ordinary is unusual or different.

circular*
[sə́:rkjulər]
a. 원형의, 둥근
Something that is circular is shaped like a circle.

revolve*
[riválv]
v. 회전하다, 빙빙 돌다 (revolving door n. 회전문)
When something revolves or when you revolve it, it moves or turns in a circle around a central point or line.

remind복습
[rimáind]
vt. 생각나게 하다, 상기시키다, 일깨우다
If someone reminds you of a fact or event that you already know about, they say something which makes you think about it.

ancient**
[éinʃənt]
a. 고대의, 옛날의; n. 고대인
Ancient means very old, or having existed for a long time.

temple*
[templ]
n. 신전, 사원
A temple is a building used for the worship of a god or gods, especially in the Buddhist and Hindu religions, and in ancient Greek and Roman times.

pillar*
[pílər]
n. 기둥; vt. 기둥으로 받치다
A pillar is a tall solid structure, which is usually used to support part of a building.

marble*
[ma:rbl]
a. 대리석으로 된; n. 대리석; 구슬
Marble is a type of very hard rock which feels cold when you touch it and which shines when it is cut and polished.

concierge^{복습}
[kànsiéərʒ]

n. (호텔의) 안내원; 수위
A concierge is a person, especially in France, who looks after a block of flats and checks people entering and leaving the building.

intimidate
[intímədèit]

vt. 겁주다, 두려워하게 만들다 (intimidating a. 위협적인)
If you intimidate someone, you deliberately make them frightened enough to do what you want them to do.

bellhop
[bélhap]

n. 벨보이(호텔에서 짐을 운반하는 사람)
A bellhop is a man or boy who works in a hotel, carrying bags or bringing things to the guests' rooms.

dial^{복습}
[dáiəl]

v. 전화를 걸다, 다이얼을 돌리다; n. 다이얼
If you dial or if you dial a number, you turn the dial or press the buttons on a telephone in order to phone someone.

operate^{복습}
[ápərèit]

v. (기계 · 장치 등을) 움직이다, 작동하다; 사업하다, 경영하다; 수술하다
(operator n. 전화 교환원)
When you operate a machine or device, or when it operates, you make it work.

note^{복습}
[nout]

n. (악기의) 음; (짧은) 기록; 짧은 편지; v. 주목하다, 알아채다; 메모하다
In music, a note is the sound of a particular pitch, or a written symbol representing this sound.

twitch^{복습}
[twitʃ]

v. (손가락 · 근육 따위가) 씰룩거리다; 홱 잡아당기다, 잡아채다; n. 씰룩거림, 경련
If something, especially a part of your body, twitches or if you twitch it, it makes a little jumping movement.

blond[*]
[bland]

a. 금발의
Blond hair can be very light brown or light yellow.

twin[*]
[twin]

n. 쌍둥이 (중의 한 명)
If two people are twins, they have the same mother and were born on the same day.

protect^{복습}
[prətékt]

v. 보호하다, 막다, 지키다
To protect someone or something means to prevent them from being harmed or damaged.

witch^{복습}
[witʃ]

n. 마녀, 여자 마법사; vt. 마법을 걸다, 황홀하게 하다
In fairy stories, a witch is a woman, usually an old woman, who has evil magic powers.

credit^{**}
[krédit]

n. 칭찬, 인정; 신용, 신뢰; vt. ~을 믿다; 명예롭게 하다
If you get the credit for something good, people praise you because you are responsible for it, or are thought to be responsible for it.

declare^{***}
[dikléər]

v. 단언하다; 선언하다, 공표하다
If you declare that something is true, you say that it is true in a firm, deliberate way.

denim
[dénəm]

n. 데님
Denim is a thick cotton cloth, usually blue, which is used to make clothes. Jeans are made from denim.

sleeve*
[sli:v]

n. 소매, 소맷자락; vt. 소매를 달다 (sleeveless a. 소매가 없는)
The sleeves of a coat, shirt, or other item of clothing are the parts that cover your arms.

belly button
[béli bʌ́tən]

n. 배꼽
Your belly button is the small round thing in the center of your stomach.

knuckle*
[nʌkl]

n. 손가락 관절[마디]
Your knuckles are the rounded pieces of bone that form lumps on your hands where your fingers join your hands, and where your fingers bend.

tan*
[tæn]

n. 황갈색; 햇볕에 그을음; vt. (피부를) 햇볕에 태우다
Something that is tan is a light brown color.

starve*
[sta:rv]

v. 굶주리다, 굶어죽다
If you say that you are starving, you mean that you are very hungry.

flight^{복습}
[flait]

n. 계단, 층계; 날기, 비행
A flight of steps or stairs is a set of steps or stairs that lead from one level to another without changing direction.

patio
[pǽtiòu]

n. 문밖 테라스; (스페인식 집의) 안뜰
A patio is an area of flat blocks or concrete next to a house, where people can sit and relax or eat.

overlook*
[òuvərlúk]

vt. 내려다보다; 못 보고 지나치다; 눈감아주다
If a building or window overlooks a place, you can see the place clearly from the building or window.

hostess*
[hóustis]

n. 여주인
The hostess at a party is the woman who has invited the guests and provides the food, drink, or entertainment.

booth*
[bu:θ]

n. (식당의) 칸막이된 자리, 작은 공간, 부스
A booth in a restaurant or cafe consists of a table with long fixed seats on two or sometimes three sides of it.

privacy^{복습}
[práivəsi]

n. 사생활; 비밀, 은밀
If you have privacy, you are in a place or situation which allows you to do things without other people seeing you or disturbing you.

aid**
[eid]

n. 구원, 구조, 원조; v. 돕다, 조력하다
(come to a person's aid idiom ~에게 원조의 손길을 뻗치다)
If you come or go to someone's aid, you try to help them when they are in danger or difficulty.

just in case^{복습}

idiom 만일에 대비하여
Just in case means so as to be prepared for what may or may not happen.

squeeze^{복습}
[skwi:z]

vt. 짜다, 압착하다; 꽉 쥐다[죄다]; 밀어 넣다, 쑤셔 넣다; n. 압착, 짜냄
If you squeeze a liquid or a soft substance out of an object, you get the liquid or substance out by pressing the object.

134

opposite ^{복습}
[ápəzit]

a. 정반대의; 반대편의, 맞은편의; ad. 정반대의 위치에
The opposite of someone or something is the person or thing that is most different from them.

dump ^{복습}
[dʌmp]

vt. 아무렇게나 내려놓다; (쓰레기를) 버리다; n. 쓰레기 더미
If you dump something somewhere, you put it or unload it there quickly and carelessly.

packet[*]
[pǽkit]

n. (1회분의 액체·가루가 든 포장용) 봉지; 소포
A packet is a small container in which a quantity of something is sold.

awkward^{**}
[ɔ́:kwərd]

a. 어색한, 불편한, 곤란한
Someone who feels awkward behaves in a shy or embarrassed way.

security ^{복습}
[sikjúərəti]

n. 보안, 경비; 안전, 보호
Security refers to all the measures that are taken to protect a place, or to ensure that only people with permission enter it or leave it.

nod ^{복습}
[nad]

v. 끄덕이다, 끄덕여 표시하다; n. (동의·인사·신호·명령의) 끄덕임
If you nod, you move your head downward and upward to show agreement, understanding, or approval.

view^{**}
[vju:]

n. 경치, 풍경; 시야, 시각; 견해, 의견; v. 보다, 고찰하다
The view from a window or high place is everything which can be seen from that place, especially when it is considered to be beautiful.

unusual ^{복습}
[ʌnjú:ʒuəl]

a. 보통이 아닌, 드문 (unusually ad. 보통이 아니게, 현저히)
If you describe someone as unusual, you think that they are interesting and different from other people.

colony ^{복습}
[káləni]

n. (동일 지역에 서식하는 동·식물의) 군집; 식민지, 거류지
A colony of birds, insects, or animals is a group of them that live together.

benefit[*]
[bénəfit]

n. 이익, 유리; v. 이득을 보다, 이익을 주다 (for one's benefit idiom ~을 위하여)
If you say that someone is doing something for the benefit of a particular person, you mean that they are doing it for that person.

manicure
[mǽnəkjùər]

vi. 손질하다; n. 손톱 손질 (manicured a. (잔디·정원 등이) 손질된)
A manicured lawn, park, or garden has very short neatly cut grass.

lawn[*]
[lɔ:n]

n. 잔디밭, 잔디
A lawn is an area of grass that is kept cut short and is usually part of someone's garden or backyard, or part of a park.

slope^{**}
[sloup]

v. 경사지(게 하)다, 비탈지다; n. 경사면, 비탈, 언덕
If a surface slopes, it is at an angle, so that one end is higher than the other.

steep[*]
[sti:p]

a. 가파른, 경사가 급한; n. 가파른 언덕
A steep slope rises at a very sharp angle and is difficult to go up.

ditch[*]
[ditʃ]

v. (사람을) 따돌리다, (물건을) 버리다; 도랑을 파다; n. 수로, 도랑
If someone ditches someone, they end a relationship with that person.

doofus ^{복습}
[dú:fəs]

n. (비격식) 멍청이, 얼간이
Doofus is a slow-witted or stupid person.

dirt복습
[dəːrt]

n. 흙, 진흙, 먼지; 가십, 스캔들
You can refer to the earth on the ground as dirt, especially when it is dusty.

brake＊
[breik]

n. 브레이크, 제동 장치; v. 브레이크를 걸어 정지시키다
(put on the brakes idiom 제동을 걸다)
You can use brake in a number of expressions to indicate that something has slowed down or stopped.

spin복습
[spin]

v. (spun–spun) 돌(리)다, 맴돌리다; 오래[질질] 끌다; n. 회전
If something spins or if you spin it, it turns quickly around a central point.

bounce복습
[bauns]

v. 튀다, 튀게 하다; 급히 움직이다, 뛰어다니다; n. 튐, 바운드
If something bounces off a surface or is bounced off it, it reaches the surface and is reflected back.

palm＊
[paːm]

n. 손바닥
The palm of your hand is the inside part.

kid복습
[kid]

v. 놀리다, 장난치다; 속이다; n. 어린이
If you are kidding, you are saying something that is not really true, as a joke.

wimp
[wimp]

n. 겁쟁이, 약골
If you call someone a wimp, you disapprove of them because they lack confidence or determination, or because they are often afraid of things.

point out복습

phrasal v. ~을 지적하다
If you point out a fact or mistake, you tell someone about it or draw their attention to it.

creepy
[kríːpi]

a. 소름이 끼치는, 오싹한; 꾸물꾸물 움직이는
If you say that something or someone is creepy, you mean they make you feel very nervous or frightened.

curious복습
[kjúəriəs]

a. 궁금한, 호기심이 많은; 별난, 특이한
If you are curious about something, you are interested in it and want to know more about it.

risk복습
[risk]

vt. 위험을 무릅쓰다; n. 위험
If you risk doing something, you do it, even though you know that it might have undesirable consequences.

blow복습
[blou]

v. (blew–blown) 폭파하다; 불다; 누설하다, 고자질하다; n. 강타, 급습
To blow something out, off, or away means to remove or destroy it violently with an explosion.

twinge
[twindʒ]

n. 찌릿한 통증; (정신적) 고통, (마음의) 가책
A twinge is a sudden sharp pain.

smooth복습
[smuːð]

a. 매끄러운; 유창한; v. 매끄럽게 하다[되다]
You use smooth to describe something that is going well and is free of problems or trouble.

136

weird^{복습}
[wiə:rd]

a. 이상한, 기묘한; 수상한
If you describe something or someone as weird, you mean that they are strange.

proposal^{복습}
[prəpóuzəl]

n. 결혼 신청, 청혼; 신청, 제안
A proposal is the act of asking someone to marry you.

claim^{복습}
[kleim]

v. 주장하다; 요구[청구]하다; n. 요구, 청구; 권리
If you say that someone claims that something is true, you mean they say that it is true but you are not sure whether or not they are telling the truth.

billionaire
[biljənέər]

n. 억만장자, 갑부
A billionaire is an extremely rich person who has money or property worth at least a thousand million pounds or dollars.

charm^{복습}
[ʧa:rm]

v. 매력이 있다; 황홀하게 하다; n. 매력, 마력; 마술 (charming a. 매력 있는)
If you say that something is charming, you mean that it is very pleasant or attractive.

lame
[leim]

a. 설득력이 없는, 믿기 힘든; 절름발이의, 절룩거리는, 불구의
If you describe something, for example an excuse, argument, or remark, as lame, you mean that it is poor or weak.

glue^{복습}
[glu:]

vt. 접착제를 바르다; ~에 꼭 붙여서 떨어지지 않게 하다; n. 접착제
If you glue one object to another, you stick them together using glue.

counsel^{복습}
[káunsəl]

v. 상의하다; 조언[충고]하다; n. 상담, 조언, 권고 (counselor n. 상담가)
If you counsel people, you give them advice about their problems.

current^{복습}
[kə́:rənt]

n. 흐름, 해류, 기류; a. 지금의, 현재의; 유행하는
A current is a steady and continuous flowing movement of some of the water in a river, lake, or sea.

knock off^{복습}

phrasal v. ~을 쳐서[두드려서] 떨어뜨리다
If you knock someone off something, you make them fall off it by hitting them.

poetic[*]
[pouétik]

a. 시적인, 시의
Something that is poetic is very beautiful and expresses emotions in a sensitive or moving way.

wash up

phrasal v. 끝나게 하다, 망쳐놓다
If you say that someone is washed up, you mean that their career or success has ended.

damsel^{복습}
[dǽmzəl]

n. 계집아이, 처녀
A damsel is a young, unmarried woman.

distress^{복습}
[distrés]

n. 고통, 곤란; 가난, 곤궁; vt. 고민하게 하다, 괴롭히다
Distress is a state of extreme sorrow, suffering, or pain.

embarrass^{복습}
[imbǽrəs]

v. 부끄럽게[무안하게] 하다; 어리둥절하게 하다; 당황하다 (embarrassment n. 당황)
If something or someone embarrasses you, they make you feel shy or ashamed.

arrange^{복습}
[əréindʒ]

v. 준비하다, 계획을 짜다; 가지런히 하다, 배열하다
If you arrange an event or meeting, you make plans for it to happen.

freak ^{복습}
[fri:k]

n. 열광자, 괴짜; 희한한 것; v. 기겁하(게 하)다
(control freak n. 만사를 자기 뜻대로 하려는 사람, 지배광)
If you say that someone is a control freak, you mean that they want to be in control of every situation they find themselves in.

bet ^{복습}
[bet]

v. 틀림없이 ~이다, 확신하다; (돈을) 걸다, 내기를 하다; n. 내기, 건 돈
You use expressions such as 'I bet' to indicate that you are sure something is true.

fire ^{복습}
[faiər]

v. 해고하다; 발사하다; 불을 지르다; n. 불; 정열, 흥분
If an employer fires you, they dismiss you from your job.

calloused
[kǽləst]

a. 못[굳은살]이 박힌, 굳어진
A foot or hand that is calloused is covered in thick skin.

condition ^{***}
[kəndíʃən]

n. 조건; (건강) 상태, 상황; v. ~을 좌우하다; 조절[조정]하다
A condition is something which must happen or be done in order for something else to be possible, especially when this is written into a contract or law.

nasty ^{복습}
[nǽsti]

a. 추잡한, 더러운; 못된, 고약한
Something that is nasty is very unpleasant to see, experience, or feel.

shrug ^{복습}
[ʃrʌg]

v. (어깨를) 으쓱하다; n. (양 손바닥을 내보이면서 어깨를) 으쓱하기
If you shrug, you raise your shoulders to show that you are not interested in something or that you do not know or care about something.

mean ^{***}
[mi:n]

① a. 성질이 나쁜, 심술궂은 ② vt. 의미하다, 뜻하다 ③ a. 평균의, 중간의
If you describe a behavior as mean, you are saying that it is very bad and evil.

shriek ^{복습}
[ʃri:k]

v. 새된 소리를 지르다, 비명을 지르다; n. 비명
When someone shrieks, they make a short, very loud cry.

pull away

phrasal v. (몸을) 빼다; 뿌리치다; (차가 발차하여) 떠나다
If you pull away from something, you move quickly away from it.

ticklish
[tíkliʃ]

a. 간지럼을 타는; 신경질적인
Someone who is ticklish is sensitive to being tickled, and laughs as soon as you tickle them.

still ^{***}
[stil]

a. 정지한, 움직이지 않는; 조용한, 고요한; ad. 여전히, 아직도
If you stay still, you stay in the same position and do not move.

poke ^{복습}
[pouk]

v. 찌르다, 쑤시다; 삐져나오다; 들이대다; n. 찌름, 쑤심
If you poke someone or something, you quickly push them with your finger or with a sharp object.

fulfill ^{복습}
[fulfíl]

vt. (의무·명령을) 이행하다, 다하다; 이루다, 달성하다
To fulfill a task, role, or requirement means to do or be what is required, necessary, or expected.

bargain ^{복습}
[bá:rgən]

n. 거래, 매매 계약; 싼 물건, 특가품, 특매품; v. 흥정하다, 거래하다
A bargain is an agreement, especially a formal business agreement, in which two people or groups agree what each of them will do, pay, or receive.

138

yuck
[jʌk]

int. 윽(역겨울 때 내는 소리)
People say 'yuck' to indicate contempt, dislike, or disgust.

sweaty^{복습}
[swéti]

a. 땀이 나는, 땀투성이의
If parts of your body or your clothes are sweaty, they are soaked or covered with sweat.

scorpion^{복습}
[skɔ́ːrpiən]

n. 전갈
A scorpion is a small creature which looks like a large insect. Scorpions have a long curved tail, and some of them are poisonous.

tiptoe
[típtòu]

n. 발끝; vi. 발끝으로 걷다, 발돋움하다
If you do something on tiptoe or on tiptoes, you do it standing or walking on the front part of your foot, without putting your heels on the ground.

pulsate
[pʌ́lseit]

vi. 진동하다, 고동치다
If something pulsates, it beats, moves in and out, or shakes with strong, regular movements.

lean^{복습}
[liːn]

① v. 상체를 굽히다, 기울다; 기대다, 의지하다 ② a. 야윈, 마른
When you lean in a particular direction, you bend your body in that direction.

exclaim^{복습}
[ikskléim]

v. 외치다, 소리치다
If you exclaim, you say or shout something suddenly because of surprise, fear and pleasure.

Check Your Reading Speed

1분에 몇 단어를 읽는지 리딩 속도를 측정해보세요.

$$\frac{1{,}856 \text{ words}}{\text{reading time ( ) sec}} \times 60 = (\quad) \text{ WPM}$$

Build Your Vocabulary

tease^{복습}
[tiːz]

v. 놀리다, 괴롭히다; 졸라대다; n. 골리기
To tease someone means to laugh at them or make jokes about them in order to embarrass, annoy, or upset them.

giggle^{복습}
[gígl]

vi. 낄낄 웃다; n. 낄낄 웃음
If someone giggles, they laugh in a childlike way, because they are amused, nervous, or embarrassed.

spoonful*
[spúːnfùl]

n. 한 숟가락 가득(한 분량); 소량
You can refer to an amount of food resting on a spoon as a spoonful of food.

ruin^{복습}
[rúːin]

v. 망치다, 못쓰게 만들다; 몰락하다; n. 폐허; 파멸
To ruin something means to severely harm, damage, or spoil it.

smooth^{복습}
[smuːð]

a. 매끄러운; 유창한; v. 매끄럽게 하다[되다]
You use smooth to describe something that is going well and is free of problems or trouble.

yell^{복습}
[jel]

v. 소리치다, 고함치다; n. 고함소리, 부르짖음
If you yell, you shout loudly, usually because you are excited, angry, or in pain.

a dime a dozen

idiom (10센트로 한 다스나 살 수 있을 만큼) 흔해 빠진, 값싼
Something is a dime a dozen is so common as to be pratically worthless.

practically^{복습}
[prǽktikəli]

ad. 거의, ~이나 마찬가지; 실지로, 실질상
Practically means almost, but not completely or exactly.

sulk
[sʌlk]

vi. 샐쭉해지다, 부루퉁해지다; n. 샐쭉함, 부루퉁함
If you sulk, you are silent and bad-tempered for a while because you are annoyed about something.

charge^{복습}
[ʧaːrʤ]

v. (지불을) 청구하다; 부담 지우다, 맡기다; 돌격하다; n. 수수료, 요금; 책임, 의무
If you charge someone an amount of money, you ask them to pay that amount for something that you have sold to them or done for them.

big deal^{복습}
[bíg díːl]

n. 대단한 것, 중대사
If you say that something is a big deal, you mean that it is important or significant in some way.

140

porch ^{복습}
[pɔːrtʃ]

n. (본 건물 입구에 달린 지붕이 있는) 현관, 포치
A porch is a sheltered area at the entrance to a building, which has a roof and sometimes has walls.

reliable ^{복습}
[riláiəbl]

a. 의지할 수 있는, 신뢰할 수 있는
People or things that are reliable can be trusted to work well or to behave in the way that you want them to.

indicator
[índikèitər]

n. (일의 현황 · 사정 변화 등을 나타내는) 지표, 방향 표시등
An indicator is a measurement or value which gives you an idea of what something is like.

exception **
[iksépʃən]

n. 예외, 이례; 제외
An exception is a particular thing, person, or situation that is not included in a general statement, judgment, or rule.

detective *
[ditéktiv]

n. 형사, 수사관; 탐정
A detective is someone whose job is to discover what has happened in a crime or other situation and to find the people involved.

department ^{복습}
[dipá:rtmənt]

n. 부분, 부, 부서
A department is one of the sections in an organization such as a government, business, or university.

struggle ^{복습}
[strʌgl]

v. 분투하다, 열심히 하다; 버둥거리다, 허덕이다; n. 노력, 분투
If you struggle to do something, you try hard to do it, even though other people or things may be making it difficult for you to succeed.

composure *
[kəmpóuʒər]

n. 침착, 냉정, 평정, 자제
Composure is the appearance or feeling of calm and the ability to control your feelings.

offer ^{복습}
[ɔ́:fər]

v. 제공하다, 제의[제안]하다; n. 제공
If you offer something to someone, you ask them if they would like to have it or use it.

decline **
[dikláin]

v. 거절하다; 쇠퇴하다, 기울다
If you decline something or decline to do something, you politely refuse to accept it or do it.

plaid
[plæd]

a. 격자 무늬의; n. 격자무늬 천
Plaid is the check design.

couch ^{복습}
[kautʃ]

n. 소파, 긴 의자
A couch is a long, comfortable seat for two or three people.

lap ^{복습}
[læp]

① n. 무릎; (트랙의) 한 바퀴 ② v. (파도가) 찰싹거리다; (할짝할짝) 핥다
If you have something on your lap, it is on top of your legs and near to your body.

glow *
[glou]

n. 홍조, 새빨간 색; 백열, 새빨간 빛; v. 붉어지다; 빛을 내다
A glow is a pink color on a person's face, usually because they are healthy or have been exercising.

blush *
[blʌʃ]

v. 얼굴을 붉히다, (얼굴이) 빨개지다; n. 얼굴을 붉힘, 홍조
When you blush, your face becomes redder than usual because you are ashamed or embarrassed.

correct ^{복습}
[kərékt]

a. 옳은; v. 정정하다, 고치다; 나무라다, 벌주다
If something is correct, it is in accordance with the facts and has no mistakes.

resist ^{복습}
[rizíst]

v. 저항하다, 반대하다, 방해하다 (resistance n. 저항)
If you resist doing something, or resist the temptation to do it, you stop yourself from doing it although you would like to do it.

conscious^{**}
[kánʃəs]

a. 의식하고 있는, 알고 있는, 지각 있는
If you are conscious of something, you notice it or realize that it is happening.

worn^{**}
[wɔːrn]

a. 닳아 해진, 낡은; 진부한; 지친, 여윈
Worn is used to describe something that is damaged or thin because it is old and has been used a lot.

shoddy
[ʃádi]

a. 조잡한; 가짜의, 모조품의; n. 가짜, 싸구려; 겉치레, 허울
Shoddy work or a shoddy product has been done or made carelessly or badly.

suspect ^{복습}
[səspékt]

n. 용의자; v. 짐작하다, 의심하다, 혐의를 두다
A suspect is a person who the police or authorities think may be guilty of a crime.

remind ^{복습}
[rimáind]

vt. 상기시키다, 일깨우다, 생각나게 하다
If someone reminds you of a fact or event that you already know about, they say something which makes you think about it.

victim ^{복습}
[víktim]

n. 피해자, 희생(자)
A victim is someone who has suffered as a result of someone else's actions or beliefs, or as a result of unpleasant circumstances.

ad ^{복습}
[æd]

n. (= advertisement) 광고; 광고 활동
An advertisement is an announcement in a newspaper, on television, or on a poster about something such as a product, event, or job.

get ahold of

idiom ~을 손에 넣다, 잡다
To get ahold of something means to have or take it in your hands.

stick ^{복습}
[stik]

① v. 달라붙다, 붙이다; 내밀다; 고수하다 ② n. 막대기, 지팡이
If one thing sticks to another, it becomes attached to it and is difficult to remove.

recycle[*]
[riːsáikl]

vt. 재활용하다, ~을 순환 처리[사용]하다
If you recycle things that have already been used, such as bottles or sheets of paper, you process them so that they can be used again.

firm ^{복습}
[fəːrm]

① a. 굳은, 단단한; 견고한 (firmly ad. 단호하게) ② n. 회사
If you describe someone as firm, you mean they behave in a way that shows that they are not going to change their mind, or that they are the person who is in control.

desperate ^{복습}
[déspərət]

a. 필사적인; 자포자기의, 절망적인
If you are desperate for something or desperate to do something, you want or need it very much indeed.

142

end up ^{복습}

phrasal v. 마침내는 (~으로) 되다; 끝나다
If you end up doing something or end up in a particular state, you do that thing or get into that state even though you did not originally intend to.

foul ^{복습}
[faul]

n. 반칙; 싫은 것, 더러운 것. **a.** 규칙 위반인, 반칙인; 더러운, 악취 나는
A foul is an act in a game or sport that is not allowed according to the rules.

mayor ^{복습}
[méiər]

n. 시장(市長); (지방 자치단체의) 행정장관
The mayor of a town or city is the person who has been elected to represent it for a fixed period of time or, in some places, to run its government.

mild ^{복습}
[maild]

a. 유순한, 부드러운; 온화한; (정도가) 심하지 않은 (mildly ad. 조심스럽게)
Mild is used to describe something such as a feeling, attitude, or illness that is not very strong or severe.

curious ^{복습}
[kjúəriəs]

a. 궁금한, 호기심이 많은; 별난, 특이한
If you are curious about something, you are interested in it and want to know more about it.

relief **
[rilíːf]

n. 안심, 안도
If you feel a sense of relief, you feel happy because something unpleasant has not happened or is no longer happening.

prior *
[práiər]

a. 전의, 먼저의; 더 중요한, 우선하는
You use prior to indicate that something has already happened, or must happen, before another event takes place.

criminal ^{복습}
[krímənl]

a. 범죄의; **n.** 범죄자, 범인
Criminal means connected with crime.

initial *
[iníʃəl]

a. 처음의, 최초의; **n.** 이니셜, 머리글자
You use initial to describe something that happens at the beginning of a process.

decipher
[disáifər]

vt. 뜻을 파악하다; (암호 · 수수께끼를) 풀다, 해독하다
If you decipher a piece of writing or a message, you work out what it says, even though it is very difficult to read or understand.

recognize ^{복습}
[rékəgnaiz]

vt. 인지하다, 알아보다
If you recognize someone or something, you know who that person is or what that thing is.

hang ^{복습}
[hæŋ]

v. 매달리다; 걸다, 달아매다; 교수형에 처하다
If something hangs in a high place or position, or if you hang it there, it is attached there so it does not touch the ground.

bargain ^{복습}
[báːrgən]

v. 흥정하다, 거래하다; **n.** 싼 물건, 특가품, 특매품; 매매 계약, 거래
When people bargain with each other, they discuss what each of them will do, pay, or receive.

curb *
[kəːrb]

n. 도로 경계석, (차도 가의) 연석; **v.** 억제[제한]하다
The curb is the raised edge of a pavement or sidewalk which separates it from the road.

jam^{복습}
[dʒæm]

v. 밀어붙이다, 가득 차다; 쑤셔 넣다, 채워 넣다; n. 혼잡; 고장
(jammed a. 빽빽히 찬)
If a lot of people jam a place, or jam into a place, they are pressed tightly together so that they can hardly move.

distinguish**
[distíŋgwiʃ]

v. 구별하다, 분별하다; 구별이 되다, 특색을 나타내다 (distinguishing a. 특징적인)
If you can distinguish one thing from another or distinguish between two things, you can see or understand how they are different.

characteristic*
[kæriktərístik]

n. 특징, 특성; a. 독특한, 특징적인
The characteristics of a person or thing are the qualities or features that belong to them and make them recognizable.

tattoo^{복습}
[tætú:]

n. 문신; v. 문신을 새기다
A tattoo is a design that is drawn on someone's skin using needles to make little holes and filling them with colored dye.

mustache*
[mʌ́stæʃ]

n. 코밑수염
A man's moustache is the hair that grows on his upper lip.

mention^{복습}
[ménʃən]

vt. 말하다, 언급하다; n. 언급, 진술
If you mention something, you say something about it, usually briefly.

shave^{복습}
[ʃeiv]

v. 면도하다, 깎다, 밀다; n. 면도
When a man shaves, he removes the hair from his face using a razor or shaver so that his face is smooth.

1. Why was X-Ray NOT worried about the police and the tickets?
   A. He said that he had the perfect alibi for Armpit and himself.
   B. He said that the police had better things than investigate them.
   C. He said that he had bribed the police officers to drop the investigation.
   D. He said that he would be moving from Austin soon.

2. How did Ginny and Armpit try to guess where Kaira would be each day?
   A. They looked at her fan site online to check her GPS posts.
   B. They called her and asked for a hint about where she was staying then.
   C. They looked at the list of tour cities on the back of their souvenir shirts.
   D. They used a map to draw a line connecting random cities across America.

3. Why did Armpit make a mistake on the job with the sprinkler system?
   A. He had never worked with sprinkler systems before and was confused.
   B. He had run out of supplies and tried to use something else instead.
   C. X-Ray came by and he was distracted while talking to him.
   D. A Kaira DeLeon song came on the radio.

4. What did Detective Newberg say that made Armpit almost drop the phone?
   A. She mentioned the name Armpit.
   B. She said that he was the main suspect in the case.
   C. She said that she had arrested X-Ray.
   D. She accused him of being a drug dealer.

5. How did Kaira describe her relation to Armpit and Ginny in the letter?
   A. She wanted to come visit them again in Austin.
   B. Armpit and Ginny were her only friends.
   C. They reminded her of her friends in San Francisco.
   D. Armpit was really kind around Ginny.

6. What was Kaira's new nickname for her bodyguard?
   A. El Doofus
   B. Mr. Doofus
   C. Dr. Doofus
   D. Doofus Junior

7. How did Kaira say that Armpit helped her with her love songs?
   A. She pictured Armpit when she sang love songs.
   B. She used his loving words to her for inspiration.
   C. She used his voice for backup vocals.
   D. She asked him for useful feedback and his opinions.

1분에 몇 단어를 읽는지 리딩 속도를 측정해보세요.

$$\frac{1{,}226 \ words}{reading \ time \ (\quad) \ sec} \times 60 = (\quad) \ WPM$$

Build Your Vocabulary

pace^{복습}
[peis]

v. 왔다 갔다 하다, 보조를 맞추어 걷다; n. 걸음걸이, 보폭; 속도
If you pace a small area, you keep walking up and down it, because you are anxious or impatient.

launch^{복습}
[lɔːnʧ]

v. 시작하다, 착수하다; 발사하다, 던지다; 내보내다; n. 개시; 발포
To launch a large and important activity, for example a military attack, means to start it.

investigate[*]
[invéstəgèit]

v. 조사하다, 수사하다; 연구하다 (investigation n. 조사)
If someone, especially an official, investigates an event, situation, or claim, they try to find out what happened or what is the truth.

phony^{복습}
[fóuni]

a. 가짜의, 엉터리의; n. 가짜, 위조품, 사기꾼
If you describe something as phony, you disapprove of it because it is false rather than genuine.

come up with^{복습}

idiom ~을 제안하다, 생각하다
If you come up with a plan or idea, you think of it and suggest it.

mention^{복습}
[ménʃən]

vt. 말하다, 언급하다; n. 언급, 진술
If you mention something, you say something about it, usually briefly.

obvious^{복습}
[ábviəs]

a. 명백한, 분명한
If something is obvious, it is easy to see or understand.

interrogate
[intérəgèit]

v. 심문하다, 질문하다
If someone, especially a police officer, interrogates someone, they question them thoroughly for a long time in order to get some information from them.

split^{복습}
[split]

v. 분배하다; 쪼개다, 찢다, 째다; n. 쪼개기, 분열
If something splits or if you split it, it is divided into two or more parts.

cop^{복습}
[kap]

n. (구어) 경찰관, 순경
A cop is a policeman or policewoman.

point out^{복습}

phrasal v. ~을 지적하다
If you point out a fact or mistake, you tell someone about it or draw their attention to it.

have one's stomach pumped^{복습}

idiom 위세척을 하다
To have someone's stomach pumped means to remove the contents of the stomach using a pump, because they have swallowed something harmful.

148

joker ^{복습}
[dʒóukər]

n. 우스갯소리를 잘하는 사람; 멍청한[골치 아픈] 사람; 조커
Someone who is a joker likes making jokes or doing amusing things.

nod ^{복습}
[nad]

v. 끄덕이다, 끄덕여 표시하다; n. (동의 · 인사 · 신호 · 명령의) 끄덕임
If you nod, you move your head downward and upward to show agreement, understanding, or approval.

fringe ^{복습}
[frindʒ]

n. (숄 · 테이블 가장자리의) 술 (장식); 가장자리, 주변; v. 술을 달다, 테를 두르다
A fringe is a decoration attached to clothes, or other objects such as curtains, consisting of a row of hanging strips or threads.

economic ^{복습}
[èkənámik]

a. 경제(상)의, 경제적인; 경제학의 (economics n. 경제학)
Economic means concerned with the organization of the money, industry, and trade of a country, region, or society.

owe ^{**}
[ou]

v. 빚이 있다, 신세를 지다
If you owe money to someone, they have lent it to you and you have not yet paid it back.

souvenir ^{복습}
[sùːvəníər]

n. 기념품
A souvenir is something which you buy or keep to remind you of a holiday, place, or event.

predict [*]
[pridíkt]

v. 예언하다, 예상하다
If you predict an event, you say that it will happen.

give a thought

idiom ~을 한 번 생각해 보다
If you give a thought to something, you consider or think about it.

practically ^{복습}
[præktikəli]

ad. 거의, ~이나 마찬가지; 실지로, 실질상
Practically means almost, but not completely or exactly.

alert ^{복습}
[əlɔ́ːrt]

n. 경보, 경계; a. 방심하지 않는; v. 경고하다
An alert is a situation in which people prepare themselves for something dangerous that might happen soon.

get around ^{복습}

phrasal v. (여기저기 · 이 사람 저 사람에게로) 돌아다니다
If you get around, you move from place to place or to go to lots of different places.

concentrate ^{복습}
[kánsəntrèit]

v. 집중하다, 전념하다
If you concentrate on something, you give all your attention to it.

sprinkler ^{복습}
[spríŋklə:r]

n. 스프링클러(물을 뿌리는 장치)
A sprinkler is a device used to spray water to plants or grass, or to put out fires in buildings.

entire ^{복습}
[intàiər]

a. 전체의; 완전한
You use entire when you want to emphasize that you are referring to the whole of something, for example, the whole of a place, time, or population.

even ^{***}
[íːvən]

a. 균등한, 고른; 같은, 동등한; 평평한; 짝수의 (evenly ad. 고르게)
If there is an even distribution or division of something, each person, group, or area involved has an equal amount.

distribute [*]
[distríbjuːt]

v. 분포시키다; 분배하다, 배포하다
To distribute a substance over something means to scatter it over it.

lawn [복습]
[lɔːn]

n. 잔디밭, 잔디
A lawn is an area of grass that is kept cut short and is usually part of someone's garden or backyard, or part of a park.

secure [*]
[sikjúər]

v. 확보하다, 얻다; 안전하게 지키다; a. 안전한, 안정된; 단단한
If you secure something that you want or need, you obtain it, often after a lot of effort.

attach [복습]
[ətǽtʃ]

vt. 붙이다, 달다
If you attach something to an object, you connect it or fasten it to the object.

rectangle [*]
[réktæŋgl]

n. 직사각형
A rectangle is a four-sided shape whose corners are all ninety degree angles.

trench [복습]
[trentʃ]

n. 깊은 도랑; 방어전선; v. 도랑을 파다, (홈 따위를) 새기다
A trench is a long narrow channel that is cut into the ground, for example in order to lay pipes or get rid of water.

screw up [복습]

phrasal v. 망치다, 엉망으로 만들다
To screw something up means to cause it to fail or be spoiled.

detective [복습]
[ditéktiv]

n. 형사, 수사관; 탐정
A detective is someone whose job is to discover what has happened in a crime or other situation and to find the people involved.

counterfeit [복습]
[káuntərfìt]

a. 가짜의, 모조의; v. (화폐 · 지폐 · 문서 등을) 위조하다
Counterfeit money, goods, or documents are not genuine, but have been made to look exactly like genuine ones in order to deceive people.

prior [복습]
[práiər]

a. 전의, 먼저의; 더 중요한, 우선하는
You use prior to indicate that something has already happened, or must happen, before another event takes place.

conviction [**]
[kənvíkʃən]

n. 유죄 판결; 신념, 확신
If someone has a conviction, they have been found guilty of a crime in a court of law.

impress [*]
[imprés]

v. 감동시키다, 좋은 인상을 주다 (impressed a. 인상 깊게 생각하는)
If something impresses you, you feel great admiration for it.

get through [복습]

phrasal v. 끝내다, 해결하다; (곤란 등을) 벗어나다, 극복하다
If you get through a task or process, you complete it.

just in case [복습]

idiom 만일에 대비하여
Just in case means so as to be prepared for what may or may not happen.

embarrass [복습]
[imbǽrəs]

v. 부끄럽게[무안하게] 하다; 어리둥절하게 하다; 당황하다
(embarrassed a. 당혹한, 창피한)
If something or someone embarrasses you, they make you feel shy or ashamed.

accuse [복습]
[əkjúːz]

v. 비난하다, 고발하다
If you accuse someone of doing something wrong or dishonest, you say or tell them that you believe that they did it.

150

dealer[*]
[díːlər]

n. 상인, 무역업자, 도매업자 (drug dealer n. 마약상)
A dealer is a person whose business involves buying and selling things.

due[복습]
[djuː]

a. ~하기로 되어 있는; ~로 인한, ~ 때문에; n. ~에게 마땅히 주어져야 하는 것
If something is due at a particular time, it is expected to happen at that time.

stuff[복습]
[stʌf]

n. 일[것](일반적으로 말하거나 생각하는 것); 물건, 물질 vt. 채워 넣다, 속을 채우다
You can use stuff to refer to things such as a substance, a collection of things, events, or ideas, or the contents of something in a general way without mentioning the thing itself by name.

prospective[*]
[prəspéktiv]

a. 미래의, 장래의; 가망이 있는, 기대되는
You use prospective to describe something that is likely to happen soon.

employer[**]
[implɔ́iər]

n. 고용주, 사장
Your employer is the person or organization that you work for.

paragraph[*]
[pǽrəgræf]

n. 단락, 절; 작은 기사
A paragraph is a section of a piece of writing.

make sense[복습]

idiom 뜻이 통하다, 도리에 맞다
If something makes sense, it has a meaning that you can easily understand.

shatter[*]
[ʃǽtər]

v. 산산이 부서지다, 산산조각 내다
If something shatters your dreams, hopes, or beliefs, it completely destroys them.

casual[복습]
[kǽʒuəl]

a. 태평스러운, 무심한; 우연한; 가벼운, 평상복의
If you are casual, you are, or you pretend to be, relaxed and not very concerned about what is happening or what you are doing.

nasal
[néizəl]

a. 콧소리의; 코의
If someone's voice is nasal, it sounds as if air is passing through their nose as well as their mouth while they are speaking.

ring a bell

idiom 들어본 적이 있는 것 같다, (들어보니) 낯이 익다
If something rings a bell, it sounds familiar and helps you remember it, but not completely.

1분에 몇 단어를 읽는지 리딩 속도를 측정해보세요.

$$\frac{520 \text{ words}}{\text{reading time ( ) sec}} \times 60 = (\quad) \text{ WPM}$$

Build Your Vocabulary

stationery*
[stéiʃənèri]

n. 편지지; 문방구, 필기 용구
Stationery is paper, envelopes, and other materials or equipment used for writing.

remarkable*
[rimá:rkəbl]

a. 주목할 만한, 눈에 띄는 (remarkably ad. 눈에 띄게, 현저히)
Someone or something that is remarkable is unusual or special in a way that makes people notice them and be surprised or impressed.

neat^{복습}
[ni:t]

a. 말끔한, 정돈된, 깨끗한
A neat place, thing, or person is tidy and smart, and has everything in the correct place.

dopey
[dóupi]

a. 바보 같은, 멍청한; 몽롱한
If you describe someone as dopey, you mean that they are rather stupid.

lame^{복습}
[leim]

a. 설득력이 없는, 믿기 힘든; 절름발이의, 절룩거리는; 불구의
If you describe something, for example an excuse, argument, or remark, as lame, you mean that it is poor or weak.

junk*
[dʒʌŋk]

n. 쓰레기, 폐물, 고물
Junk is old and used goods that have little value and that you do not want any more.

dumb*
[dʌm]

a. 우둔한, 어리석은; 말을 못하는, 벙어리인
If you call a person dumb, you mean that they are stupid or foolish.

pathetic*
[pəθétik]

a. 불쌍한, 애처로운
If you describe someone or something as pathetic, you mean that they make you feel impatient or angry, often because they are weak or not very good.

beat^{복습}
[bi:t]

v. 더 낫다, 능가하다; 이기다, 패배시키다; 치다, 두드리다; n. 치기, 때리기; 박자
If you say that one thing beats another, you mean that it is better than it.

shrink*
[ʃriŋk]

n. (속어) 정신과 의사; v. 오그라들다, 줄다; 축소시키다
A shrink is a psychiatrist.

slot*
[slat]

n. (동전) 투입구, 가늘고 긴 홈; 위치, 자리, 장소, 시간대
(mail slot n. 우편물 투입구)
A slot is a narrow opening in a machine or container, for example a hole that you put coins in to make a machine work.

152

cliff**
[klif]

n. 낭떠러지, 절벽
A cliff is a high area of land with a very steep side, especially one next to the sea.

insane^{복습}
[inséin]

a. 미친, 정신 이상의
Someone who is insane has a mind that does not work in a normal way, with the result that their behavior is very strange.

freak^{복습}
[fri:k]

v. 기겁하(게 하)다; n. 열광자, 괴짜; 희한한 것
(freak out phrasal v. 질겁하다, 놀라다)
If somebody freaks out or if something freaks them out, they react very strongly to something that shocks, angers, excites or frightens them.

goosey
[gú:si]

a. 소름이 잘 끼치는, 간지럼 잘 타는; 거위 같은; 바보의
Goosey means ticklish or reacting very quickly to touch.

1. Why did Detective Newberg ask Armpit to come to the police station?
   A. She had a suspect that she wanted to have Armpit see.
   B. She wanted to give him back his money for the tickets.
   C. She wanted him to bring the counterfeit ticket stubs.
   D. She wanted to question Armpit as a suspect.

2. Who did Detective Newberg say was behind the two-way mirror to X-Ray?
   A. Armpit
   B. X-Ray's mother
   C. The police chief
   D. A criminal psychologist

3. How did X-Ray tell Detective Newberg that he met Armpit?
   A. He had known Armpit for a long time as coworkers.
   B. He had never seen Armpit until he met in the ticket line.
   C. He called a number that he saw in a newspaper ad.
   D. He had already seen Armpit a couple of times before at concerts.

4. What did X-Ray tell Armpit about his meeting with Detective Newberg?

   A. Everything was fine but maybe they should avoid each other for a while.
   B. He was almost arrested and was never so afraid.
   C. He knew X-Ray was behind the two-way mirror the whole time.
   D. Armpit should be careful because Newberg wanted to question him next.

5. How did Kaira feel about Armpit not bragging about their relationship?

   A. She felt that he didn't care enough about her.
   B. She felt that he was phony.
   C. She felt that he was real and down-to-earth.
   D. She felt that he was after her fame and money.

6. What embarrassing thing did Armpit share with Kaira?

   A. He told her the story about how a scorpion stung his arm.
   B. He told her that it sounded like she sang his name Armpit in one of her songs.
   C. He told her that he might not be able to graduate from high school.
   D. He told her that his older brother was in jail.

7. Where did Kaira invite Armpit and why?

   A. She invited him to San Francisco to spend time with her between concerts.
   B. She invited him to Los Angeles to help her work on new songs.
   C. She invited him to Philadelphia to be part of her crew.
   D. She invited him to Sacramento to relax while not on tour.

1분에 몇 단어를 읽는지 리딩 속도를 측정해보세요.

$$\frac{2{,}548 \text{ words}}{\text{reading time (\quad) sec}} \times 60 = (\quad) \text{ WPM}$$

Build Your Vocabulary

envelope^{복습}
[énvəlòup]

n. 봉투, 봉지
An envelope is the rectangular paper cover in which you send a letter to someone through the post.

slot^{복습}
[slat]

n. (동전) 투입구, 가늘고 긴 홈; 위치, 자리, 장소, 시간대
(mail slot n. 우편물 투입구)
A slot is a narrow opening in a machine or container, for example a hole that you put coins in to make a machine work.

get in touch

idiom ~와 연락을 하다
If you get in touch with someone, you make contact with them by phone, letter, or visit.

grab^{복습}
[græb]

v. 부여잡다, 움켜쥐다; n. 부여잡기
If you grab something, you take it or pick it up suddenly and roughly.

detective^{복습}
[ditéktiv]

n. 형사, 수사관; 탐정
A detective is someone whose job is to discover what has happened in a crime or other situation and to find the people involved.

suspect^{복습}
[səspékt]

n. 용의자; v. 짐작하다, 의심하다, 혐의를 두다
A suspect is a person who the police or authorities think may be guilty of a crime.

station^{복습}
[stéiʃən]

n. 부, 부서; 방송 채널, 방송국; 역, 정류장; 지역 본부, 사업소
A station is a facility equipped with special equipment and personnel for a particular purpose.

patrolman
[pətróulmən]

n. 순찰 경찰관
A patrolman is a policeman who patrols a particular area.

hang up^{복습}

phrasal v. 전화를 끊다
To hang up means to end a telephone conversation, often very suddenly, by putting down the part of the telephone that you speak into or switching the telephone off.

pull into^{복습}

phrasal v. ~에 도착하다, 들다
If a train or a bus pulls into, it arrives somewhere and stops.

arrest^{복습}
[ərést]

vt. 체포하다, 저지하다; (주의 · 이목 · 흥미 등을) 끌다; n. 체포, 검거, 구속
If the police arrest you, they take charge of you and take you to a police station, because they believe you may have committed a crime.

156

escape^{**}
[iskéip]

v. (말 · 웃음 · 한숨 등이) 저절로 새어나오다; 도망치다, 벗어나다
If a sound or utterance escapes your lips, it slips from or is expressed by the lips unknowingly.

hop in

phrasal v. (자동차에) 뛰어 올라타다
If you hop in to a vehicle, you jump into it.

criminal^{복습}
[krímənl]

a. 범죄의; n. 범죄자, 범인
Criminal means connected with crime.

story^{**}
[stɔ́ːri]

① n. (건물의) 층 ② n. 이야기
A story of a building is one of its different levels, which is situated above or below other levels.

recognize^{복습}
[rékəgnaiz]

vt. 인지하다, 알아보다
If you recognize someone or something, you know who that person is or what that thing is.

subject^{**}
[sʌ́bdʒikt]

a. ~을 받기 쉬운, 면할 수 없는; ~을 조건으로 하는; vt. 복종시키다
If someone is subject to a particular set of rules or laws, they have to obey those rules or laws.

detector
[ditéktər]

n. 탐지기; 발견자, 탐지하는 사람
A metal detector is a device that gives an audible or visual signal when its search head comes close to a metallic object embedded in food or buried in the ground.

identical^{복습}
[aidéntikəl]

a. 동일한, 꼭 같은
Things that are identical are exactly the same.

light^{***}
[lait]

v. (lit/lighted–lit/lighted) 밝게 하다, 비추다, 밝아지다; 점화하다; n. 빛, 광선; 불
If a place or object is lit by something, it has light shining on it.

drum^{**}
[drʌm]

v. 계속 두드리다; 북을 치다; n. 북, 드럼
If something drums on a surface, or if you drum something on a surface, it hits it regularly, making a continuous beating sound.

tap^{복습}
[tæp]

① v. 가볍게 두드리다; n. 가볍게 두드리기 ② n. 주둥이, (수도 등의) 꼭지
If you tap something, you hit it with a quick light blow or a series of quick light blows.

definite^{복습}
[défənit]

a. 확실한, 확고한; 분명한, 뚜렷한 (definitely ad. 확실히, 명확히)
If something such as a decision or an arrangement is definite, it is firm and clear, and unlikely to be changed.

strike a chord

idiom 생각나게 하다; 들은 적이 있다
To stirke a chord means to say or do something which speaks directly to someone's emotions or memories.

pad[*]
[pæd]

n. (한 장씩 떼어 쓰는) 필기첩; 덧대는 것; vt. 완충제를 덧대다, 속을 채우다
A pad of paper is a number of pieces of paper which are fixed together along the top or the side, so that each piece can be torn off when it has been used.

briefcase
[brí:fkèis]

n. 서류 가방
A briefcase is a case used for carrying documents in.

attorney
[ətə́ːrni]

n. 변호사; 대리인
An attorney or attorney at law is a lawyer.

cooperate^{**}
[kouápərèit]

vi. 협력하다, 협동하다 (cooperative a. 협조적인)
If you cooperate with someone, you work or act with them together.

flash a smile

idiom (~에게) 미소를 보내다
If you flash a smile at someone, you suddenly smile at them.

telepathic
[tèləpǽθik]

a. 텔레파시를 이용한; 이심전심의 (telepathically ad. 텔레파시로)
If you believe that someone is telepathic, you believe that they have mental powers which cannot be explained by science, such as being able to communicate with other people's minds, and know what other people are thinking.

nod^{복습}
[nad]

v. 끄덕이다, 끄덕여 표시하다; n. (동의 · 인사 · 신호 · 명령의) 끄덕임
If you nod, you move your head downward and upward to show agreement, understanding, or approval.

audible
[ɔ́ːdəbl]

a. 들리는, 들을 수 있는 (audibly ad. 들리도록, 들을 수 있게)
A sound that is audible is loud enough to be heard.

affirmative
[əfə́ːrmətiv]

n. 긍정, 동의; a. 긍정의, 찬성하는
If you reply to a question in the affirmative, you say 'yes' or make a gesture that means 'yes'.

evidence
[évədəns]

n. 증거, 증언; 근거, 증명; vt. 증거가 되다, 입증하다
Evidence is the information which is used in a court of law to try to prove something.

court^{**}
[kɔːrt]

n. 법원, 법정; 궁정, 왕실; 뜰, 안뜰; (테니스 · 배구 등의) 코트
A court is a place where legal matters are decided by a judge and jury or by a magistrate.

knowing^{복습}
[nóuiŋ]

a. 아는 체하는; 지식이 있는, 박식한 (knowingly ad. 아는 체하고)
A knowing gesture or remark is one that shows that you understand something, for example the way that someone is feeling or what they really mean, even though it has not been mentioned directly.

license^{복습}
[láisəns]

n. 면허(증), 허가(증); v. 면허를 주다 (license plate n. (자동차의) 번호판)
A license plate is a sign on the front and back of a vehicle that shows its license number.

reassure
[rìːəʃúər]

vt. 안심시키다
If you reassure someone, you say or do things to make them stop worrying about something.

hesitate^{복습}
[hézətèit]

v. 주저하다, 머뭇거리다, 망설이다
If you hesitate, you do not speak or act for a short time, usually because you are uncertain, embarrassed, or worried about what you are going to say or do.

figure^{복습}
[fígjər]

v. 생각하다, 판단하다; 계산하다; n. 수치, 숫자; 형태, 형상; 작은 조각상
If you figure that something is the case, you think or guess that it is the case.

158

worth [wəːrθ] ^{복습}

a. 가치가 있는; n. 가치, 값어치

If you say that something is worth having, you mean that it is pleasant or useful, and therefore a good thing to have.

charge [ʧɑːrdʒ] ^{복습}

v. (지불을) 청구하다; 부담 지우다; 맡기다; 돌격하다; n. 수수료, 요금; 책임, 의무

If you charge someone an amount of money, you ask them to pay that amount for something that you have sold to them or done for them.

illegal [iliːgəl] *

a. 불법의, 비합법적인

If something is illegal, the law says that it is not allowed.

enterprise [éntərpràiz] *

n. 기업, 회사; 사업, 일의 계획
(free enterprise n. (정부의 간섭을 받지 않는) 자유 기업)

An enterprise is a company or business, often a small one.

protect [prətékt] ^{복습}

v. 보호하다, 막다, 지키다

To protect someone or something means to prevent them from being harmed or damaged.

constitution [kὰnstətjúːʃən] *

n. 헌법; 체질, 체격

The constitution of a country or organization is the system of laws which formally states people's rights and duties.

twist [twist] ^{복습}

v. 비틀다, 꼬다, 돌리다, 감기다; n. 뒤틀림, 엉킴

If you twist something, especially a part of your body, or if it twists, it moves into an unusual, uncomfortable, or bent position, for example because of being hit or pushed, or because you are upset.

fair [fɛər] ^{복습}

a. 공평한, 공정한; 상당한; n. 박람회, 전시회

Something or someone that is fair is reasonable, right, and just.

expense [ikspéns] ^{복습}

n. (pl.) 소요 경비; 비용, 지출

Expenses are amounts of money that you spend while doing something in the course of your work, which will be paid back to you afterward.

profit [práfit] ^{복습}

n. 이익, 수익; v. 이익을 얻다; 득이 되다

A profit is an amount of money that you gain when you are paid more for something than it cost you to make, get, or do it.

ad [æd] ^{복습}

n. (= advertisement) 광고; 광고 활동

An advertisement is an announcement in a newspaper, on television, or on a poster about something such as a product, event, or job.

independent [ìndipéndənt] ^{복습}

a. 독자적인, 독립한; n. 독립한 사람[것]

If one thing or person is independent of another, they are separate and not connected, so the first one is not affected or influenced by the second.

flinch [flinʧ] ^{복습}

v. (고통 · 공포로) 주춤하다, 위축되다

If you flinch, you make a small sudden movement, especially when something surprises you or hurts you.

apparent [əpǽrənt] ^{복습}

a. 또렷한, 명백한; 외관상의 (apparently ad. 명백하게, 보아하니)

If something is apparent to you, it is clear and obvious to you.

chuckle*
[tʃʌkl]

v. 킬킬 웃다, 소리 없이 웃다; n. 빙그레 웃음
When you chuckle, you laugh quietly.

acquire**
[əkwáiər]

vt. 얻다, 획득하다; 습득하다, 배우다
If you acquire something, you buy or obtain it for yourself, or someone gives it to you.

mention복습
[ménʃən]

vt. 말하다, 언급하다; n. 언급, 진술
If you mention something, you say something about it, usually briefly.

arena복습
[ərí:nə]

n. 경기장, 시합장
An arena is a place where sports, entertainments, and other public events take place.

rip-off복습
[ríp-ɔ̀f]

n. 폭리, 바가지 (물품); 속임수, 도둑질
If you say that something that you bought was a rip-off, you mean that you were charged too much money or that it was of very poor quality.

strict**
[strikt]

a. 엄격한, 엄한; 정확한, 주의 깊은
A strict rule or order is very clear and precise or severe and must always be obeyed completely.

prevent복습
[privént]

vt. 막다, 방해하다; 예방[방지]하다
To prevent someone from doing something means to make it impossible for them to do it.

scalper복습
[skǽlpər]

n. 암표상
A scalper is someone who sells tickets outside a sports ground or theater, usually for more than their original value.

row복습
[rou]

① n. 열, (좌석) 줄 ② vi. (노를 써서) 배를 젓다; (배가) 저어지다
A row of things or people is a number of them arranged in a line.

crime**
[kraim]

n. 죄, 범죄
A crime is an illegal action or activity for which a person can be punished by law.

false**
[fɔːls]

a. 틀린, 정확하지 않은; 가짜의, 모조의
If something is false, it is incorrect, untrue, or mistaken.

prior복습
[práiər]

a. 전의, 먼저의; 더 중요한, 우선하는
You use prior to indicate that something has already happened, or must happen, before another event takes place.

offense*
[əféns]

n. 범죄, 위법 행위; 공격
An offense is a crime that breaks a particular law and requires a particular punishment.

probation
[proubéiʃən]

n. [법률] 보호 관찰 (기간), 근신 (기간)
Probation is a period of time during which a person who has committed a crime has to obey the law and be supervised by a probation officer, rather than being sent to prison.

makeup복습
[méikʌp]

n. 화장, 분장; 조립, 구성
Makeup consists of things such as lipstick, eye shadow, and powder which some women put on their faces to make themselves look more attractive or which actors use to change or improve their appearance.

160

expert*
[ékspə:rt]

n. 전문가, 숙련가; a. 전문적인, 전문(가)의
An expert is a person who is very skilled at doing something or who knows a lot about a particular subject.

psychologist*
[saiká_lədʒist]

n. 심리학자
A psychologist is a person who studies the human mind and tries to explain why people behave in the way that they do.

inflection
[inflékʃən]

n. 억양, 어조
An inflection in someone's voice is a change in its tone or pitch as they are speaking.

correct^{복습}
[kərékt]

v. 정정하다, 고치다; 나무라다, 벌주다; a. 옳은 (correction n. 정정, 수정)
If you correct someone, you say something which you think is more accurate or appropriate than what they have just said.

dude^{복습}
[dju:d]

n. 사내, 녀석; (구어) 형씨, 친구
A dude is a man.

swear^{복습}
[swɛər]

v. 맹세하다, 증언하다
If you say that you swear that something is true or that you can swear to it, you are saying very firmly that it is true.

offer^{복습}
[ɔ́:fər]

v. 제의[제안]하다; 제공하다; n. 제공
If you offer something to someone, you ask them if they would like to have it or use it.

buck^{복습}
[bʌk]

① n. (속어) 달러 ② n. 수사슴, 수컷
A buck is a US or Australian dollar.

insist^{복습}
[insist]

v. 우기다, 주장하다; 요구하다
If you insist that something is the case, you say so very firmly and refuse to say otherwise, even though other people do not believe you.

testify*
[téstəfài]

v. 증언하다, 증명하다, 입증하다
When someone testifies in a court of law, they give a statement of what they saw someone do or what they know of a situation, after having promised to tell the truth.

witness**
[wítnis]

n. 증인, 목격자; 증언, 증명; v. 목격하다; 증언[증명]하다
A witness is someone who appears in a court of law to say what they know about a crime or other event.

arrange^{복습}
[əréindʒ]

v. 준비하다, 계획을 짜다; 가지런히 하다, 배열하다 (arrangement n. 준비, 계획)
If you arrange an event or meeting, you make plans for it to happen.

split^{복습}
[split]

v. 분배하다; 쪼개다, 찢다, 째다; n. 쪼개기, 분열
If something splits or if you split it, it is divided into two or more parts.

rip off

phrasal v. 속이다; 빼앗다, 훔치다
To rip someone off means to cheat them, for example by charging them too much for something, or selling them something of poor quality.

latch^{복습}
[lætʃ]

v. 걸쇠를 걸다, 잠그다; n. 걸쇠, 빗장 (unlatch vi. 빗장을 벗기다)
If you latch a door or gate, you fasten it with a metal bar.

clasp*
[klæsp]

n. 걸쇠; 꽉 잡기; v. (걸쇠가) 잠기다; 걸쇠로 채우다; 꽉 쥐다
A clasp is a small device that fastens something.

foul^{복습}
[faul]

n. 반칙; 싫은 것, 더러운 것; a. 규칙 위반인, 반칙인; 더러운, 악취 나는
A foul is an act in a game or sport that is not allowed according to the rules.

mustache^{복습}
[mʌ́stæʃ]

n. 코밑수염
A man's moustache is the hair that grows on his upper lip.

shave^{복습}
[ʃeiv]

v. 면도하다, 깎다, 밀다; n. 면도
When a man shaves, he removes the hair from his face using a razor or shaver so that his face is smooth.

sigh^{복습}
[sai]

v. 한숨 쉬다; n. 한숨, 탄식
When you sigh, you let out a deep breath, as a way of expressing feelings such as disappointment, tiredness, or pleasure.

escort[*]
[éskɔ:rt]

vt. 호위하다, 호송하다; 안내하다; n. 경호, 안내
If you escort someone somewhere, you accompany them there, usually in order to make sure that they leave a place or get to their destination.

phony^{복습}
[fóuni]

a. 가짜의, 엉터리의; n. 가짜, 위조품, 사기꾼
If you describe something as phony, you disapprove of it because it is false rather than genuine.

gullible
[gʌ́ləbl]

a. 남을 잘 믿는, 잘 속아 넘어가는
If you describe someone as gullible, you mean they are easily tricked because they are too trusting.

shrug^{복습}
[ʃrʌg]

v. (어깨를) 으쓱하다; n. (양 손바닥을 내보이면서 어깨를) 으쓱하기
If you shrug, you raise your shoulders to show that you are not interested in something or that you do not know or care about something.

appetite[*]
[ǽpətàit]

n. 식욕; 욕구, 욕망
Your appetite is your desire to eat.

have nothing to do with^{복습}

idiom ~와 관계가 없다
To have nothing to do with something means not to be connected or concerned with it.

wasp[*]
[wɑsp]

n. [동물] 장수말벌; 성질 잘 내는 사람
A wasp is an insect with wings and yellow and black stripes across its body. Wasps have a painful sting like a bee but do not produce honey.

sting^{복습}
[stiŋ]

vt. (stung–stung) 찌르다, 쏘다; n. 찌름, 쏨
If a plant, animal, or insect stings you, a sharp part of it, usually covered with poison, is pushed into your skin so that you feel a sharp pain.

162

1분에 몇 단어를 읽는지 리딩 속도를 측정해보세요.

$$\frac{971 \text{ words}}{\text{reading time ( ) sec}} \times 60 = (\qquad) \text{ WPM}$$

Build Your Vocabulary

sweat^{복습}
[swet]

v. 땀 흘리다; 습기가 차다; n. 땀
When you sweat, sweat comes through your skin.

dirt^{복습}
[dəːrt]

n. 흙, 진흙, 먼지; 가십, 스캔들
You can refer to the earth on the ground as dirt, especially when it is dusty.

shrub^{복습}
[ʃrʌb]

n. 키 작은 나무, 관목
A shrub is a small bush with several woody stems.

end up^{복습}

phrasal v. 마침내는 (~으로) 되다; 끝나다
If you end up doing something or end up in a particular state, you do that thing or get into that state even though you did not originally intend to.

normal^{복습}
[nɔ́ːrməl]

a. 보통의, 정상적인; n. 보통; 표준, 기준
Something that is normal is usual and ordinary, and is what people expect.

back up

phrasal v. 뒷받침하다
If you back someone up, you support or help them and show that what they say is true.

confirm[*]
[kənfə́ːrm]

vt. (남의 의견 등을) 굳히다, 입증하다; 승인하다
If something confirms what you believe, suspect, or fear, it shows that it is definitely true.

chat[*]
[ʧæt]

n. 이야기, 잡담; v. 이야기하다, 잡담하다
When people chat, they talk to each other in an informal and friendly way.

just in case^{복습}

idiom 만일에 대비하여
Just in case means so as to be prepared for what may or may not happen.

owe^{복습}
[ou]

v. 빚이 있다, 신세를 지다
If you owe money to someone, they have lent it to you and you have not yet paid it back.

dumb^{복습}
[dʌm]

a. 우둔한, 어리석은; 말을 못하는, 벙어리인
If you call a person dumb, you mean that they are stupid or foolish.

match**
[mætʃ]

n. 성냥; 경기, 시합; 경쟁 상대; v. 필적하다, 대등하다; 경쟁시키다
A match is a small wooden stick with a substance on one end that produces a flame when you rub it along the rough side of a matchbox.

complain^{복습}
[kəmpléin]

v. 불평하다, 투덜거리다
If you complain about a situation, you say that you are not satisfied with it.

reliable^{복습}
[riláiəbl]

a. 의지할 수 있는, 신뢰할 수 있는 (unreliablity n. 신뢰할 수 없음)
People or things that are reliable can be trusted to work well or to behave in the way that you want them to.

postal*
[póustl]

a. 우편의, 우체국의
Postal is used to describe things or people connected with the public service of carrying letters and packages from one place to another.

lamebrain
[léimbrèin]

n. 바보, 멍청이, 얼간이
A lamebrain indicates a stupid or slow-witted person.

goosey^{복습}
[gúːsi]

a. 소름이 잘 끼치는, 간지럼 잘 타는; 거위 같은; 바보의
Goosey means ticklish or reacting very quickly to touch.

brag
[bræg]

v. 자랑하다, 뽐내다; n. 자랑, 허풍 (braggy a. (심하게) 자랑하는, 떠벌리는)
If you brag, you say in a very proud way that you have something or have done something.

down-to-earth
[dáun-tə-əːrθ]

a. 현실적인, 실제적인; 철저한, 더할 나위 없는
If you say that someone is down-to-earth, you approve of the fact that they concern themselves with practical things and actions, rather than with abstract theories.

force^{복습}
[fɔːrs]

v. (힘 · 목소리를) 무리하게 내다, 짜내다; 강요하다, 억지로 시키다; n. 힘; 영향력
If you force a smile or a laugh, you manage to smile or laugh, but with an effort because you are unhappy.

fake^{복습}
[feik]

a. 가짜의, 위조의; v. 가장하다, 꾸며내다, 위조하다
A fake fur or a fake painting, for example, is a fur or painting that has been made to look valuable or genuine, usually in order to deceive people.

embarrass^{복습}
[imbǽrəs]

v. 부끄럽게[무안하게] 하다; 어리둥절하게 하다; 당황하다
(embarrassing a. 난처하게 하는)
If something or someone embarrasses you, they make you feel shy or ashamed.

even^{복습}
[íːvən]

a. 같은, 동등한; 균등한, 고른; 평평한; 짝수의
If there is an even distribution or division of something, each person, group, or area involved has an equal amount.

damsel^{복습}
[dǽmzəl]

n. 계집아이, 처녀
A damsel is a young, unmarried woman.

distress^{복습}
[distrés]

n. 고통, 곤란; 가난, 곤궁; vt. 고민하게 하다, 괴롭히다
Distress is a state of extreme sorrow, suffering, or pain.

164

sarcastic[복습]
[sɑːrkǽstik]

a. 빈정대는. 비꼬는. 풍자적인 (sarcastically ad. 비꼬는 투로, 풍자적으로)
Someone who is sarcastic says or does the opposite of what they really mean in order to mock or insult someone.

exclaim[복습]
[ikskléim]

v. 외치다, 소리치다
If you exclaim, you say or shout something suddenly because of surprise, fear and pleasure.

make sense[복습]

idiom 뜻이 통하다, 도리에 맞다
If something makes sense, it has a meaning that you can easily understand.

delusion
[dilúːʒən]

n. 망상, 착각 (delusional a. 망상의)
A delusion is a false idea.

humor[**]
[hjúːmər]

vt. (님을) 어르다, 만족시키다, 비위를 맞주다; n. 기분, 비위; 유머, 익살
If you humor someone who is behaving strangely, you try to please them or pretend to agree with them, so that they will not become upset.

recite[*]
[risáit]

v. 낭독하다, 암송하다; (상세히) 말하다; 열거하다; 인용하다
When someone recites a poem or other piece of writing, they say it aloud after they have learned it.

pause[복습]
[pɔːz]

vi. 중단하다, 잠시 멈추다; n. 멈춤, 중지
If you pause while you are doing something, you stop for a short period and then continue.

arrange[복습]
[əréindʒ]

v. 준비하다, 계획을 짜다; 가지런히 하다, 배열하다
If you arrange an event or meeting, you make plans for it to happen.

incomprehensible
[ìnkamprihénsəbl]

a. 이해할 수 없는
Something that is incomprehensible is impossible to understand.

might as well[복습]

idiom ~하는 것이 좋겠다
Might as well is used for saying that you will do something because it seems best in the situation that you are in, although you may not really want to do it.

1. What was Armpit's impression of Aileen when she called him?

   A. He thought that she was not a very nice person to be around.

   B. He thought that she was unbelievably disorganized.

   C. He thought that she was jealous of Kaira's fame.

   D. He thought that she was incredibly efficient.

2. What did Aileen do with Kaira's trust account?

   A. She made sure it was safe and sound.

   B. She added her own money to raise the interest rates.

   C. She had taken about three million dollars from the account.

   D. She had set aside some money for special charities for disabled children.

3. What was Jerome's plan involving Kaira?

   A. He wanted her to turn eighteen so that he could be free to live with just her mother.

   B. He could find someone else to easily replace her while he still oversaw her money.

   C. He would gladly hand over the trust account to her when she turned eighteen.

   D. He would try hard to treat Kaira kindly like his own daughter.

4. How did Armpit find the leak in the sprinkler system so quickly?
   A. He noticed a new mountain laurel and started digging there.
   B. He used a special detector to find the leak.
   C. He noticed where the ground was the wettest.
   D. He asked if anyone else had recently worked in the yard.

5. In what condition did X-Ray arrive with Felix and Moses?
   A. He looked like he was hungry.
   B. He looked injured.
   C. He looked like he had been crying.
   D. He looked like he hadn't slept much.

6. What did Felix want Armpit to do in order to fix the damages?
   A. He wanted him to pay a thousand dollars.
   B. He wanted him to work for him selling more tickets.
   C. He wanted him to sell Kaira's letter to him.
   D. He wanted Armpit to admit his crime to the police.

7. What did Jack Dunley offer X-Ray?
   A. He offered him a ride back to his home.
   B. He offered him a landscaping job with Armpit.
   C. He offered him a job managing sprinkler systems.
   D. He offered him a chance to clean his criminal record.

1분에 몇 단어를 읽는지 리딩 속도를 측정해보세요.

$$\frac{1,010 \text{ words}}{\text{reading time (\quad) sec}} \times 60 = (\quad) \text{ WPM}$$

Build Your Vocabulary

distance**
[dístəns]

n. (시간 · 공간적) 거리, 간격; 원거리; vt. 멀리 떨어지게 하다
(in the distance idiom 먼 곳에, 저 멀리)
In the distance means far away but still able to be seen or heard.

earthquake**
[ə́ːrθkwèik]

n. 지진; 대변동, 격동
An earthquake is a shaking of the ground caused by movement of the earth's crust.

airline*
[ɛ́ərlain]

n. (pl.) 항공 회사; 항공 노선
An airline is a company which provides regular services carrying people or goods in airplanes.

frequent**
[fríːkwənt]

a. 자주[빈번히] 일어나는; 흔한, 보통의; v. 자주 가다
If something is frequent, it happens often.

nonstop
[nánstap]

a., ad. (교통 기관이) 도중에 멈추지 않고[않는], 중단 없이[없는]
Nonstop means to be done without any pauses or interruptions.

enroll
[inróul]

v. 등록하다, 명단에 기재하다
If you enroll or are enrolled at an institution or on a course, you officially join it and pay a fee for it.

incredible*
[inkrédəbl]

a. 놀랄 만한, 믿을 수 없을 정도의; 믿어지지 않는
(incredibly ad. 믿을 수 없을 만큼, 엄청나게)
You use incredible to emphasize the degree, amount, or intensity of something.

efficient^{복습}
[ifíʃənt]

a. 유능한, 실력 있는; 능률적인, 효과가 있는
If something or someone is efficient, they are able to do tasks successfully, without wasting time or energy.

rattle off

phrasal v. (기억하고 있는 내용을) 줄줄 말하다
To rattle something off means to say or repeat it from memory, quickly and without any effort.

departure*
[dipáːrtʃər]

n. 출발; 이탈, 벗어남
Departure or a departure is the act of going away from somewhere.

struggle^{복습}
[strʌgl]

v. 분투하다, 열심히 하다; 버둥거리다, 허덕이다; n. 노력, 분투
If you struggle to do something, you try hard to do it, even though other people or things may be making it difficult for you to succeed.

keep up^{복습}

phrasal v. 뒤떨어지지 않도록 따라가다
If you keep up with something, you continue to pay or do something regularly.

168

traffic [복습]
[trǽfik]

n. 교통(량), 통행, 왕래; 거래, 무역; v. 매매하다, 거래하다
Traffic refers to the movement of ships, trains, or aircraft between one place and another.

layover
[léiòuvər]

n. 도중하차, (비행기를 갈아타기 위해서) 기다리는 곳
Layover is a break in a journey by plane, especially in waiting for a connention.

hang up [복습]

phrasal v. 전화를 끊다
To hang up means to end a telephone conversation, often very suddenly, by putting down the part of the telephone that you speak into or switching the telephone off.

occur[**]
[əkɔ́:r]

vi. 문득 생각나다, 떠오르다; 생기다, 일어나다
If a thought or idea occurs to you, you suddenly think of it or realize it.

economic [복습]
[èkənámik]

a. 경제(상)의, 경제적인; 경제학의 (economics n. 경제학)
Economic means concerned with the organization of the money, industry, and trade of a country, region, or society.

antique[*]
[æntí:k]

a. 골동품의; 구식의; n. 골동품
An antique is an old object such as a piece of china or furniture which is valuable because of its beauty or rarity.

offer [복습]
[ɔ́:fər]

v. 제공하다, 제의[제안]하다; n. 제공
If you offer something to someone, you ask them if they would like to have it or use it.

charm [복습]
[ʧɑ:rm]

n. 매력, 마력; 마술; v. 매력이 있다; 황홀하게 하다
Charm is the quality of being pleasant or attractive.

serenity
[sirénəti]

n. 고요함, 평온; 맑음, 화창함
Serenity is the state or quality of being serene or calm.

lack[**]
[læk]

v. ~이 없다, ~이 결핍되다; n. 부족
If you say that someone or something lacks a particular quality or that a particular quality is lacking in them, you mean that they do not have any or enough of it.

reception[*]
[risépʃən]

n. 수신 (상태); 수용, 받아들이기; 환영(회), 응접
If you get good reception from your radio or television, the sound or picture is clear because the signal is strong.

click [복습]
[klik]

n. 딸깍[찰깍]하는 소리; v. 딸깍 소리를 내다; (불현듯) 딱 분명해지다[이해가 되다]
If something clicks or if you click it, it makes a short, sharp sound.

poke [복습]
[pouk]

v. 들이대다; 찌르다, 쑤시다; 삐져나오다; n. 찌름, 쑤심
If you poke one thing into another, you push the first thing into the second thing.

arrange [복습]
[əréindʒ]

v. 준비하다, 계획을 짜다; 가지런히 하다, 배열하다 (arrangement n. 준비, 계획)
If you arrange an event or meeting, you make plans for it to happen.

glance [복습]
[glæns]

v. 흘끗 보다, 잠깐 보다; n. 흘끗 봄
If you glance at something or someone, you look at them very quickly and then look away again immediately.

criminal ^{복습}
[krímənl]

a. 범죄의; n. 범죄자, 범인
Criminal means connected with crime.

assault *
[əsɔ́ːlt]

n. 폭행; 습격; vt. 폭행하다; 맹렬히 공격하다
An assault on a person is a physical attack on them.

battery *
[bǽtəri]

n. [법률] 구타; 건전지
Assault and battery is the crime of attacking someone and causing them physical harm.

genius ^{복습}
[dʒíːnjəs]

n. 천재; 특수한 재능
A genius is a highly talented, creative, or intelligent person.

tiptoe ^{복습}
[típtòu]

n. 발끝; vi. 발끝으로 걷다, 발돋움하다
If you do something on tiptoe or on tiptoes, you do it standing or walking on the front part of your foot, without putting your heels on the ground.

whisper ^{복습}
[hwíspəːr]

v. 속삭이다, 작은 소리로 말하다; n. 속삭임
When you whisper, you say something very quietly.

intelligence **
[intélədʒəns]

n. 지능, 총명
Intelligence is the quality of being intelligent or clever.

opportunity ^{복습}
[àpərtjúːnəti]

n. 기회
An opportunity is a situation in which it is possible for you to do something that you want to do.

secure ^{복습}
[sikjúər]

a. 안전한, 안정된; 단단한; v. 확보하다, 얻다; 안전하게 지키다
(insecure a. 믿을 수 없는, 불안한)
If you feel secure, you feel safe and happy and are not worried about life.

constant ^{복습}
[kánstənt]

a. 끊임없이 계속되는, 변함없는, 불변의 (constantly ad. 끊임없이)
You use constant to describe something that happens all the time or is always there.

impress ^{복습}
[imprés]

v. 감동시키다, 좋은 인상을 주다 (impressed a. 인상 깊게 생각하는)
If something impresses you, you feel great admiration for it.

extract *
[ikstrǽkt]

v. 뽑다, 빼다; 인용하다, 발췌하다; 추출하다
If you extract something from a place, you take it out or pull it out.

account ^{복습}
[əkáunt]

n. (은행) 계좌, 예금(액); 기술, 설명; 계산; v. 설명하다; 책임지다; 생각하다
If you have an account with a bank or a similar organization, you have an arrangement to leave your money there and take some out when you need it.

extent ^{복습}
[ikstént]

n. 범위, 정도; 넓이, 크기
You use expressions such as to a large extent, to some extent, or to a certain extent in order to indicate that something is partly true, but not entirely true.

embezzle
[imbézl]

vi. 횡령하다 (embezzlement n. 횡령)
If someone embezzles money that their organization or company has placed in their care, they take it and use it illegally for their own purposes.

170

pace ^{복습}
[peis]

v. 왔다 갔다 하다, 보조를 맞추어 걷다; n. 걸음걸이, 보폭; 속도
If you pace a small area, you keep walking up and down it, because you are anxious or impatient.

ramble
[ræmbl]

vi. 두서없이 말하다; (어슬렁어슬렁) 거닐다, 산책하다; n. 산책
If you say that a person rambles in their speech or writing, you mean they do not make much sense because they keep going off the subject in a confused way.

fire ^{복습}
[faiər]

v. 해고하다; 발사하다; 불을 지르다; n. 불; 정열, 흥분
If an employer fires you, they dismiss you from your job.

inherit *
[inhérit]

v. 물려받다, 상속하다
If you inherit money or property, you receive it from someone who has died.

oversee
[óuvərsi:]

vt. 감독하다, 감시하다
If someone in authority oversees a job or an activity, they make sure that it is done properly.

financial ^{복습}
[fainǽnʃəl]

a. 재정(상)의, 재무의, 금융의
Financial means relating to or involving money.

declare ^{복습}
[dikléər]

v. 단언하다; 선언하다, 공표하다
If you declare that something is true, you say that it is true in a firm, deliberate way.

choir *
[kwaiər]

n. 합창단, 성가대; vi. 합창하다
A choir is a group of people who sing together, for example in a church or school.

suspicion *
[səspíʃən]

n. 의심, 의혹, 혐의
Suspicion or a suspicion is a belief or feeling that someone has committed a crime or done something wrong.

divorce ^{복습}
[divɔ́:rs]

v. 이혼하다; n. 이혼, 별거
If a man and woman divorce or if one of them divorces the other, their marriage is legally ended.

intend ^{복습}
[inténd]

v. ~할 작정이다; 의도하다, 꾀하다 (intention n. 의지, 의도)
If you intend to do something, you have decided or planned to do it.

self-absorbed
[self-æbsɔ́:rbd]

a. 자신에게만 몰두한[관심이 있는]
Someone who is self-absorbed thinks so much about things concerning themselves that they do not notice other people or the things around them.

maniac ^{복습}
[méiniæk]

n. 미치광이, 광적인 열중가; a. 광적인, 광란의
A maniac is a mad person who is violent and dangerous.

amphitheater
[ǽmfəθì:ətər]

n. 원형 극장; (극장의 반원형) 계단식 관람석
An amphitheater is a large open area surrounded by rows of seats sloping upward.

nestle *
[nesl]

v. (집 등이) 아늑하게 자리 잡다, 아담한 장소에 있다; 기분좋게 드러눕다[앉다]
If something such as a building nestles somewhere or if it is nestled somewhere, it is in that place and seems safe or sheltered.

foothill
[fúthil]

n. (큰 산 · 산맥 기슭의) 작은 언덕[산]
The foothills of a mountain or a range of mountains are the lower hills or mountains around its base.

patio^{복습}
[pǽtiòu]

n. 문밖 테라스; (스페인식 집의) 안뜰
A patio is an area of flat blocks or concrete next to a house, where people can sit and relax or eat.

offstage
[ɔ́:fstéidʒ]

n. 무대 뒤; a. 무대 뒤에서
When an actor or entertainer goes offstage, they go into the area behind or to the side of the stage, so that the audience no longer sees them.

foggy
[fɔ́:gi]

a. 안개가 낀[자욱한]; 흐릿한, 뚜렷하지 않은
When it is foggy, there is fog.

bloom[*]
[blu:m]

v. 꽃이 피다, 개화하다; 번영하다; n. 꽃; 개화(기)
When a plant or tree blooms, it produces flowers. When a flower blooms, it opens.

admit^{복습}
[ædmít]

v. 인정하다, 시인하다; 들이다, 허락하다
If you admit that something bad, unpleasant, or embarrassing is true, you agree, often unwillingly, that it is true.

bluster
[blʌ́stər]

n. 허세; 거세게 몰아침; v. 고함 지르다; 거세게[사납게] 몰아치다
Bluster is the vain and empty boasting.

float^{**}
[flout]

v. 뜨다, 떠다니다, 띄우다; 헤매다, 표류하다
Something that floats in or through the air hangs in it or moves slowly and gently through it.

damsel^{복습}
[dǽmzəl]

n. 계집아이, 처녀
A damsel is a young, unmarried woman.

distress^{복습}
[distrés]

n. 고통, 곤란; 가난, 곤궁; vt. 고민하게 하다, 괴롭히다
Distress is a state of extreme sorrow, suffering, or pain.

Check Your Reading Speed

1분에 몇 단어를 읽는지 리딩 속도를 측정해보세요.

$$\frac{1,376 \text{ words}}{\text{reading time (} \quad \text{) sec}} \times 60 = (\quad) \text{ WPM}$$

Build Your Vocabulary

characteristic ^{복습}
[kæriktərístik]

a. 독특한, 특징적인; n. 특징, 특성 (uncharacteristically ad. 특징 없이)
A quality or feature that is characteristic of someone or something is one which is often seen in them and seems typical of them.

grumble ^{복습}
[grʌmbl]

v. 투덜거리다, 불평하다; n. 투덜댐, 불평
If someone grumbles, they complain about something in a bad-tempered way.

mayor ^{복습}
[méiər]

n. 시장(市長); (지방 자치단체의) 행정장관
The mayor of a town or city is the person who has been elected to represent it for a fixed period of time or, in some places, to run its government.

install ^{복습}
[instɔ́:l]

vt. 설치하다, 장치하다
If you install a piece of equipment, you fit it or put it somewhere so that it is ready to be used.

sprinkler ^{복습}
[spríŋklə:r]

n. 스프링클러(물을 뿌리는 장치)
A sprinkler is a device used to spray water to plants or grass, or to put out fires in buildings.

leak [*]
[li:k]

n. (물·공기·빛 등이) 새는 구멍[곳]; 누수, 누출; v. 새(게 하)다; 누설하다
A leak is a crack, hole, or other gap that a substance such as a liquid or gas can pass through.

edgy
[édʒi]

a. 초조한, 화를 잘 내는; 날카로운
If someone is edgy, they are nervous and anxious, and seem likely to lose control of themselves.

gash ^{복습}
[gæʃ]

n. 깊은 상처; (지면의) 갈라진 틈; vt. 상처를 입히다
A gash is a long, deep cut in your skin or in the surface of something.

shovel ^{복습}
[ʃʌ́vəl]

n. 삽; v. ~을 삽으로 뜨다[파다], 삽으로 일하다
A shovel is a tool with a long handle that is used for lifting and moving earth, coal, or snow.

saw [*]
[sɔ:]

① v. 톱으로 켜다, 톱질하다; n. 톱 ② v. SEE의 과거 ③ n. 속담, 격언
If you saw something, you cut it with a saw.

section ^{복습}
[sékʃən]

n. 조각, 잘라낸 부분; 구역, 지역; (신문 등의) 난; vt. 구분하다, 구획하다
A section of something is one of the parts into which it is divided or from which it is formed.

attach [복습]
[ətǽtʃ]

vt. 붙이다, 달다
If you attach something to an object, you connect it or fasten it to the object.

glue [복습]
[glu:]

n. 접착제; vt. 접착제를 바르다; ~에 꼭 붙여서 떨어지지 않게 하다
Glue is a sticky substance used for joining things together, often for repairing broken things.

shade [복습]
[ʃeid]

n. 그늘, 음영; 색조; (pl.) 선글라스; vt. 그늘지게 하다
Shade is an area of darkness under or next to an object such as a tree, where sunlight does not reach.

pull up [복습]

phrasal v. (차 등이) 서다, 차를 세우다
When a vehicle or driver pulls up, the vehicle slows down and stops.

assume [복습]
[əsjú:m]

vt. 추정하다, 가정하다; 가장하다, 꾸미다; (역할 · 임무 등을) 맡다
If you assume that something is true, you imagine that it is true, sometimes wrongly.

register [복습]
[rédʒistər]

vt. 기재하다, 등록하다; n. 기록, 등록(부)
If you register to do something, you put your name on an official list, in order to be able to do that thing or to receive a service.

bruise*
[bru:z]

n. 멍, 타박상; v. 멍들게 하다, 타박상을 입히다
A bruise is an injury which appears as a purple mark on your body, although the skin is not broken.

rip [복습]
[rip]

v. 찢다, 벗겨내다; 잡아채다; 돌진하다; n. 찢어진 틈, 잡아 찢음
When something rips or when you rip it, you tear it forcefully with your hands or with a tool such as a knife.

rise to one's feet [복습]

idiom 벌떡 일어서다
If you get or rise to your feet, you stand up.

shove*
[ʃʌv]

v. (뒤에서 난폭하게) 밀다, 밀어넣다; n. 떠밀기
If you shove someone or something, you push them with a quick, violent movement.

lawn [복습]
[lɔ:n]

n. 잔디밭, 잔디
A lawn is an area of grass that is kept cut short and is usually part of someone's garden or backyard, or part of a park.

counterfeit [복습]
[káuntərfit]

a. 가짜의, 모조의; v. (화폐 · 지폐 · 문서 등을) 위조하다
Counterfeit money, goods, or documents are not genuine, but have been made to look exactly like genuine ones in order to deceive people.

cop [복습]
[kap]

n. (구어) 경찰관, 순경
A cop is a policeman or policewoman.

phony [가짜]
[fóuni]

a. 가짜의, 엉터리의; n. 가짜, 위조품, 사기꾼
If you describe something as phony, you disapprove of it because it is false rather than genuine.

buck [복습]
[bʌk]

① n. (속어) 달러 ② n. 수사슴, 수컷
A buck is a US or Australian dollar.

174

whack[복습]
[wæk]

v. 후려치다, 세게 때리다; n. 구타, 강타
If you whack someone or something, you hit them hard.

unusual[복습]
[ʌnjúːʒuəl]

a. 보통이 아닌, 드문 (unusually ad. 보통이 아니게, 현저히)
If you describe someone as unusual, you think that they are interesting and different from other people.

lately[복습]
[léitli]

ad. 요즘에, 최근에, 근래
You use lately to describe events in the recent past, or situations that started a short time ago.

charge up

phrasal v. 청중·군중을 선동하다, 흥분하게 하다
If you charge up someone, you make them be excited or roused.

concierge[복습]
[kɑ̀nsiέərʒ]

n. (호텔의) 안내원; 수위
A concierge is a person, especially in France, who looks after a block of flats and checks people entering and leaving the building.

scalp[복습]
[skælp]

v. 암표를 팔다; n. 두피, 머리가죽
If someone scalps tickets, they sell them outside a sports ground or theater, usually for more than their original value.

illegal[복습]
[ilíːgəl]

a. 불법의, 비합법적인
If something is illegal, the law says that it is not allowed.

constitution[복습]
[kɑ̀nstətjúːʃən]

n. 헌법; 체질, 체격 (unconstitutional a. 헌법에 위배되는)
The constitution of a country or organization is the system of laws which formally states people's rights and duties.

put up with

phrasal v. ~을 참고 견디다, 참다
If you put up with something, you tolerate or accept it, even though you find it unpleasant or unsatisfactory.

dude[복습]
[djuːd]

n. 사내, 녀석; (구어) 형씨, 친구
A dude is a man.

appreciate[복습]
[əpríːʃieit]

vt. 고맙게 생각하다; 진가를 알아보다, 인정하다
If you appreciate something that someone has done for you or is going to do for you, you are grateful for it.

demand[복습]
[dimǽnd]

n. [경제] 수요(량), 요구; vt. 묻다, 요구하다, 청구하다
If you refer to demand, or to the demand for something, you are referring to how many people want to have it, do it, or buy it.

figure[복습]
[fígjər]

v. 생각하다, 판단하다; 계산하다; n. 수치, 숫자; 형태, 형상; 작은 조각상
If you figure that something is the case, you think or guess that it is the case.

challenge**
[ʧǽlindʒ]

v. ~에 도전하다, (해보라고) 요구[권유]하다; n. 도전; 요구; 문제, 난문
If you challenge someone, you invite them to fight or compete with you in some way.

settle down[복습]

phrasal v. 진정하다; 정착하다, 자리잡다
To settle down means to become or to make someone become calmer or less excited.

detective ^{복습}
[ditéktiv]

n. 형사, 수사관; 탐정
A detective is someone whose job is to discover what has happened in a crime or other situation and to find the people involved.

firm ^{복습}
[fəːrm]

① a. 굳은, 단단한; 견고한 (firmly ad. 단호하게) ② n. 회사
If you describe someone as firm, you mean they behave in a way that shows that they are not going to change their mind, or that they are the person who is in control.

pickup truck ^{복습}
[píkʌp trʌ̀k]

n. 소형 오픈 트럭
A pickup truck is a light motor vehicle with an open-top rear cargo area.

frame ^{**}
[freim]

n. (안경) 테, 액자, 테두리; 뼈대, 골조; v. 테를 두르다; 세우다, 고안하다; 모함하다
The frames of a pair of glasses are all the metal or plastic parts of it, but not the lenses.

pop out ^{복습}

phrasal v. 튀어나오다, 갑자기 뛰어나가다; 갑자기 꺼지다, 급사하다
If something pops out, it suddenly comes out from a place.

relative ^{**}
[rélətiv]

a. 상대적인, 비교상의; 관계가 있는; n. 친척, 집안 (relatively ad. 비교적)
You use relative when you are comparing the quality or size of two things.

undisturbed
[ʌ̀ndistəːrbd]

a. 그대로 있는, 방해받지 않은, 영향을 받지 않는
If you are undisturbed in something that you are doing, you are able to continue doing it and are not affected by something that is happening.

raise ^{***}
[reiz]

n. (임금 · 물가 등의) 인상, 상승; 올리기, 높이기; v. 올리다, 일으키다; 기르다
A raise is an increase in your wages or salary.

promotion [*]
[prəmóuʃən]

n. 승진, 승격; 조장, 촉진
If you are given promotion or a promotion in your job, you are given a more important job or rank in the organization that you work for.

contract ^{**}
[kántrækt]

n. 계약; v. 계약하다; 수축시키다
A contract is a legal agreement, usually between two companies or between an employer and employee, which involves doing work for a stated sum of money.

landscape ^{복습}
[lǽndskeip]

v. (나무를 심거나 지형을 바꾸어) 미화[조경]하다; n. 풍경, 경치, 조망
If an area of land is landscaped, it is changed to make it more attractive, for example by adding streams or ponds and planting trees and bushes.

hire ^{복습}
[haiər]

vt. 고용하다; 빌리다, 빌려주다; n. 고용
If you hire someone, you employ them or pay them to do a particular job for you.

bunch ^{복습}
[bʌntʃ]

n. 떼, 한패; 다발, 송이; 다량
A bunch of people is a group of people who share one or more characteristics or who are doing something together.

kid ^{복습}
[kid]

v. 놀리다, 장난치다; 속이다
If you are kidding, you are saying something that is not really true, as a joke.

176

crew^{복습}
[kru:]

n. 팀, 그룹; 동료, 패거리; 승무원, 선원
A crew is a group of people with special technical skills who work together on a task or project.

up-front
[ʌ́p-frʌnt]

a. 솔직한, 정직한; 선행 투자의, 선불의
If you are up-front about something, you act openly or publicly so that people know what you are doing or what you believe.

straight off

idiom 서슴없이[망설이지 않고], 즉시
If you do something straight off, you do it without hesitating.

consider^{복습}
[kənsídər]

v. 고려하다, 숙고하다
If you consider something, you think about it carefully.

1. What did Armpit assume Felix would do with the letter?
   A. He would probably try to embarrass Armpit as revenge.
   B. He would probably sell it on eBay.
   C. He would probably donate it to a charity auction.
   D. He would probably frame it and put it in his room.

2. Why did Armpit compare his life situation to the donkey starving between two stacks of hay?
   A. Armpit could not decide what to do.
   B. Armpit was very hungry and couldn't find anything to eat.
   C. Armpit was gradually losing weight due to all of the hard work he had done.
   D. Armpit's landscaping job required him to move stacks of hay.

3. Why did Felix and Moses come to Armpit's house before he left?
   A. They knew he was trying to escape to San Francisco.
   B. They wanted to tell him that they had beaten up X-Ray again.
   C. They wanted to give Armpit more time to think about giving them the letter.
   D. They wanted the letter right then and there.

4. How did the fight between Moses and Armpit end?
   A. The limo driver honked his horn and said that he called the police.
   B. Armpit knocked Moses out in the middle of the road.
   C. Moses agreed to give him until Tuesday to give the letter to them.
   D. Moses broke Armpit's legs and took the letter from him.

5. How did the limo driver initially react to Armpit?
   A. He knew it was Theodore Johnson immediately and warmly welcomed him.
   B. He drove away after Armpit tried to open the door.
   C. He got inside and locked the doors.
   D. He called an ambulance to bring him to the hospital.

6. What did Armpit do to Moses's cowboy hat?
   A. He took it as a souvenir from Texas for Kaira.
   B. He took it inside to bring it back to him later.
   C. He stepped on it just like Moses had stepped on X-Ray's glasses.
   D. He gave it to the limo driver to show his gratitude for helping him.

7. Which of the following did Armpit NOT do before leaving his house?
   A. He took a shower.
   B. He put a Band-Aid on his hand.
   C. He put some clean clothes into a backpack.
   D. He left a note for his parents.

1분에 몇 단어를 읽는지 리딩 속도를 측정해보세요.

$$\frac{256 \text{ words}}{\text{reading time ( ) sec}} \times 60 = (\quad) \text{ WPM}$$

Build Your Vocabulary

identical^{복습}
[aidéntikəl]

a. 동일한, 꼭 같은
Things that are identical are exactly the same.

haystack
[héistæk]

n. 건초 더미
A haystack is a large, solid pile of hay, often covered with a straw roof to protect it, which is left in the field until it is needed.

argue^{복습}
[á:rgju:]

v. 논쟁하다; 주장하다
If one person argues with another, they speak angrily to each other about something that they disagree about.

make sense^{복습}

idiom 뜻이 통하다, 도리에 맞다
If something makes sense, it has a meaning that you can easily understand.

get rid of^{복습}

idiom 제거하다, 없애다
If you get rid of something, you make yourself free of it that is annoying you or that you do not want.

droop[*]
[dru:p]

v. 축 처지다, 수그러지다; 의기소침해지다, 기운이 빠지다
If something droops, it hangs or leans downward with no strength or firmness.

hang^{복습}
[hæŋ]

v. (hung-hung) 매달리다; 걸다, 달아매다; 교수형에 처하다
If something hangs in a high place or position, or if you hang it there, it is attached there so it does not touch the ground.

chew^{복습}
[tʃu:]

v. 씹다, 씹어서 으깨다
If you chew gum, you keep biting it and moving it around your mouth to taste the flavor of it.

personal^{복습}
[pə́rsənl]

a. 개인의, 사사로운; 자신이 직접 하는
A personal opinion, quality, or thing belongs or relates to one particular person rather than to other people.

paralyze^{복습}
[pǽrəlaiz]

vt. 무력[무능]하게 만들다; 마비시키다 (paralyzed a. 무기력한)
If a person, place, or organization is paralyzed by something, they become unable to act or function properly.

indecision
[indisídʒən]

n. 주저, 망설임; 우유부단
If you say that someone suffers from indecision, you mean that they find it very difficult to make decisions.

1분에 몇 단어를 읽는지 리딩 속도를 측정해보세요.

$$\frac{1{,}118 \text{ words}}{\text{reading time ( ) sec}} \times 60 = (\quad) \text{ WPM}$$

Build Your Vocabulary

ridiculous^{복습}
[ridíkjuləs]

a. 터무니없는; 웃기는, 우스꽝스러운 (ridiculously ad. 터무니없이)
If you say that something or someone is ridiculous, you mean that they are very foolish.

multiple*
[mʌ́ltəpl]

a. 많은 부분[요소]로 이루어진, 복합의; n. 배수 (multiple choice a. 선다식의)
In a multiple choice test or question, you have to choose the answer that you think is right from several possible answers that are listed on the question paper.

false^{복습}
[fɔːls]

a. 틀린, 정확하지 않은; 가짜의, 모조의
If something is false, it is incorrect, untrue, or mistaken.

economic^{복습}
[èkənάmik]

a. 경제(상)의, 경제적인; 경제학의 (economics n. 경제학)
Economic means concerned with the organization of the money, industry, and trade of a country, region, or society.

stick^{복습}
[stik]

① v. 고수하다; 달라붙다, 붙이다; 내밀다 ② n. 막대기, 지팡이
If you stick to something, you continue doing it even if it is difficult of you have problems.

let down^{복습}

phrasal v. ~을 실망시키다, 기대를 저버리다
If you let someone down, you fail to help or support them in the way that they hoped or expected.

complain^{복습}
[kəmpléin]

v. 불평하다, 투덜거리다
If you complain about a situation, you say that you are not satisfied with it.

fair^{복습}
[fɛər]

a. 공평한, 공정한; 상당한; n. 박람회, 전시회
Something or someone that is fair is reasonable, right, and just.

rearview mirror^{복습}
[ríərvjuː mírər]

n. (자동차의) 백미러
Inside a car, the rearview mirror is the mirror that enables you to see the traffic behind when you are driving.

graduate^{복습}
[grǽdʒueit]

vi. 졸업하다; n. 졸업생; 대학원생
When a student graduates, they complete their studies successfully and leave their school or university.

a heck of

idiom 대단한, 엄청난
People use a heck of to emphasize how big something is or how much of it there is.

horn ^{복습}
[hɔːrn]

n. (자동차 등의) 경적; 뿔
On a vehicle such as a car, the horn is the device that makes a loud noise as a signal or warning.

honk
[hɔːŋk]

v. 경적을 울리다; (거위 · 기러기가) 울다
If you honk the horn of a vehicle or if the horn honks, you make the horn produce a short loud sound.

stick out ^{복습}

phrasal v. 돌출하다, 불쑥 내밀다[나오다]
If something sticks out, it is further out than something else or is partly outside something such as a container.

angle ^{복습}
[æŋgl]

n. 각도, 관점; 귀퉁이; vt. (어떤 각도로) 기울이다, 굽다, 움직이다
An angle is the difference in direction between two lines or surfaces.

appreciate ^{복습}
[əpríːʃieit]

vt. 고맙게 생각하다; 진가를 알아보다, 인정하다
If you appreciate something that someone has done for you or is going to do for you, you are grateful for it.

string along ^{복습}

phrasal v. (~을) 속이다
To string someone along means to allow them to believe something that is not true for a long time, especially when you encourage them to have false hopes.

fist[*]
[fist]

n. (쥔) 주먹
Your hand is referred to as your fist when you have bent your fingers in toward the palm in order to hit someone.

slam ^{복습}
[slæm]

v. 세게 치다; (문 따위를) 탕 닫다; 털썩 내려놓다; n. 쾅 (하는 소리)
If one thing slams into or against another, it crashes into it with great force.

palm ^{복습}
[paːm]

n. 손바닥
The palm of your hand is the inside part.

duck
[dʌk]

① v. (머리나 몸을) 휙 숙이다, 피하다, 급히 움직이다 ② n. 오리
If you duck, you move your head or the top half of your body quickly downward to avoid something that might hit you, or to avoid being seen.

swing ^{복습}
[swiŋ]

v. 휘두르다; 빙 돌다, 흔들다; n. 휘두르기; 그네; 짧은 여행, (정치인의) 유세
If something swings in a particular direction or if you swing it in that direction, it moves in that direction with a smooth, curving movement.

charge ^{복습}
[ʧɑːrdʒ]

v. 돌격하다; (지불을) 청구하다; 부담 지우다, 맡기다; n. 수수료, 요금; 책임, 의무
If you charge toward someone or something, you move quickly and aggressively toward them.

bull ^{복습}
[bul]

n. 황소; 수컷; 허풍, 거짓말; v. 밀고 나아가다; 허풍 떨다
A bull is a male animal of the cow family.

headfirst
[hédfɔ̀ːrst]

ad. 저돌적으로, 무턱대고; 거꾸로, 곤두박질로
If you move headfirst, you move rashly or carelessly.

crack ^{복습}
[kræk]

v. 금이 가다, 깨다, 부수다; n. 갈라진 금[틈]; 갑작스런 날카로운 소리
If something hard cracks, or if you crack it, it becomes slightly damaged, with lines appearing on its surface.

182

get to one's feet^{복습}
idiom 벌떡 일어서다
If you get or rise to your feet, you stand up.

rub**
[rʌb]
v. 문지르다, 맞비비다; 닦다, 윤내다; 쓰다듬다; n. 닦기, 마찰
If you rub a part of your body, you move your hand or fingers backward and forward over it while pressing firmly.

fake^{복습}
[feik]
v. 가장하다, 꾸며내다, 위조하다; a. 가짜의, 위조의
If you fake a feeling, emotion, or reaction, you pretend that you are experiencing it when you are not.

gut
[gʌt]
n. 배; 장, 창자; 용기; 결단력
You can refer to someone's stomach as their gut, especially when it is very large and sticks out.

double over
phrasal v. (웃음 · 고통으로) 몸을 구부리다; 접어서 겹치다
If you double over, you suddenly bend forward and down, usually because of pain or laughter.

fend
[fend]
v. (타격 · 질문 등을) 받아넘기다, 피하다; 꾸려가다, 부양하다
If you fend off someone who is attacking you, you use your arms or something such as a stick to defend yourself from their blows.

blow^{복습}
[blou]
n. 강타, 급습; v. 폭파하다; 불다; 누설하다, 고자질하다
If someone receives a blow, they are hit with a fist or weapon.

gutter
[gʌ́tər]
n. (도로의) 배수로; (지붕의) 홈통; v. 도랑이 생기다
The gutter is the edge of a road next to the pavement, where rain water collects and flows away.

trade^{복습}
[treid]
v. 교환하다; 장사하다; n. 교환, 무역; 직업
If someone trades one thing for another or if two people trade things, they agree to exchange one thing for the other thing.

stuff^{복습}
[stʌf]
n. 일[것](일반적으로 말하거나 생각하는 것); 물건, 물질; vt. 채워 넣다, 속을 채우다
You can use stuff to refer to things such as a substance, a collection of things, events, or ideas, or the contents of something in a general way without mentioning the thing itself by name.

doubtful*
[dáutfəl]
a. 불확실한; 확신이 없는, 의심을 품은
If it is doubtful that something will happen, it seems unlikely to happen or you are uncertain whether it will happen.

drip^{복습}
[drip]
v. 방울방울[뚝뚝] 떨어지다; 가득[넘칠 듯이] 지니고 있다
When something drips, drops of liquid fall from it.

tear**
[tɛər]
v. (tore-torn) 찢다, 잡아뜯다; n. 찢기, 갈라진 금
If you tear paper, cloth, or another material, or if it tears, you pull it into two pieces or you pull it so that a hole appears in it.

splash^{복습}
[splæʃ]
v. (물 · 흙탕물 등을) 끼얹다, 튀기다; n. 첨벙 하는 소리
If you splash a liquid somewhere or if it splashes, it hits someone or something and scatters in a lot of small drops.

knuckle^{복습}
[nʌkl]
n. 손가락 관절[마디]; (pl.) 주먹; v. 주먹으로 치다
Your knuckles are the rounded pieces of bone that form lumps on your hands where your fingers join your hands, and where your fingers bend.

bleed^{복습}
[bli:d]

v. 피가 나다, 출혈하다
When you bleed, you lose blood from your body as a result of injury or illness.

drawer^{**}
[drɔ́:ər]

n. 서랍
A drawer is part of a desk, chest, or other piece of furniture that is shaped like a box and is designed for putting things in.

pad^{복습}
[pæd]

n. (한 장씩 떼어 쓰는) 필기첩; 덧대는 것; vt. 완충제를 덧대다, 속을 채우다
A pad of paper is a number of pieces of paper which are fixed together along the top or the side, so that each piece can be torn off when it has been used.

cover^{***}
[kʌ́vər]

v. (자리를 비운 사람의 일을) 대신하다; 씌우다, 가리다; n. 덮개, 커버
If you cover for someone who is ill or away, you do their work for them while they are not there.

grab^{복습}
[græb]

v. 부여잡다, 움켜쥐다; n. 부여잡기
If you grab something, you take it or pick it up suddenly and roughly.

point out^{복습}

phrasal v. ~을 지적하다
If you point out a fact or mistake, you tell someone about it or draw their attention to it.

panel^{복습}
[pǽnl]

n. (자동차 · 비행기 등의) 계기판; (넓은 직사각형의) 합판, 벽판
A control panel or instrument panel is a board or surface which contains switches and controls to operate a machine or piece of equipment.

temperature^{복습}
[témpəritʃər]

n. 온도, 기온
The temperature of something is a measure of how hot or cold it is.

knob[*]
[nab]

n. 손잡이; 혹, 마디; (작은) 덩이
A knob is a round handle on a door or drawer which you use in order to open or close it.

envelope^{복습}
[énvəlòup]

n. 봉투, 봉지
An envelope is the rectangular paper cover in which you send a letter to someone through the post.

apparent^{복습}
[əpǽrənt]

a. 뚜렷한, 명백한, 외관상의 (apparently ad. 명백하게, 보아하니)
If something is apparent to you, it is clear and obvious to you.

clown^{복습}
[klaun]

n. 어릿광대, 익살꾼; 쓸모없는 사람; v. 익살부리다, 어릿광대짓을 하다
A clown is a performer in a circus who wears funny clothes and bright make-up, and does silly things in order to make people laugh.

inspire^{**}
[inspáiər]

vt. 영감을 주다, 고무하다, 불어넣다
If someone or something inspires you, they give you new ideas and a strong feeling of enthusiasm.

spangle
[spǽŋgl]

vt. (번쩍이는 것을) 박아 넣다; n. 스팽글, 반짝거리는 장식
Something that is spangled is covered with small shiny objects.

trapeze
[træpí:z]

n. (곡예 · 체조용의) 그네
A trapeze is a bar of wood or metal hanging from two ropes on which people in a circus swing and perform skillful movements.

184

floppy 복습
[flápi]

a. 축 늘어진, 느슨한; 기운 없는
Something that is floppy is loose rather than stiff, and tends to hang downward.

attire
[ətáiər]

n. 옷차림새, 복장; vt. 차려 입히다
Your attire is the clothes you are wearing.

admire 복습
[ædmáiər]

v. 감탄하다, 칭찬하다, 존경하다
If you admire someone or something, you like and respect them very much.

perspire 복습
[pərspáiər]

vi. 땀을 흘리다, 땀이 나다
When you perspire, a liquid comes out on the surface of your skin, because you are hot or frightened.

1. How did Armpit describe San Francisco weather?
   A. It was hot and humid just like Texas.
   B. It was cloudy and depressing.
   C. It was cool and fresh.
   D. It was like a tropical paradise.

2. What did Jerome show Armpit?
   A. A baseball glove
   B. A baseball bat
   C. A baseball cap
   D. A baseball

3. How did Armpit greet Kaira in the hotel lobby?
   A. He greeted her with a kiss.
   B. He greeted her with a hug.
   C. He greeted her with flowers.
   D. He greeted her with a handshake.

4. Why did Kaira tell Armpit not to worry about the price of the jacket?
   A. He could ask for a discount when he was ready to pay for it.
   B. Kaira was going to buy it as a present using her own pocket money.
   C. Kaira was famous and could get anything she wanted for free.
   D. He could just charge it to his room and the tour would pay for it.

5. How did Armpit and Kaira manage to get away from Fred?
   A. They changed their clothes in a park.
   B. They paid the taxi driver to quickly let them out when he stopped in traffic.
   C. They called Fred's cell phone and told them they were going back to the hotel.
   D. They paid Fred's taxi driver to take him the wrong way.

6. Which of the following did Jerome NOT do in Armpit's room?
   A. He took some hair from the hairbrush.
   B. He took the used Band-Aid with blood on it.
   C. He placed a key to Kaira's room on the couch.
   D. He called for room service for a fruit and cheese plate.

7. What did Armpit buy for Ginny in Chinatown?
   A. A silk scarf
   B. Green beans
   C. Silk slippers
   D. A sweatshirt

1분에 몇 단어를 읽는지 리딩 속도를 측정해보세요.

$$\frac{1,555 \text{ words}}{\text{reading time ( ) sec}} \times 60 = (\quad) \text{ WPM}$$

Build Your Vocabulary

breeze^{복습}
[bri:z]

v. 거침없이[경쾌하게] 걷다; n. 산들바람, 미풍
If you breeze into a place or a position, you enter it in a very casual or relaxed manner.

passenger^{복습}
[pǽsəndʒər]

n. 승객, 여객
A passenger in a vehicle such as a bus, boat, or plane is a person who is traveling in it, but who is not driving it or working on it.

agent^{복습}
[éidʒənt]

n. 대리인, 중개인; 행위자
An agent is a person who looks after someone else's business affairs or does business on their behalf.

security^{복습}
[sikjúərəti]

n. 보안, 경비; 안전, 보호
Security refers to all the measures that are taken to protect a place, or to ensure that only people with permission enter it or leave it.

bald^{복습}
[bɔ:ld]

a. (머리 등이) 벗어진, 대머리의; vi. 머리가 벗어지다
Someone who is bald has little or no hair on the top of their head.

earthquake^{복습}
[ɔ́:rθkwèik]

n. 지진; 대변동, 격동
An earthquake is a shaking of the ground caused by movement of the earth's crust.

duck^{복습}
[dʌk]

① v. (머리나 몸을) 휙 숙이다, 피하다, 급히 움직이다 ② n. 오리
If you duck, you move your head or the top half of your body quickly downward to avoid something that might hit you, or to avoid being seen.

doorway[*]
[dɔ́:rwèi]

n. 문간, 현관, 출입구
A doorway is a space in a wall where a door opens and closes.

cower
[káuər]

vi. (추위 · 공포 등으로) 움츠리다, 위축되다
If you cower, you bend forward and downward because you are very frightened.

plaster[*]
[plǽstər]

n. 회반죽, 석고; 고약; vt. 더덕더덕 바르다; 회반죽을 바르다
Plaster is a smooth paste made of sand, lime, and water, and is used to cover walls and ceilings and is also used to make sculptures.

brick^{**}
[brik]

n. 벽돌; vt. 벽돌로 막다
Bricks are rectangular blocks of baked clay used for building walls, which are usually red or brown.

crash** [kræʃ]	vt. 충돌하다, 추락하다; (굉음과 함께) 부딪치다; n. 쿵 하는 소리; 충돌, 추락 If something crashes somewhere, it moves and hits something else violently, making a loud noise.
gap** [gæp]	n. 갈라진 틈, 구멍; 큰 차이, 격차; v. (사이가) 벌어지다, 깨지다 A gap is a space between two things or a hole in the middle of something solid.
baggage* [bǽgidʒ]	n. 여행용 수하물 Your baggage consists of the bags that you take with you when you travel.
claim^{복습} [kleim]	n. 청구, 요구; 권리; v. 주장하다; 요구[청구]하다 A claim is a demand for something that you think you have a right to.
spot^{복습} [spat]	vt. 발견하다, 분별하다; n. 장소, 지점; 반점, 얼룩 If you spot something or someone, you notice them.
oppressive [əprésiv]	a. 답답한, 불쾌한; 압박적인, 가혹한 If you describe the weather or the atmosphere in a room as oppressive, you mean that it is unpleasantly hot and damp.
temperature^{복습} [témpəritʃər]	n. 온도, 기온 The temperature of something is a measure of how hot or cold it is.
downright [dáunrait]	a. 순전한, 완전한 You use downright to emphasize unpleasant or bad qualities or behavior.
air- conditioned [έər-kəndiʃənd]	a. 냉난방이 된 If a room or vehicle is air-conditioned, the air in it is kept cool and dry by means of a special machine.
humid^{복습} [hjúːmid]	a. 습한, 눅눅한, 축축한 You use humid to describe an atmosphere or climate that is very damp, and usually very hot.
stale* [steil]	a. 퀴퀴한, 고약한 냄새가 나는; (음식 등이) 상한, 신선하지 않은 Stale air or a stale smells is unpleasant because it is no longer fresh.
stagnant [stǽgnənt]	a. (물 · 공기 등이) 흐르지 않는, 괴어 있는; 불경기의, 부진한 Stagnant water is not flowing, and therefore often smells unpleasant and is dirty.
luggage^{복습} [lʌ́gidʒ]	n. 여행 가방, (여행자의) 수하물 Luggage is the suitcases and bags that you take with you when travel.
revolve^{복습} [riválv]	v. 회전하다, 빙빙 돌다 (revolving door n. 회전문) When something revolves or when you revolve it, it moves or turns in a circle around a central point or line.
spectacular* [spektǽkjulər]	a. 호화로운, 장관을 이루는, 눈부신 Something that is spectacular is very impressive or dramatic.

chandelier
[ʃændəlíər]

n. 샹들리에(천장에서 내리 드리운 호화로운 장식등)
A chandelier is a large, decorative frame which holds light bulbs or candles and hangs from the ceiling.

ornate
[ɔːrnéit]

a. 화려하게 장식한, 잘 꾸민
An ornate building, piece of furniture, or object is decorated with complicated patterns or shapes.

attractive**
[ətrǽktiv]

a. 매력 있는; 마음을 끌어당기는
A person who is attractive is pleasant to look at.

approach^{복습}
[əpróutʃ]

v. 접근하다, 다가오다; n. 접근, 가까움
When you approach something, you get closer to it.

brass*
[bræs]

n. 놋쇠, 황동
Brass is a yellow-colored metal made from copper and zinc.

attach^{복습}
[ətǽtʃ]

vt. 붙이다, 달다
If you attach something to an object, you connect it or fasten it to the object.

bellman
[belmən]

n. 벨보이(호텔에서 짐을 운반하는 사람)
A bellman is a man or boy who works in a hotel, carrying bags or bringing things to the guests' rooms.

restrict*
[ristríkt]

vt. 제한하다, 한정하다 (restricted a. 제한된)
If you restrict something to a particular place, it is allowed only in that place.

wimp^{복습}
[wimp]

n. 겁쟁이, 약골
If you call someone a wimp, you disapprove of them because they lack confidence or determination, or because they are often afraid of things.

in the first place

idiom 우선, 먼저
You say in the first place when you are talking about the beginning of a situation or about the situation as it was before a series of events.

confuse^{복습}
[kənfjúːz]

v. 어리둥절하게 하다, 혼동하다 (confusing a. 당황하게 하는)
To confuse someone means to make it difficult for them to know exactly what is happening or what to do.

sarcastic^{복습}
[sɑːrkǽstik]

a. 빈정대는, 비꼬는, 풍자적인 (sarcasm n. 빈정거림)
Someone who is sarcastic says or does the opposite of what they really mean in order to mock or insult someone.

insert*
[insɔ́ːrt]

v. 삽입하다, 끼워 넣다; n. 삽입물; 삽화
If you insert an object into something, you put the object inside it.

slot^{복습}
[slat]

n. (동전) 투입구, 가늘고 긴 홈; 위치, 자리, 장소, 시간대
A slot is a narrow opening in a machine or container, for example a hole that you put coins in to make a machine work.

access*
[ǽkses]

n. 접근(할 수 있는 기회), 이용(하는 권리); vt. 접근하다, 이용하다
If you have access to a building or other place, you are able or allowed to go into it.

190

turn out ^{복습}

phrasal v. 결국은 ~이 되다, 결국은 ~임이 밝혀지다
To turn out means to happen in a particular way or to have a particular result.

suite ^{복습}
[swi:t]

n. 호텔의 스위트 룸; (물건의) 한 벌
A suite is a set of rooms in a hotel or other building.

compliment ^{복습}
[kámpləmənt]

n. (pl.) 존경을 나타내는 인사말; 찬사, 칭찬의 말; v. 경의를 표하다, 칭찬하다
You can refer to your compliments when you want to express thanks, good wishes, or respect to someone in a formal way.

taste ^{복습}
[téist]

v. 맛보다, 맛이 나다; n. 맛, 미각; 취향, 기호
If food or drink tastes of something, it has that particular flavor, which you notice when you eat or drink it.

figure ^{복습}
[fígjər]

v. 생각하다, 판단하다; 계산하다; n. 수치, 숫자; 형태, 형상; 작은 조각상
If you figure that something is the case, you think or guess that it is the case.

pop ^{복습}
[pap]

v. 불쑥 움직이다; 뻥 하고 소리를 내다, 터뜨리다; n. 뻥[탁] 하는 소리; 발포
If you pop something somewhere, you put it there quickly.

class ^{***}
[klæs]

n. 최고, 고급; 학급, 반; 수업; 계급, 등급; v. 분류하다
If you say that someone or something has class, you mean that they are elegant and sophisticated.

complimentary
[kàmpləméntəri]

a. 무료의; 칭찬하는
A complimentary seat, ticket, or book is given to you free.

get rid of ^{복습}

idiom 제거하다, 없애다
If you get rid of something, you make yourself free of it that is annoying you or that you do not want.

extend ^{복습}
[iksténd]

v. (손·발 등을) 뻗다, 늘이다; 넓히다, 확장하다
If someone extends their hand, they stretch out their arm and hand to shake hands with someone.

appreciate ^{복습}
[əprí:ʃieit]

vt. 고맙게 생각하다; 진가를 알아보다, 인정하다
If you appreciate something that someone has done for you or is going to do for you, you are grateful for it.

identical ^{복습}
[aidéntikəl]

a. 동일한, 꼭 같은
Things that are identical are exactly the same.

closet ^{복습}
[klázit]

n. 벽장; 작은 방
A closet is a very small room for storing things, especially one without windows.

initial ^{복습}
[iníʃəl]

n. 이니셜, 머리글자; a. 처음의, 최초의
Initials are the capital letters which begin each word of a name.

swing ^{복습}
[swiŋ]

n. 휘두르기; 그네; 짧은 여행, (정치인의) 유세; v. 휘두르다; 빙 돌다, 흔들다
A swing is a movement of back and forth or in one particular direction.

exaggerate [*]
[igzǽdʒərèit]

v. 과장하다 (exaggeration n. 과장)
If you exaggerate, you indicate that something is, for example, worse or more important than it really is.

allow^{복습}
[əláu]

v. 허락하다, ~하게 두다; 인정하다
If someone is allowed to do something, it is all right for them to do it and they will not get into trouble.

roster
[rástər]

n. 선수 명단; 근무 명부[표], 등록부
A roster is a list of the sports players who are available for a particular team, or of the people who work for a particular organization or are available to do a particular job.

so-called
[sə-kɔ:ld]

a. 소위, 이른바
You use so-called to indicate that you think a word or expression used to describe someone or something is in fact wrong.

physical^{복습}
[fízikəl]

a. 신체의, 육체의; 물리적인, 물질의
Physical qualities, actions, or things are connected with a person's body, rather than with their mind.

pitch^{복습}
[pitʃ]

n. (공의) 투구; 던지기; 최고도, 정점; v. 던지다; 고정시키다
In the game of baseball or rounders, when you pitch the ball, you throw it to the batter for them to hit it.

work out

phrasal v. (일이) 잘되어가다, (문제가) 해결되다
If something works out, it happens or develops in a paticular way, especially a successful way.

ballplayer
[bɔ́:lplèiər]

n. 직업 야구 선수
A ballplayer is a baseball player.

be better off^{복습}

idiom (~하는 것이) 더 낫다
Be better off is used to say that someone would be happier or more satisfied if they were in a particular position or did a particular thing.

mean^{***}
[mi:n]

vt. ~할 작정이다, ~하려고 생각하다; 의미하다; a. 비열한, 음흉한; 뒤떨어진
If you mean to do something, you intend or plan to do it.

weird^{복습}
[wiə:rd]

a. 이상한, 기묘한; 수상한
If you describe something or someone as weird, you mean that they are strange.

denim^{복습}
[dénəm]

n. 데님, 두꺼운 면포
Denim is a thick cotton cloth, usually blue, which is used to make clothes. Jeans are made from denim.

lumberjack
[lʌ́mbərdʒæk]

n. 나무꾼, 벌목꾼
A lumberjack is a person whose job is to cut down trees.

linger[*]
[líŋgər]

vi. 오래 머물다, 남아 있다, 계속되다
When something lingers, it continues to exist for a long time, often much longer than expected.

worth^{복습}
[wə:rθ]

a. 가치가 있는; n. 가치, 값어치
If you say that something is worth having, you mean that it is pleasant or useful, and therefore a good thing to have.

whisper^{복습}
[hwíspə:r]

v. 속삭이다, 작은 소리로 말하다; n. 속삭임
When you whisper, you say something very quietly.

192

1분에 몇 단어를 읽는지 리딩 속도를 측정해보세요.

$$\frac{1{,}144 \text{ words}}{\text{reading time (} \quad \text{) sec}} \times 60 = (\quad) \text{ WPM}$$

Build Your Vocabulary

freeze[**]
[frí:z]
v. 얼다, 얼리다; n. (임금·가격 등의) 동결
If you freeze, you feel extremely cold.

boutique
[bu:tí:k]
n. 부티크(여자용 고급 유행복이나 액세서리를 파는 가게)
A boutique is a small shop that sells fashionable clothes, shoes, or jewelry.

cutesy
[kjú:tsi]
a. 귀엽게 보이도록 한
If you describe someone or something as cutesy, you dislike them because you think they are unpleasantly pretty and sentimental.

charcoal
[ʧɑ́:rkòul]
n. 숯, 목탄 (charcoal gray n. 짙은 회색)
Charcoal is a black substance obtained by burning wood without much air.

hang[복습]
[hæŋ]
v. 매달리다; 걸다, 달아매다; 교수형에 처하다
If something hangs in a high place or position, or if you hang it there, it is attached there so it does not touch the ground.

display[복습]
[displéi]
n. 진열(품), 전시; 표시; v. 보이다, 나타내다, 진열(전시)하다
A display is an arrangement of things that have been put in a particular place, so that people can see them easily.

fabric[*]
[fǽbrik]
n. 직물, 천; 구조, 구성
Fabric is cloth or other material produced by weaving together cotton, nylon, wool, silk, or other threads.

charge[복습]
[ʧɑ:rdʒ]
v. (지불을) 청구하다; 부담 지우다, 맡기다; 돌격하다; n. 수수료, 요금; 책임, 의무
If you charge someone an amount of money, you ask them to pay that amount for something that you have sold to them or done for them.

hood[*]
[hud]
n. 두건, 후드; (자동차의) 보닛 (hooded a. 두건이 있는)
A hood is a part of a coat which you can pull up to cover your head.

cable[복습]
[kéibl]
n. 케이블 (전선), 굵은 밧줄
A cable is a thick wire, or a group of wires inside a rubber or plastic covering, which is used to carry electricity or electronic signals.

whistle[**]
[hwísl]
v. 휘파람을 불다; 획획 소리를 내다; n. 휘파람; 호각; 경적
When someone whistles, they make a sound by forcing their breath out between their lips or their teeth.

snuggle
[snʌgl]

v. 바싹 파고들다, 달라붙다; 끌어안다
If you snuggle somewhere, you settle yourself into a warm, comfortable position, especially by moving closer to another person.

cab ^{복습}
[kæb]

n. 택시; (버스 · 기차 · 트럭의) 운전석
A cab is a taxi.

cuddle
[kʌdl]

v. 꼭 껴안다, 포옹하다; 바싹 달라붙다 (cuddly a. 꼭 껴안고 싶은)
If you cuddle someone, you put your arms round them and hold them close as a way of showing your affection.

stuffed ^{복습}
[stʌft]

a. 속을 채운; 배가 너무 부른 (stuffed animal n. 봉제 동물인형)
Stuffed animals are toys that are made of cloth filled with a soft material and which look like animals.

pull away ^{복습}

phrasal v. (차가 발차하여) 떠나다; (몸을) 빼다, 뿌리치다
When a vehicle pulls away, it begins to move.

apparent ^{복습}
[əpǽrənt]

a. 또렷한, 명백한, 외관상의 (apparently ad. 명백하게, 보아하니)
If something is apparent to you, it is clear and obvious to you.

doofus ^{복습}
[dúːfəs]

n. (비격식) 멍청이, 얼간이
Doofus is a slow-witted or stupid person.

ditch ^{복습}
[ditʃ]

v. (사람을) 따돌리다, (물건을) 버리다; 도랑을 파다; n. 수로, 도랑
If someone ditches someone, they end a relationship with that person.

spot ^{복습}
[spat]

n. 장소, 지점; 반점, 얼룩; vt. 발견하다, 분별하다 (on the spot idiom 즉석에서)
You can refer to a particular place as a spot.

remark **
[rimάːrk]

v. 말하다, 언급하다; n. 의견, 발언
If you remark that something is the case, you say that it is the case.

swerve ^{복습}
[swəːrv]

v. 휙 방향을 틀다, 벗어나다, 빗나가다; n. 벗어남, 빗나감
If a vehicle or other moving thing swerves or if you swerve it, it suddenly changes direction, often in order to avoid hitting something.

lane *
[lein]

n. (도로의) 차선; 좁은 길, 골목, 작은 길
A lane is a part of a main road which is marked by the edge of the road and a painted line, or by two painted lines.

traffic ^{복습}
[trǽfik]

n. 교통(량), 통행, 왕래; 거래, 무역; v. 매매하다, 거래하다
Traffic refers to the movement of ships, trains, or aircraft between one place and another.

lap ^{복습}
[læp]

① n. 무릎; (트랙의) 한 바퀴 ② v. (파도가) 찰싹거리다; (할짝할짝) 핥다
If you have something on your lap, it is on top of your legs and near to your body.

ease ^{복습}
[iːz]

v. 살짝 움직이다[옮기다]; (고통 · 고민 등을) 진정[완화]시키다; n. 편함, 안정
If you ease your way somewhere or ease somewhere, you move there slowly, carefully, and gently.

pavement *
[péivmənt]

n. 포장 도로
The pavement is the hard surface of a road.

194

| **hit the gas** | idiom 액셀러레이터를 밟다. 속도를 내다 |
| | If a driver hit the gas, the driver puts his foot on the accelarator and goes faster. |

swing^{복습}
[swiŋ]

v. (swung–swung) 휘두르다; 빙 돌다, 흔들다;
n. 휘두르기; 그네; 짧은 여행, (정치인의) 유세
If something swings in a particular direction or if you swing it in that direction, it moves in that direction with a smooth, curving movement.

grab^{복습}
[græb]

v. 부여잡다, 움켜쥐다; n. 부여잡기
If you grab something, you take it or pick it up suddenly and roughly.

crouch[*]
[krautʃ]

v. 몸을 쭈그리다, 쪼그리고 앉다; 웅크리다; n. 웅크림
If you are crouching, your legs are bent under you so that you are close to the ground and leaning forward slightly.

slip^{복습}
[slip]

v. 살짝 들어가(게 하)다; 미끄러지다, 미끄러지듯이 움직이다
If you slip something somewhere, you put it there quickly in a way that does not attract attention.

slot^{복습}
[slat]

n. (동전) 투입구, 가늘고 긴 홈; 위치, 자리, 장소, 시간대
A slot is a narrow opening in a machine or container, for example a hole that you put coins in to make a machine work.

hallway
[hɔ́:lwei]

n. 복도, 통로
A hallway in a building is a long passage with doors into rooms on both sides of it.

suite^{복습}
[swi:t]

n. 호텔의 스위트 룸; (물건의) 한 벌
A suite is a set of rooms in a hotel or other building.

surgeon[*]
[sə́:rdʒən]

n. 외과의사, 외과 전문의
A surgeon is a doctor who is specially trained to perform surgery.

layer[*]
[léiər]

n. 층; 계층; 지층; v. 층지게 하다, 층을 이루다
A layer of a material or substance is a quantity or piece of it that covers a surface or that is between two other things.

strew
[stru:]

vt. (strewed–strewn) 온통 뒤덮다; 뿌리다, 흩뿌리다
If a place is strewn with things, they are lying scattered there.

sweat^{복습}
[swet]

n. 땀; v. 땀 흘리다; 습기가 차다
Sweat is the salty colorless liquid which comes through your skin when you are hot, ill, or afraid.

soak[*]
[souk]

v. 젖다, 적시다; 스며들다, 흡수하다 (soaked a. 흠뻑 젖은)
If a liquid soaks something or if you soak something with a liquid, the liquid makes the thing very wet.

consider^{복습}
[kənsídər]

v. 고려하다, 숙고하다
If you consider something, you think about it carefully.

heap[*]
[hi:p]

n. 더미, 쌓아올린 것; 많음, 다수; vt. 쌓아올리다; 축적하다
A heap of things is a pile of them, especially a pile arranged in a rather untidy way.

robe^{복습}
[roub]

n. 길고 헐거운 겉옷(실내복이나 휴식 때의 옷); 예복, 관복
A robe is a piece of clothing, usually made of toweling, which people wear in the house, especially when they have just got up or had a bath.

leak^{복습}
[liːk]

v. 새(게 하)다; 누설하다; n. (물·공기·빛 등이) 새는 구멍[곳]; 누수, 누출
If a container leaks, there is a hole or crack in it which lets a substance such as liquid or gas escape.

strand
[strænd]

n. (실·전선·머리카락 등의) 가닥, 꼰 줄
A strand of something such as hair, wire, or thread is a single thin piece of it.

stick^{복습}
[stik]

① v. (stuck–stuck) 달라붙다, 붙이다; 내밀다; 고수하다 ② n. 막대기, 지팡이
If one thing sticks to another, it becomes attached to it and is difficult to remove.

bristle
[brisl]

n. (솔의 짧은) 털; 짧고 뻣뻣한 털; v. 벌컥 화내다; 곤두세우다
The bristles of a brush are the thick hairs or hair-like pieces of plastic which are attached to it.

envelope^{복습}
[énvəlòup]

n. 봉투, 봉지
An envelope is the rectangular paper cover in which you send a letter to someone through the post.

crusted
[krʌstid]

a. 겉껍질이 생긴; 굳은, 융통성 없는
If something is crusted with a substance, it is covered with a hard or thick layer of that substance.

couch^{복습}
[kautʃ]

n. 소파, 긴 의자
A couch is a long, comfortable seat for two or three people.

rack^{복습}
[ræk]

n. 선반, 걸이; vt. 괴롭히다
A rack is a frame or shelf, usually with bars or hooks, that is used for holding things or for hanging things on.

grocery^{복습}
[gróusəri]

n. 식료 잡화점; (pl.) 식료 잡화류
A grocery or a grocery store is a shop selling foods such as flour, sugar, and tinned foods.

block^{복습}
[blak]

vt. 막다, 방해하다; n. (도시의) 블록, 한 구획; 덩어리; 방해물
If you block someone's way, you prevent them from going somewhere or entering a place by standing in front of them.

sidewalk[*]
[sáidwɔ̀ːk]

n. (포장한) 보도, 인도
A sidewalk is a path with a hard surface by the side of a road.

standstill
[stǽndstil]

n. 정지, 정체; a. 정지된 (be at a standstill idiom 정체되어 있다)
If movement or activity comes to or is brought to a standstill, it stops completely.

pagoda
[pəgóudə]

n. (아시아 여러 나라의 사찰의) 탑
A pagoda is a tall building which is used for religious purposes, especially by Buddhists, in China, Japan, and South-East Asia.

grumble^{복습}
[grʌmbl]

v. 투덜거리다, 불평하다; n. 투덜댐, 불평
If someone grumbles, they complain about something in a bad-tempered way.

196

veggie
[védʒi]

n. (= vegetable) 채소; (= vegitarian) 채식주의자
Veggies are plants such as cabbages, potatoes, and onions which you can cook and eat.

exotic
[igzátik]

a. 이국풍의, 외래의, 외국의
Something that is exotic is unusual and interesting, usually because it comes from a distant country.

gross^{복습}
[grous]

a. 역겨운, 기분 나쁜; 큰, 비대한; 전체의 (gross out idiom 역겹게 하는)
If you describe something as gross, you think it is very unpleasant.

string^{복습}
[striŋ]

n. 일련, 한 줄; 끈, 실; (악기의) 현[줄]; v. 묶다, 매달다
A string of things is a number of them on a piece of string, thread, or wire.

souvenir^{복습}
[sùːvəníər]

n. 기념품
A souvenir is something which you buy or keep to remind you of a holiday, place, or event.

point out^{복습}

phrasal v. ~을 지적하다
If you point out a fact or mistake, you tell someone about it or draw their attention to it.

go through^{복습}

idiom 자세히 검토하다; 통과하다; 겪다
To go through something means to look at, check or examine it closely and carefully, especially in order to find something.

identical^{복습}
[aidéntikəl]

a. 동일한, 꼭 같은
Things that are identical are exactly the same.

end up^{복습}

phrasal v. 마침내는 (~으로) 되다; 끝나다
If you end up doing something or end up in a particular state, you do that thing or get into that state even though you did not originally intend to.

stretch^{복습}
[stretʃ]

v. 뻗다, 쭉 펴다, 늘이다; n. (특히 길게 뻗은) 길, 구간; 뻗침
Something that stretches over an area or distance covers or exists in the whole of that area or distance.

1. Where did Armpit and Kaira go after Chinatown and why?
   A. They went back to the hotel because they were tired.
   B. They went to a restaurant because they were hungry.
   C. They went back to the Golden Gate Bridge because Armpit wanted to take a picture.
   D. They went to a coffeehouse in North Beach because Kaira wanted coffee.

2. Which of the following was NOT something that Kaira said about the stage at the coffeehouse?
   A. Beatniks used to read poetry there.
   B. She would like to sing on a stage like that.
   C. Armpit should play the drums there.
   D. Beatniks used to play bongos there.

3. How did Kaira say she felt about visiting the girl with a disease?
   A. She felt creeped out by around people with diseases.
   B. She felt happy that she could make a little girl glad.
   C. She felt comfortable around disabled children.
   D. She felt angry that she was forced to talk to people.

4. Why did the man in the coffeehouse interrupt Armpit and Kaira?
   A. He wanted an autograph from Kaira.
   B. He was curious if Armpit was Kaira's boyfriend.
   C. He thought they were talking too loudly and wanted them to be quiet.
   D. He bought Kaira a pastry as a gift from a music fan.

5. How did Kaira react to Armpit asking her to write a letter for him to sell?
   A. She would do anything for Armpit and gladly agreed.
   B. She got angry with him and threw her coffee at him.
   C. She thought it was a great idea for Armpit to become rich too.
   D. She reluctantly agreed to help Armpit because his friend was in trouble.

6. How did Armpit feel about being alone in Chinatown?
   A. He thought there was something special about being in a strange place.
   B. He felt lonely and wanted to go back to Austin.
   C. He felt scared and vulnerable.
   D. He felt like he wanted to live in Chinatown forever.

7. How did Fred feel when he lost Kaira?
   A. It had happened before so he knew how to handle it.
   B. He felt that he might be fired if something bad happened to Kaira.
   C. He knew that he could completely trust Kaira with Armpit.
   D. It had never happened before and he was worried.

Check Your Reading Speed

1분에 몇 단어를 읽는지 리딩 속도를 측정해보세요.

$$\frac{1,428 \text{ words}}{\text{reading time (\quad) sec}} \times 60 = (\quad) \text{ WPM}$$

Build Your Vocabulary

section^{복습}
[sékʃən]

n. 구역, 지역; 조각, 잘라낸 부분; (신문 등의) 난; vt. 구분하다, 구획하다
A section of something is one of the parts into which it is divided or from which it is formed.

basement**
[béismənt]

n. 지하층, 지하실
The basement of a building is a floor built partly or completely below ground level.

intersperse
[intərspə́:rs]

vt. 배치하다, 흩뿌리다, 산재시키다
If you intersperse one group of things with another or among another, you put or include the second things between or among the first things.

vertical*
[və́:rtikəl]

a. 수직의, 세로의; n. 수직선, 수직면
Something that is vertical stands or points straight up.

beam*
[bi:m]

n. [건축] 들보; 광선, 빔; 빛남; v. 빛나다, 빛을 발하다
A beam is a long thick bar of wood, metal, or concrete, especially one used to support the roof of a building.

absorb*
[æbsɔ́:rb]

vt. 흡수하다, 받아들이다; 열중시키다
If something absorbs a liquid, gas, or other substance, it soaks it up or takes it in.

teardrop
[tíərdràp]

n. 눈물 방울 모양; 한 방울의 눈물
A teardrop is a large tear that comes from your eye when you are crying quietly.

tattoo^{복습}
[tætú:]

n. 문신; v. 문신을 새기다
A tattoo is a design that is drawn on someone's skin using needles to make little holes and filling them with colored dye.

whip*
[hwip]

v. 휘저어 거품을 일게 하다; 채찍질하다, 세차게 때리다; 갑자기 움직이다
(whipped cream n. 거품을 낸 크림)
When you whip something liquid such as cream or an egg, you stir it very fast until it is thick or stiff.

dumb^{복습}
[dʌm]

a. 우둔한, 어리석은; 말을 못하는, 벙어리인
If you call a person dumb, you mean that they are stupid or foolish.

serve^{복습}
[sə:rv]

v. 제공하다; 시중들다, 접대하다; (교도소에서) 복역하다; 근무하다, 복무하다
When you serve food and drink, you give people food and drink.

200

eternal[*]
[itə́:rnəl]

a. 끝없는; 영원한, 불멸의; n. 신 (eternally ad. 끊임없이, 계속)
If you describe something as eternal, you mean that it seems to last forever, often because you think it is boring or annoying.

sprinkle[*]
[spríŋkl]

vt. (액체 · 분말 등을) 뿌리다, 끼얹다; n. 소량, 조금
If you sprinkle a thing with something such as a liquid or powder, you scatter the liquid or powder over it.

twist[복습]
[twist]

v. 꼬다, 비틀다, 돌리다, 감기다; n. 뒤틀림, 엉킴
If you twist something, you turn it to make a spiral shape, for example by turning the two ends of it in opposite directions.

pastry[*]
[péistri]

n. 빵과자; 가루 반죽
A pastry is a small cake made with dough of flour and water and shortening.

cheerful[***]
[tʃíərfəl]

a. 발랄한, 쾌활한
Someone who is cheerful is happy and shows this in their behavior.

jar[**]
[dʒa:r]

① n. 병, 단지 ② v. 삐걱거리다; n. 삐걱거리는 소리, 잡음
A jar is a glass container with a lid that is used for storing food.

packet[복습]
[pǽkit]

n. (1회분의 액체 · 가루가 든 포장용) 봉지; 소포
A packet is a small container in which a quantity of something is sold.

puddle
[pʌdl]

n. 웅덩이, 액체가 괸 것; v. 물웅덩이를 만들다; 흙탕물을 휘젓다
A puddle is a small, shallow pool of liquid that has spread on the ground.

triangular[*]
[traiǽŋgjulər]

a. 삼각형의
Something that is triangular is in the shape of a triangle.

attach[복습]
[ətǽtʃ]

vt. 붙이다, 달다
If you attach something to an object, you connect it or fasten it to the object.

advertise[**]
[ǽdvərtàiz]

v. 광고하다, 선전하다, 알리다
If you advertise something, you tell people about it in newspapers, on television, or on posters.

various[복습]
[véəriəs]

a. 여러 가지의, 다양한; 많은
If you say that there are various things, you mean there are several different things of the type mentioned.

poet[**]
[póuit]

n. 시인
A poet is a person who writes poems.

earthquake[복습]
[ə́:rθkwèik]

n. 지진; 대변동, 격동
An earthquake is a shaking of the ground caused by movement of the earth's crust.

sip[복습]
[sip]

n. 한 모금; vt. (음료를) 홀짝거리다, 조금씩 마시다
A sip is a small amount of drink that you take into your mouth.

figure out[복습]

phrasal v. ~을 생각해내다, 발견하다
If you figure out a solution to a problem or the reason for something, you succeed in solving it or understanding it.

bloodsucking
[blʌ́dsʌkiŋ]

a. 착취하는; 흡혈하는
A bloodsucking thing is something drawing blood from the body of another.

agent ^{복습}
[éidʒənt]

n. 대리인, 중개인; 행위자
An agent is a person who looks after someone else's business affairs or does business on their behalf.

pass around the hat

idiom (모자를 돌려서) 기부를 청하다, 기부금을 모으다
If you pass around the hat, you collect money from a group of people, for example in order to give someone a present.

light ^{복습}
[lait]

v. (lit/lighted–lit/lighted) 밝아지다, 밝게 하다, 비추다; 점화하다; n. 빛, 광선; 불
If a place or object is lit by something, it has light shining on it.

tear ^{복습}
[tɛər]

v. (tore–torn) 찢다, 잡아뜯다; n. 찢기, 갈라진 금
If you tear paper, cloth, or another material, or if it tears, you pull it into two pieces or you pull it so that a hole appears in it.

dip*
[dip]

v. 담그다, 적시다; 가라앉다, 내려가다; n. (가격 등의) 일시적 하락
If you dip something in a liquid, you put it into the liquid for a short time, so that only part of it is covered, and take it out again.

taste ^{복습}
[téist]

v. 맛보다, 맛이 나다; n. 취향, 기호; 맛, 미각
If you taste some food or drink, you eat or drink a small amount of it in order to try its flavor, for example to see if you like it or not.

admire ^{복습}
[ædmáiər]

v. 감탄하다, 칭찬하다, 존경하다
If you admire someone or something, you like and respect them very much.

handicapped ^{복습}
[hǽndikæpt]

a. (신체적·정신적) 장애가 있는; n. (pl.) 장애인들
Someone who is handicapped has a physical or mental disability that prevents them living a totally normal life.

foundation*
[faundéiʃən]

n. 재단, 사회 사업단; 기초, 기반; 설립
A foundation is an organization that is established to provide money for a particular purpose, for example for scientific research or charity.

dread*
[dred]

v. 겁내다, 두려워하다; a. 대단히 무서운; n. 공포; 불안
If you dread something which may happen, you feel very anxious and unhappy about it because you think it will be unpleasant or upsetting.

awful ^{복습}
[ɔ́:fəl]

a. 몹시 나쁜, 무서운, 지독한
If you say that something is awful, you mean that it is extremely unpleasant, shocking, or bad.

creep out

phrasal v. 소름끼치게 하다
To creep someone out means to make them feel frightened and not safe.

publicity*
[pʌblísəti]

n. 광고, 홍보; 평판, 널리 알려져 있음
Publicity is information or actions that are intended to attract the public's attention to someone or something.

cancer *
[kǽnsər]

n. 암
Cancer is a serious disease in which cells in a person's body increase rapidly in an uncontrolled way, producing abnormal growths.

counterfeit 복습
[káuntərfit]

a. 가짜의, 모조의; v. (화폐 · 지폐 · 문서 등을) 위조하다
Counterfeit money, goods, or documents are not genuine, but have been made to look exactly like genuine ones in order to deceive people.

approach 복습
[əpróutʃ]

v. 접근하다, 다가오다; n. 접근, 가까움
When you approach something, you get closer to it.

admit 복습
[ædmít]

v. 인정하다, 시인하다; 들이다, 허락하다
If you admit that something bad, unpleasant, or embarrassing is true, you agree, often unwillingly, that it is true.

glance 복습
[glæns]

v. 흘끗 보다, 잠깐 보다; n. 흘끗 봄
If you glance at something or someone, you look at them very quickly and then look away again immediately.

niece *
[ni:s]

n. 조카딸, 질녀
Someone's niece is the daughter of their sister or brother.

fountain 복습
[fáuntən]

n. 분수; 샘
A fountain is an decorative feature in a pool or lake which consists of a long narrow stream of water that is forced up into the air.

youth 복습
[ju:θ]

n. 젊음, 청춘; 청년(층), 젊은이들
Youth is the quality or state of being young.

overproduce
[óuvərprədjú:s]

v. 과잉 생산하다
over (접두사: 한도를 넘어서) + produce (동사: 생산하다)

commercial **
[kəmə́:rʃəl]

a. 영리적인, 돈벌이 위주의; 상업의, 무역의; n. 광고
Commercial means involving or relating to the buying and selling of goods.

pap
[pæp]

n. 아무 가치 없는 것[어린애 장난 같은 것]
If you describe something such as information, writing, or entertainment as pap, you mean that you consider it to be of no worth, value, or serious interest.

stretch 복습
[stretʃ]

v. 쭉 펴다, 뻗다, 늘이다; n. (특히 길게 뻗은) 길, 구간; 뻗침
When you stretch, you put your arms or legs out straight and tighten your muscles.

honor 복습
[ánər]

n. 명예, 영예; vt. 존경하다, 공경하다 (honored a. 영광으로 생각하여)
If you describe doing or experiencing something as an honor, you mean you think it is something special and desirable.

shrug 복습
[ʃrʌg]

v. (어깨를) 으쓱하다; n. (양 손바닥을 내보이면서 어깨를) 으쓱하기
If you shrug, you raise your shoulders to show that you are not interested in something or that you do not know or care about something.

prompt *
[prampt]

vt. 잊은 말을 생각나게 하다; 일으키다, 자극하다; a. 즉석의, 즉각의
If you prompt someone when they stop speaking, you encourage or help them to continue.

embarrass 복습
[imbǽrəs]

v. 부끄럽게[무안하게] 하다; 어리둥절하게 하다; 당황하다
(embarrassing a. 난처하게 하는)
If something or someone embarrasses you, they make you feel shy or ashamed.

lean 복습
[li:n]

① v. 상체를 굽히다, 기울다; 기대다, 의지하다 ② a. 야윈, 마른
When you lean in a particular direction, you bend your body in that direction.

whisper 복습
[hwíspə:r]

v. 속삭이다, 작은 소리로 말하다; n. 속삭임
When you whisper, you say something very quietly.

scalper 복습
[skǽlpər]

n. 암표상
A scalper is someone who sells tickets outside a sports ground or theater, usually for more than their original value.

technically
[téknikəli]

ad. 엄밀히 말해서; 전문적으로, 기술적으로
Technically means according to an exact understanding of rules or facts.

make sense 복습
idiom 뜻이 통하다, 도리에 맞다
If something makes sense, it has a meaning that you can easily understand.

scalp 복습
[skælp]

v. 암표를 팔다; n. 두피, 머리가죽
If someone scalps tickets, they sell them outside a sports ground or theater, usually for more than their original value.

split 복습
[split]

v. 분배하다; 쪼개다, 찢다, 째다; n. 쪼개기, 분열
If something splits or if you split it, it is divided into two or more parts.

phony 복습
[fóuni]

a. 가짜의, 엉터리의; n. 가짜, 위조품, 사기꾼
If you describe something as phony, you disapprove of it because it is false rather than genuine.

hustler
[hʌ́slər]

n. 사기꾼
If you refer to someone as a hustler, you mean that they try to earn money or gain an advantage from situations they are in by using dishonest or illegal methods.

clue 복습
[klu:]

n. 실마리, 단서; vt. 암시를 주다, 귀띔하다
A clue to a problem or mystery is something that helps you to find the answer to it.

toss 복습
[tɔ:s]

v. 던지다; 흔들(리)다; n. 던지기
If you toss something somewhere, you throw it there lightly, often in a rather careless way.

content *
[kántent]

n. (용기 속의) 내용물; (표현의) 내용
The contents of a container such as a bottle, box, or room are the things that are inside it.

splatter 복습
[splǽtə:r]

v. 튀기다, 튀다; n. 튀기기; 칠벅철벅 소리
If a thick wet substance splatters on something or is splattered on it, it drops or is thrown over it.

204

applaud^{복습}
[əplɔ́ːd]

v. 박수를 보내다, 성원하다

When a group of people applaud, they clap their hands in order to show approval, for example when they have enjoyed a play or concert.

leather**
[léðər]

n. 가죽 (제품)

Leather is treated animal skin which is used for making shoes, clothes, bags, and furniture.

1분에 몇 단어를 읽는지 리딩 속도를 측정해보세요.

$$\frac{696 \text{ words}}{\text{reading time ( ) sec}} \times 60 = (\quad) \text{ WPM}$$

Build Your Vocabulary

general**
[dʒénərəl]

a. 대체적인, 대강의; 일반적인, 전반적인
If you talk about the general situation somewhere or talk about something in general terms, you are describing the situation as a whole rather than considering its details or exceptions.

steep복습
[sti:p]

a. 가파른, 경사가 급한; n. 가파른 언덕
A steep slope rises at a very sharp angle and is difficult to go up.

stain*
[stein]

v. 얼룩지(게 하)다, 더러워(지게 하)다; n. 얼룩, 오염 (stained a. 얼룩진)
If a liquid stains something, the thing becomes colored or marked by the liquid.

weird복습
[wiərd]

a. 이상한, 기묘한; 수상한
If you describe something or someone as weird, you mean that they are strange.

lame복습
[leim]

a. 설득력이 없는, 믿기 힘든; 절름발이의, 절룩거리는, 불구의
If you describe something, for example an excuse, argument, or remark, as lame, you mean that it is poor or weak.

detective복습
[ditéktiv]

n. 형사, 수사관; 탐정
A detective is someone whose job is to discover what has happened in a crime or other situation and to find the people involved.

eventually복습
[ivéntʃuəli]

ad. 결국, 마침내
Eventually means at the end of a situation or process or as the final result of it.

current복습
[kə́:rənt]

n. 흐름, 해류, 기류; a. 지금의, 현재의; 유행하는
A current is a steady and continuous flowing movement of some of the water in a river, lake, or sea.

knock off복습

phrasal v. ~을 쳐서[두드려서] 떨어뜨리다
If you knock someone off something, you make them fall off it by hitting them.

whim
[hwim]

n. 변덕, 일시적 기분; v. 일시적인 기분으로 바라다
A whim is a wish to do or have something which seems to have no serious reason or purpose behind it, and often occurs suddenly.

hook**
[huk]

v. 유혹하다, 꾀다; (갈고리로) 걸다, 달다; n. 갈고리, 고리; 함정
(hooked a. ~에 푹 빠진)
If you are hooked into something, or hook into something, you get involved with it.

mock[*]
[mak]

vt. 조롱하다, 비웃다; n. 조롱, 놀림감; a. 가짜의, 모의의
If someone mocks you, they show or pretend that they think you are foolish or inferior, for example by saying something funny about you, or by imitating your behavior.

charge[복습]
[ʧɑːrdʒ]

v. (지불을) 청구하다; 부담 지우다, 맡기다; 돌격하다; n. 수수료, 요금; 책임, 의무
If you charge someone an amount of money, you ask them to pay that amount for something that you have sold to them or done for them.

highfalutin
[hàifəlúːtn]

a. 허세를 부리는, 거만한
People sometimes use highfalutin to describe something that they think is being made to sound complicated or important in order to impress people.

exotic[복습]
[igzátik]

a. 이국풍의, 외래의, 외국의
Something that is exotic is unusual and interesting, usually because it comes from a distant country.

screw up[복습]
[복습]

phrasal v. 망치다, 엉망으로 만들다
To screw something up means to cause it to fail or be spoiled.

steam[**]
[stiːm]

v. (식품 등을) 찌다; 증기가 발생하다; n. 증기
If you steam food or if it steams, you cook it in steam rather than in water.

bun
[bʌn]

n. (작고 둥글납작한) 빵
Buns are small bread rolls. They are sometimes sweet and may contain dried fruit or spices.

piping hot

idiom 따끈따끈 한, 갓 구워낸
Food or water that is piping hot is very hot.

vendor[*]
[véndər]

n. 상인, 행상인
A vendor is someone who sells things such as newspapers, cigarettes, or food from a small stall or cart.

dough
[dou]

n. 반죽 덩어리; 굽지 않는 빵, 가루 반죽
Dough is a fairly firm mixture of flour, water, and sometimes also fat and sugar.

flour[**]
[flauər]

n. (곡물의) 가루, 밀가루
Flour is a white or brown powder that is made by grinding grain.

spongy[복습]
[spándʒi]

a. 푹신푹신한; 흡수성의; 작은 구멍이 많은
Something that is spongy is soft and can be pressed in, like a sponge.

roast[*]
[roust]

a. 구운, 볶은; v. 굽다, 구워지다; 볶다
Roast meat has been cooked by dry heat in an oven or over a fire.

remind[복습]
[rimáind]

vt. 생각나게 하다, 상기시키다, 일깨우다
If someone reminds you of a fact or event that you already know about, they say something which makes you think about it.

bring about[복습]

phrasal v. 야기하다, 초래하다
If you bring something about, you make it happen.

ruin^{복습}
[ru:in]

v. 망치다, 못쓰게 만들다; 몰락하다; n. 폐허; 파멸
To ruin something means to severely harm, damage, or spoil it.

determination*
[ditə́:rmənéiʃən]

n. 결정, 결심
Determination is the quality that you show when you have decided to do something and you will not let anything stop you.

pedestrian*
[pədéstriən]

n. 보행자; a. 도보의
A pedestrian is a person who is walking, especially in a town or city, rather than traveling in a vehicle.

oblivious*
[əblíviəs]

a. 의식하지 못하는, 안중에 없는
If you are oblivious to something or oblivious of it, you are not aware of it.

glance^{복습}
[glæns]

n. 흘끗 봄; v. 흘끗 보다, 잠깐 보다
A glance is a quick look at someone or something.

elbow**
[élbou]

v. 팔꿈치로 찌르다[밀다], 밀어젖히고 나아가다; n. 팔꿈치
If you elbow people aside or elbow your way somewhere, you push people with your elbows in order to move somewhere.

urgent
[ə́:rdʒənt]

a. 긴급한, 절박한 (urgency n. 위급)
If something is urgent, it needs to be dealt with as soon as possible.

represent^{복습}
[rèprizént]

vt. 나타내다, 표시하다; 대표하다
To represent an idea or quality means to be a symbol or an expression of that idea or quality.

violent^{복습}
[váiələnt]

a. 난폭한, 폭력적인; 격렬한, 맹렬한
If someone is violent, or if they do something which is violent, they use physical force or weapons to hurt, injure, or kill other people.

criminal^{복습}
[krímənl]

a. 범죄의; n. 범죄자, 범인
Criminal means connected with crime.

view^{복습}
[vju:]

n. 경치, 풍경; 시야, 시각; 견해, 의견; v. 보다, 고찰하다
The view from a window or high place is everything which can be seen from that place, especially when it is considered to be beautiful.

spy*
[spai]

v. 찾아내다, 발견하다; 몰래 조사[감시]하다; n. 스파이, 탐정
If you spy someone or something, you notice them.

1. How did Armpit get back to the hotel?
   A. He took a taxi back.
   B. He called the hotel and had someone send a car.
   C. He walked all the way back alone.
   D. He took the city bus.

2. What happened when Kaira left the shower?
   A. She slipped on a puddle and hit her head.
   B. She accidentally walked into her bodyguard.
   C. She screamed when she saw Jerome come at her with a knife.
   D. She was hit with a baseball bat by Jerome.

3. What did Jerome do to Fred?
   A. He locked him in the bathroom.
   B. He beat him unconscious with the baseball bat.
   C. He stabbed him in the stomach with a knife.
   D. He fired him from his job as Kaira's bodyguard.

4. How did Kaira manage to get Armpit's attention?
   A. She called his name out loud.
   B. She pulled the lamp off the nightstand.
   C. She turned off the lights in the hallway.
   D. She hit Jerome and caused him to scream.

5. Why did Armpit leave San Francisco immediately?
   A. He didn't want to be a suspect in the attack on Kaira.
   B. He didn't want the police to arrest him.
   C. He didn't want to ever see Kaira again.
   D. He didn't want to be stuck with the bill for the hotel.

6. Why could Armpit and Ginny not take their usual walk?
   A. The road was under construction.
   B. The road was crowded with news vans and camera crews.
   C. There was a party outside next door.
   D. Armpit had injured his legs in the fight with Jerome.

7. What did Detective Newberg tell Armpit about the investigation?
   A. There was a new suspect in the case.
   B. She was ending the investigation and he could stop worrying.
   C. She had managed to find a man named Habib.
   D. They were assigning even more resources to the investigation.

1분에 몇 단어를 읽는지 리딩 속도를 측정해보세요.

$$\frac{1{,}327 \text{ words}}{\text{reading time (} \quad \text{) sec}} \times 60 = (\quad) \text{ WPM}$$

Build Your Vocabulary

moisture*
[mɔ́istʃər]

n. 수분, 습기; 수증기
Moisture is tiny drops of water in the air, on a surface, or in the ground.

nozzle
[nazl]

n. 노즐, 분사구
The nozzle of a hose or pipe is a narrow piece fitted to the end to control the flow of liquid or gas.

lose oneself in

idiom ~에 몰두하다, ~에 넋을 잃다
If you lose yourself in something, you give a lot of attention to it and do not think about anything else.

betray^{복습}
[bitréi]

vt. 배반하다; 누설하다, 드러내다 (betrayal n. 배신, 배반)
If you betray someone who loves or trusts you, your actions hurt and disappoint them.

conjure
[kándʒər]

v. 상기시키다[떠올리게 하다]; 주문·주술로 불러내다
If you conjure something up, you make it appear in you mind.

suite^{복습}
[swi:t]

n. 호텔의 스위트 룸; (물건의) 한 벌
A suite is a set of rooms in a hotel or other building.

slip^{복습}
[slip]

v. 살짝 들어가(게 하)다; 미끄러지다, 미끄러지듯이 움직이다
If you slip something somewhere, you put it there quickly in a way that does not attract attention.

stick^{복습}
[stik]

① v. (stuck-stuck) 내밀다; 달라붙다, 붙이다; 고수하다 ② n. 막대기, 지팡이
If something is sticking into a surface or object, it is partly in it.

fireplace*
[faiərplèis]

n. (벽)난로
In a room, the fireplace is the place where a fire can be lit and the area on the wall and floor surrounding this place.

bug**
[bʌg]

vt. 괴롭히다, 귀찮게 굴다; n. 곤충; 결함
If someone or something bugs you, they worry or annoy you.

yell^{복습}
[jel]

v. 소리치다, 고함치다; n. 고함소리, 부르짖음
If you yell, you shout loudly, usually because you are excited, angry, or in pain.

pound^{복습}
[paund]

① v. 고동치다; 쿵쿵 울리다; 마구 치다, 세게 두드리다; n. 타격
② n. 파운드 (무게의 단위) ③ n. 울타리, 우리
If your heart is pounding, it is beating with an unusually strong and fast rhythm, usually because you are afraid.

212

blur
[blə:r]

v. 흐릿해지다, 몽롱해지다; n. 흐림, 침침함; 더러움, 얼룩
When a thing blurs or when something blurs it, you cannot see it clearly because its edges are no longer distinct.

momentary*
[móumantèri]

a. 순간의, 찰나의 (momentarily ad. 잠시, 즉시)
Something that is momentary lasts for a very short period of time, for example for a few seconds or less.

intellectual**
[intəlékʧuəl]

a. 지적인, 지성을 지닌; n. 지식인
Intellectual means involving a person's ability to think and to understand ideas and information.

grab복습
[græb]

v. 부여잡다, 움켜쥐다; n. 부여잡기
If you grab something, you take it or pick it up suddenly and roughly.

bedpost
[bedpòust]

n. (네 귀의) 침대 기둥, 침대다리
A bedpost is one of the four vertical supports at the corners of a bed with an old-fashioned wooden or iron frame.

steady**
[stédi]

v. 안정시키다, 침착해지다; a. 확고한, 고정된; 안정된, 흔들리지 않는
If you steady yourself, you control your voice or expression, so that people will think that you are calm and not nervous.

rattle**
[rǽtl]

v. 왈각달각 소리 나다, 덜걱덜걱 움직이다; 당황하게 하다; n. 덜거덕거리는 소리
When something rattles or when you rattle it, it makes short sharp knocking sounds because it is being shaken or it keeps hitting against something hard.

winded
[wíndid]

a. 숨이 찬
If you are winded by something such as a blow, the air is suddenly knocked out of your lungs so that you have difficulty breathing for a short time.

steep복습
[sti:p]

a. 가파른, 경사가 급한; n. 가파른 언덕
A steep slope rises at a very sharp angle and is difficult to go up.

compare복습
[kəmpéər]

v. ~와 비교하다, 견주다; 비유하다
When you compare things, you consider them and discover the differences or similarities between them.

sidewalk복습
[sáidwɔ̀:k]

n. (포장한) 보도, 인도
A sidewalk is a path with a hard surface by the side of a road.

blink*
[bliŋk]

v. (빛이) 깜박거리다, (눈을) 깜박이다; 눈을 부시게 하다; n. 깜박임
When a light blinks, it flashes on and off.

splash복습
[splæʃ]

v. (물 · 흙탕물 등을) 끼얹다, 튀기다; n. 첨벙 하는 소리
If you splash a liquid somewhere or if it splashes, it hits someone or something and scatters in a lot of small drops.

rapid**
[rǽpid]

a. 빠른, 신속한; 민첩한 (rapidly ad. 급속히)
A rapid movement is one that is very fast.

edge복습
[edʒ]

n. 끝, 가장자리, 모서리
The edge of something is the place or line where it stops, or the part of it that is furthest from the middle.

embarrass^{복습}
[imbǽrəs]

v. 부끄럽게[무안하게] 하다; 어리둥절하게 하다; 당황하다
(embarrassed a. 당혹한, 창피한)
If something or someone embarrasses you, they make you feel shy or ashamed.

clue^{복습}
[klu:]

n. 실마리, 단서; vt. 암시를 주다, 귀띔하다
A clue to a problem or mystery is something that helps you to find the answer to it.

hang up^{복습}

phrasal v. 전화를 끊다
To hang up means to end a telephone conversation, often very suddenly, by putting down the part of the telephone that you speak into or switching the telephone off.

robe^{복습}
[roub]

n. 길고 헐거운 겉옷(실내복이나 휴식 때의 옷); 예복, 관복
A robe is a piece of clothing, usually made of toweling, which people wear in the house, especially when they have just got up or had a bath.

compete^{복습}
[kəmpíːt]

vi. 겨루다, 경쟁하다
If you compete with someone for something, you try to get it for yourself and stop the other person getting it.

swing^{복습}
[swiŋ]

v. (swung–swung) 휘두르다; 빙 돌다, 흔들다;
n. 휘두르기; 그네; 짧은 여행, (정치인의) 유세
If something swings in a particular direction or if you swing it in that direction, it moves in that direction with a smooth, curving movement.

carom
[kǽrəm]

v. (~에) 부딪쳐 튀어나오다
If something moving caroms someone or something else off, it hits them by accident and with great force and then goes off in a different direction.

slam^{복습}
[slæm]

v. 세게 치다; (문 따위를) 탕 닫다; 털썩 내려놓다; n. 쾅 (하는 소리)
If one thing slams into or against another, it crashes into it with great force.

throat^{**}
[θrout]

n. 목구멍, 목
Your throat is the front part of your neck.

figure out^{복습}

phrasal v. ~을 생각해내다, 발견하다
If you figure out a solution to a problem or the reason for something, you succeed in solving it or understanding it.

strike^{***}
[straik]

v. (struck–stricken) 치다, 때리다; 충돌하다; 부딪치다; 생각나다, 떠오르다;
n. 치기, 구타; 파업
If you strike someone or something, you deliberately hit them.

crawl^{**}
[krɔːl]

vi. 기어가다, 느릿느릿 가다; 우글거리다, 들끓다; n. 서행; 기어감
When you crawl, you move forward on your hands and knees.

partial[*]
[páːrʃəl]

a. 부분적인, 일부의; 편파적인 (partially ad. 부분적으로)
You use partial to refer to something that is not complete or whole.

protect^{복습}
[prətékt]

v. 보호하다, 막다, 지키다
To protect someone or something means to prevent them from being harmed or damaged.

214

block^{복습}
[blak]

vt. 막다, 방해하다; n. (도시의) 블록, 한 구획; 덩어리; 방해물
If you block something off, you close a road or another place by placing a barrier across it to stop the thing going in or coming out.

smash[*]
[smæʃ]

v. 세게 부딪치다, 충돌하다; 산산이 부수다, 박살내다
If something smashes or is smashed against something solid, it moves very fast and with great force against it.

skull[*]
[skʌl]

n. 두개골, 해골
Your skull is the bony part of your head which encloses your brain.

vague[*]
[veig]

a. 어렴풋한, 막연한 (vaguely ad. 모호하게, 막연하게)
If you have a vague memory or idea of something, the memory or idea is not clear.

aware^{복습}
[əwéər]

a. 알고 있는, 의식하고 있는, 알아차린
If you are aware of something, you know about it.

ankle[*]
[ǽŋkl]

n. 발목
Your ankle is the joint where your foot joins your leg.

drag[*]
[dræg]

v. 끌(리)다, 잡아 당기다; 느릿느릿 나아가다
If someone drags you somewhere, they pull you there, or force you to go there by physically threatening you.

eerie
[íəri]

a. 기분 나쁜, 무시무시한, 섬뜩한
If you describe something as eerie, you mean that it seems strange and frightening, and makes you feel nervous.

split^{복습}
[split]

v. 쪼개다, 찢다, 째다; 분배하다; n. 쪼개기, 분열
If something splits or if you split it, it is divided into two or more parts.

lunge
[lʌndʒ]

v. 돌진하다; 내밀다, 찌르다; n. 돌입, 돌진
If you lunge in a particular direction, you move in that direction suddenly and clumsily.

crack^{복습}
[kræk]

v. 금이 가다, 깨다, 부수다; n. 갈라진 금[틈]; 갑작스런 날카로운 소리
If something hard cracks, or if you crack it, it becomes slightly damaged, with lines appearing on its surface.

anguish[*]
[ǽŋgwiʃ]

v. 괴로워하다, 괴롭히다; n. 괴로운, 고뇌, 번민 (anguished a. 괴로운)
Anguish is great mental suffering or physical pain.

groan[*]
[groun]

n. 신음, 끙끙거리는 소리; v. 신음하다, 끙끙거리다; 불평하다
If you groan, you make a long, low sound because you are in pain, or because you are upset or unhappy about something.

glance^{복습}
[glæns]

v. 흘끗 보다, 잠깐 보다; n. 흘끗 봄
If you glance at something or someone, you look at them very quickly and then look away again immediately.

retrieve
[ritríːv]

v. 되찾다, 회수하다; 만회하다, 회복하다; n. 되찾기, 회복
If you retrieve something, you get it back from the place where you left it.

stomach^{복습}
[stʌ́mək]

n. 배, 위
You can refer to the front part of your body below your waist as your stomach.

entrance 복습
[éntrəns]

n. 입구, 현관; 입학, 입장
The entrance to a place is the way into it, for example a door or gate.

frequent 복습
[frí:kwənt]

a. 자주[빈번히] 일어나는; 흔한, 보통의; v. 자주 가다 (frequently ad. 자주)
If something is frequent, it happens often.

host*
[houst]

v. 주최하다, 주인 노릇을 하다; 접대하다; n. 주인
If someone hosts a party, dinner, or other function, they have invited the guests and provide the food, drink, or entertainment.

freeze 복습
[fri:z]

v. (froze-frozen) 얼다, 얼리다; n. (임금·가격 등의) 동결
If someone who is moving freezes, they suddenly stop and become completely still and quiet.

condition 복습
[kəndíʃən]

n. (건강) 상태, 상황; 조건; v. ~을 좌우하다; 조절[조정]하다
If you talk about the condition of a person or thing, you are talking about the state that they are in, especially how good or bad their physical state is.

complicate*
[kǽmpləkèit]

v. 복잡하게 하다, 곤란하게 하다; 복잡해지다; a. 복잡한, 뒤얽힌
To complicate something means to make it more difficult to understand or deal with.

retain*
[ritéin]

vt. 계속 유지하다, 보유하다, 간직하다
To retain something means to continue to have that thing.

conscious 복습
[kάnʃəs]

a. 의식하고 있는, 알고 있는, 지각 있는 (consciousness n. 의식, 자각)
If you are conscious of something, you notice it or realize that it is happening.

electric 복습
[iléktrik]

a. 전기의; 전기를 이용하는 (electrical a. 전기의[에 의한])
An electric device works by means of electricity, rather than using some other source of power.

cord 복습
[kɔːrd]

n. (전기) 코드, 끈, 줄; 굴레, 속박; vt. 끈으로 묶다
Cord is wire covered in rubber or plastic which connects electrical equipment to an electricity supply.

crash 복습
[kræʃ]

n. 쿵 하는 소리; 충돌, 추락; vt. 충돌하다, 추락하다; (굉음과 함께) 부딪치다
A crash is a sudden, loud noise.

dine*
[dain]

v. 식사를 하다 (dining n. 식사하기)
When you dine, you have dinner.

collapse*
[kəlǽps]

v. 쓰러지다, 맥없이 주저앉다; 무너지다, 붕괴하다; n. 무너짐, 붕괴
If you collapse, you suddenly faint or fall down because you are very ill or weak.

spin 복습
[spin]

v. (spun-spun) 돌(리)다, 맴돌리다; 오래[질질] 끌다; n. 회전
If something spins or if you spin it, it turns quickly around a central point.

left-handed
[léft-hǽndid]

a. 왼손잡이의, 왼손용의
Someone who is left-handed uses their left hand rather than their right hand for activities such as writing and sports and for picking things up.

216

explode[*]
[iksplóud]

v. 폭발하다, 파열하다, 터지다
If an object such as a bomb explodes or if someone or something explodes it, it bursts loudly and with great force, often causing damage or injury.

fist[복습]
[fist]

n. (쥔) 주먹
Your hand is referred to as your fist when you have bent your fingers in toward the palm in order to hit someone.

momentum
[mouméntəm]

n. 힘, 기세; 탄력[가속도]
If a process or movement gains momentum, it keeps developing or happening more quickly and keeps becoming less likely to stop.

floor[***]
[flɔːr]

v. (스포츠 경기에서) 때려눕히다; n. (방의) 바닥
If you floor someone, you knock them to the floor or ground.

motion[복습]
[móuʃən]

n. 움직임, 운동; 몸짓, 신호; vt. 몸짓으로 신호하다 (motionless a. 움직이지 않는)
Motion is the activity or process of continually changing position or moving from one place to another.

hairdresser[*]
[héərdrèsər]

n. 미용사, 헤어 디자이너
A hairdresser is a person who cuts, colors, and arranges people's hair.

1분에 몇 단어를 읽는지 리딩 속도를 측정해보세요.

$$\frac{1,348 \text{ words}}{\text{reading time ( ) sec}} \times 60 = (\quad) \text{ WPM}$$

Build Your Vocabulary

amid ^{복습}
[əmíd]

pre. ~의 한 복판에, 한창 ~할 때에
If something happens amid noises or events of some kind, it happens while the other things are happening.

chaos[*]
[kéias]

n. 혼란, 무질서 (상태), 혼돈
Chaos is a state of complete disorder and confusion.

crew^{복습}
[kru:]

n. 팀, 그룹; 동료, 패거리; 승무원, 선원
A crew is a group of people with special technical skills who work together on a task or project.

hysterical[*]
[histérikəl]

a. 병적으로 흥분한, 이성을 잃은; 히스테리(성)의
Someone who is hysterical is in a state of violent and disturbed emotion that is usually a result of shock.

figure out^{복습}

phrasal v. ~을 생각해내다, 발견하다
If you figure out a solution to a problem or the reason for something, you succeed in solving it or understanding it.

retrieve^{복습}
[ritríːv]

v. 되찾다, 회수하다; 만회하다, 회복하다; n. 되찾기, 회복
If you retrieve something, you get it back from the place where you left it.

toss^{복습}
[tɔːs]

v. 던지다; 흔들(리)다; n. 던지기
If you toss something somewhere, you throw it there lightly, often in a rather careless way.

fireplace^{복습}
[faiərplèis]

n. (벽)난로
In a room, the fireplace is the place where a fire can be lit and the area on the wall and floor surrounding this place.

stretcher[*]
[strétʃər]

n. (부상자를 싣는) 들것
A stretcher is a long piece of canvas with a pole along each side, which is used to carry an injured or sick person.

conscious^{복습}
[kánʃəs]

a. 의식하고 있는, 알고 있는, 지각 있는 (unconscious a. 의식을 잃은)
If you are conscious of something, you notice it or realize that it is happening.

pass out

phrasal v. 기절하다, 의식을 잃다
If someone passes out, they become unconscious or faint.

dizzy[*]
[dízi]

a. 현기증 나는, 어지러운; vt. 어지럽게 하다
If you feel dizzy, you feel as if everything is spinning round and being unable to balance.

218

handcuff^{복습} [hǽndkʌf]	vt. 수갑을 채우다; n. 수갑 If you handcuff someone, you put two metal rings around their wrists.
confirm^{복습} [kənfɔ́:rm]	vt. 입증하다; (남의 의견 등을) 굳히다; 승인하다 If something confirms what you believe, suspect, or fear, it shows that it is definitely true.
innocence[*] [ínəsəns]	n. 결백, 무죄; 순결; 때 묻지 않음 If someone proves their innocence, they prove that they are not guilty of a crime.
beat^{복습} [bi:t]	v. 치다, 두드리다; 더 낫다, 능가하다; 이기다, 패배시키다; n. 치기, 때리기; 박자 If you beat someone or something, you hit them very hard.
assume^{복습} [əsjú:m]	vt. 추정하다, 가정하다; 가장하다, 꾸미다; (역할·임무 등을) 맡다 If you assume that something is true, you imagine that it is true, sometimes wrongly.
demeanor [dimí:nər]	n. 처신, 거동, 행실; 태도, 몸가짐 Your demeanor is the way you behave, which gives people an impression of your character and feelings.
whirl[*] [hwə:rl]	v. 빙글 돌다, 선회하다; 어지럽다, 현기증이 나다 If something or someone whirls around or if you whirl them around, they move around or turn around very quickly.
blur^{복습} [blə:r]	n. 흐림, 침침함; 더러움, 얼룩; v. 흐릿해지다, 몽롱해지다 A blur is a shape or area which you cannot see clearly because it has no distinct outline or because it is moving very fast.
confuse^{복습} [kənfjú:z]	v. 어리둥절하게 하다, 혼동하다 (confusion n. 혼란, 당황) To confuse someone means to make it difficult for them to know exactly what is happening or what to do.
charge^{복습} [ʧɑ:rdʒ]	n. 책임, 의무; 수수료, 요금; v. (지불을) 청구하다; 부담 지우다, 맡기다; 비난하다 (in charge idiom ~을 관리하는, 담당하는) If you are in charge in a particular situation, you are the most senior person and have control over something or someone.
bass^{복습} [beis]	n. 베이스, 저음; a. 베이스의 In popular music, a bass is a bass guitar or a double bass.
stamp^{복습} [stæmp]	v. 발을 구르다, 쿵쿵거리며 걷다; 짓밟다 If you stamp or stamp your foot, you lift your foot and put it down very hard on the ground, for example because you are angry or because your feet are cold.
murder^{**} [mə́:rdər]	v. 죽이다, 살해하다; n. 살인, 살해 To murder someone means to commit the crime of killing them deliberately.
desperate^{복습} [déspərət]	a. 필사적인; 자포자기의, 절망적인 (desperately ad. 필사적으로) If you are desperate for something or desperate to do something, you want or need it very much indeed.
stub^{복습} [stʌb]	n. (표·입장권의) 반쪽, 보관용 부분; 토막, 그루터기 A ticket stub is the part that you keep when you go in to watch a performance.

suite^{복습}
[swi:t]

n. 호텔의 스위트 룸: (물건의) 한 벌
A suite is a set of rooms in a hotel or other building.

emergency room
[imə́:rdʒənsi rù:m]

n. (병원의) 응급실
The emergency room is the room or department in a hospital where people who have severe injuries or sudden illnesses are taken for emergency treatment.

statement^{**}
[stéitmənt]

n. 진술서, 성명서; 말함, 진술
A statement is something that you say or write which gives information in a formal or definite way.

associate^{복습}
[əsóuʃieit]

v. 연합시키다, 제휴하다; 연결지어 생각하다, 연상하다; 교제하다; n. 동료, 한패
If you say that someone is associating with another person or group of people, you mean they are spending a lot of time in the company of people you do not approve of.

enormous^{복습}
[inɔ́:rməs]

a. 엄청난, 거대한, 막대한
You can use enormous to emphasize the great degree or extent of something.

normal^{복습}
[nɔ́:rməl]

a. 보통의, 정상적인; n. 보통; 표준, 기준 (normally ad. 보통은, 일반적으로)
Something that is normal is usual and ordinary, and is what people expect.

somewhat^{복습}
[sʌ́mhwʌt]

ad. 어느 정도, 약간, 다소
You use somewhat to indicate that something is the case to a limited extent or degree.

tongue-in-cheek
[tʌ́ŋ-in-tʃí:k]

a. 놀림조의, 비꼬는
If you say something with your tongue-in-cheek, you are not being serious and mean it as a joke.

stick^{복습}
[stik]

① v. (stuck–stuck) 달라붙다, 붙이다; 내밀다; 고수하다 ② n. 막대기, 지팡이
If one thing sticks to another, it becomes attached to it and is difficult to remove.

cab^{복습}
[kæb]

n. 택시; (버스 · 기차 · 트럭의) 운전석
A cab is a taxi.

available^{**}
[əvéiləbl]

a. 이용할 수 있는, 쓸모 있는
If something you want or need is available, you can find it or obtain it.

dismay[*]
[disméi]

n. 실망, 낙담, 경악; vt. 당황하게 하다, 깜짝 놀라게 하다
Dismay is a strong feeling of fear, worry, or sadness that is caused by something unpleasant and unexpected.

passenger^{복습}
[pǽsəndʒər]

n. 승객, 여객
A passenger in a vehicle such as a bus, boat, or plane is a person who is traveling in it, but who is not driving it or working on it.

nudge
[nʌdʒ]

vt. (주의를 끌기 위해 팔꿈치로) 슬쩍 찌르다; 주의를 끌다
If you nudge someone, you push them gently, usually with your elbow, in order to draw their attention to something.

220

moisten
[mɔ́isn]

v. 젖다, 축축해지다; 적시다
To moisten something means to make it slightly wet.

dab
[dæb]

v. 가볍게 두드리다; 살짝 누르다; n. 가볍게 두드림
If you dab a substance onto a surface, you put it there using quick, light movements.

odd**
[ad]

a. 이상한, 기묘한; 홀수의 (oddly ad. 이상하게)
If you describe someone or something as odd, you think that they are strange or unusual.

cast***
[kæst]

n. [의학] 깁스 붕대; 던지기; v. 던지다; 배정하다
A cast is a cover made of plaster which is used to protect a broken bone by keeping part of the body stiff.

shoo
[ʃuː]

v. 쉬이 하고 쫓다; 쉬이 하다; int. 쉬, 훳 (새 등을 쫓는 소리)
If you shoo an animal or a person away, you make them go away by waving your hands or arms at them.

respect복습
[rispékt]

v. 소중히 여기다, 존경하다; n. 존중, 주의, 관심
If you respect someone's wishes, rights, or customs, you avoid doing things that they would dislike or regard as wrong.

headline*
[hedlain]

n. (신문 등의) 큰 표제, (pl.) (뉴스 방송 서두에 말하는) 중요 항목
A headline is the title of a newspaper story, printed in large letters at the top of the story, especially on the front page.

article**
[ɑ́ːrtikl]

n. (신문·책·잡지 등의) 기사, 논설; 물품, 물건; 조항, 항목
An article is a piece of writing that is published in a newspaper or magazine.

rendezvous
[rɑ́ːndəvùː]

n. (약속에 의하여) 만나기, 집합; 만나기로 한 장소
A rendezvous is a meeting, often a secret one, that you have arranged with someone for a particular time and place.

occur복습
[əkə́ːr]

vi. 생기다, 일어나다; 문득 생각나다, 떠오르다
When something occurs, it happens.

rush복습
[rʌʃ]

v. 서두르다, 돌진하다, 급히 움직이다
If you rush something, you do it in a hurry, often too quickly and without much care.

wild-goose chase
[wáild-guːs ʧèis]

n. 막막한 추적; 부질없는 시도
If you are on a wild-goose chase, you waste a lot of time searching for something that you have little chance of finding, because you have been given incorrect information.

in bad shape

idiom 컨디션이 나쁘다
If someone is in bad shape, they are in a bad state of health or in a bad condition.

exasperate
[igzǽspərèit]

vt. 성나게 하다, 격분시키다 (exasperated a. 화가 치민, 짜증스러운)
If something exasperates you, they annoy you and make you feel frustrated or upset.

detective복습
[ditéktiv]

n. 형사, 수사관; 탐정
A detective is someone whose job is to discover what has happened in a crime or other situation and to find the people involved.

figure ^{복습}
[fígjər]

v. 생각하다, 판단하다; 계산하다; n. 수치, 숫자; 형태, 형상; 작은 조각상
If you figure that something is the case, you think or guess that it is the case.

flush *
[flʌʃ]

v. (얼굴 등을) 붉히다, 붉어지게 하다; (물이) 왈칵 흘러나오다; n. (볼 등의) 홍조
If you flush, your face goes red because you are hot or ill, or because you are feeling a strong emotion such as embarrassment or anger.

shrug ^{복습}
[ʃrʌg]

v. (어깨를) 으쓱하다; n. (양 손바닥을 내보이면서 어깨를) 으쓱하기
If you shrug, you raise your shoulders to show that you are not interested in something or that you do not know or care about something.

assign *
[əsáin]

v. 할당하다, 부여하다; 선정하다; 양도하다
If you assign a piece of work to someone, you give them the work to do.

superior *
[səpíəriər]

n. 상관, 상사; 뛰어난 사람; a. 위의, 높은; 뛰어난, 우수한
Your superior in an organization that you work for is a person who has a higher rank than you.

lead ***
[li:d]

n. 실마리, 단서; 지도(력); 선두, 우세; v. 인도하다, 앞장서다, 안내하다
A lead is a piece of information or an idea which may help people to discover the facts in a situation where many facts are not known, for example in the investigation of a crime or in a scientific experiment.

counterfeit ^{복습}
[káuntərfit]

a. 가짜의, 모조의; v. (화폐 · 지폐 · 문서 등을) 위조하다
Counterfeit money, goods, or documents are not genuine, but have been made to look exactly like genuine ones in order to deceive people.

worth ^{복습}
[wə:rθ]

a. 가치가 있는; n. 가치, 값어치
If you say that something is worth having, you mean that it is pleasant or useful, and therefore a good thing to have.

scalper ^{복습}
[skǽlpər]

n. 암표상
A scalper is someone who sells tickets outside a sports ground or theater, usually for more than their original value.

slip ^{복습}
[slip]

v. 미끄러지다, 미끄러지듯이 움직이다; 살짝 들어가(게 하)다[나오다]
If something slips, it slides out of place or out of your hand.

poker face
[póukər fèis]

n. 무표정한 얼굴, 포커페이스
A poker face is an expression on your face that shows none of your feelings.

genuine *
[dʒénjuin]

a. 진짜의; 성실한, 순수한 (genuinely ad. 진실로)
Genuine refers to things such as emotions that are real and not pretended.

come up with ^{복습}

idiom ~을 생각하다, 제안하다
If you come up with a plan or idea, you think of it and suggest it.

reluctant *
[rilʌ́ktənt]

a. 마음이 내키지 않는, 마지못해 하는
If you are reluctant to do something, you are unwilling to do it and hesitate before doing it, or do it slowly and without enthusiasm.

jack around

phrasal v. 시간을 헛되이 쓰다, 어리석은 짓을 하고 있다
To jack someone around means to treat them in a way that is deliberately not helpful to them or wastes their time.

foul ^{복습}
[faul]

n. 반칙; 싫은 것, 더러운 것; a. 규칙 위반인, 반칙인; 더러운, 악취 나는
A foul is an act in a game or sport that is not allowed according to the rules.

dot *
[dat]

v. 점을 찍다, 점으로 그리다; 여기저기 흩어 놓다; n. 점, 반점, 얼룩
To dot something means to mark it with a very small circular shape.

blur ^{복습}
[bləːr]

v. 흐릿해지다, 몽롱해지다; n. 흐림, 침침함; 더러움, 얼룩 (blurry a. 흐릿한)
When a thing blurs or when something blurs it, you cannot see it clearly because its edges are no longer distinct.

bandage *
[bǽndidʒ]

v. 붕대를 감다; n. 붕대, 안대; 묶는 물건
If you bandage a wound or part of someone's body, you tie a long strip of cloth around it.

nourishment
[nɔ́ːriʃmənt]

n. 음식물, 영양분
If something provides a person, animal, or plant with nourishment, it provides them with the food that is necessary for life, growth, and good health.

raspy ^{복습}
[rǽspi]

a. 거친, 목이 쉰 듯한, 쇳소리의
If someone has a raspy voice, they make rough sounds as if they have a sore throat or have difficulty in breathing.

whisper ^{복습}
[hwíspəːr]

n. 속삭임; v. 속삭이다, 작은 소리로 말하다
A whisper is soft speech produced without full voice.

lean ^{복습}
[liːn]

① v. 상체를 굽히다, 기울다; 기대다, 의지하다 ② a. 야윈, 마른
When you lean in a particular direction, you bend your body in that direction.

grab ^{복습}
[græb]

v. 부여잡다, 움켜쥐다; n. 부여잡기
If you grab something, you take it or pick it up suddenly and roughly.

doofus ^{복습}
[dúːfəs]

n. (비격식) 멍청이, 얼간이
Doofus is a slow-witted or stupid person.

chapters thirty-five & thirty-six

1. Which of the following was NOT evidence that could
   have been used against Armpit?
   A. His fingerprints were on the bat.
   B. There was a video showing him yelling at Kaira in the elevator.
   C. There were traces of his hair and blood in the next letter from
      Billy Boy.
   D. The knife came from his room.

2. After X-Ray analyzed the crime, what did Ginny say he
   should be?
   A. A lawyer
   B. A judge
   C. A police officer
   D. A detective

3. Why was Armpit disappointed that there might not be a
   trial?
   A. He wanted Jerome to be publicly humiliated.
   B. He wanted to testify as a witness against Jerome.
   C. He wanted to go back to San Francisco and see Kaira again.
   D. He had never seen a trial before and thought it might be
      interesting.

4. What happened to Kaira's money after the attack?
   A. She received more money from fans out of sympathy.
   B. She became broke after Aileen stole most of it.
   C. She was still rich but she now had expensive medical bills.
   D. She gave half of it to Armpit for saving her life.

5. What did the doctors tell Kaira after the attack?
   A. She might not be able to walk again.
   B. She might not be able to see again.
   C. She might not be able to dance again.
   D. She might not be able to sing again.

6. How did Kaira's voice sound later on the radio?
   A. It sounded ever stronger than before.
   B. It sounded rough and scratchy.
   C. It sounded fragile but clear.
   D. It sounded nervous and scared.

7. How did Armpit feel about Kaira in the end?
   A. He thought her new song meant that she wanted to see him again.
   B. He was still mad at her for throwing coffee on him and ruining his sweatshirt.
   C. He planned on going to visit her soon after she called him and asked him to come.
   D. He couldn't let his life revolve around Kaira and focused on his own small steps.

Check Your Reading Speed

1분에 몇 단어를 읽는지 리딩 속도를 측정해보세요.

$$\frac{644 \text{ words}}{\text{reading time ( ) sec}} \times 60 = (\qquad) \text{ WPM}$$

Build Your Vocabulary

cast^{복습}
[kæst]

n. [의학] 깁스 붕대; 던지기; v. 던지다; 배정하다
A cast is a cover made of plaster which is used to protect a broken bone by keeping part of the body stiff.

decorate**
[dékərèit]

v. 장식하다, 꾸미다
If you decorate something, you make it more attractive by adding things to it.

economic^{복습}
[èkənάmik]

a. 경제(상)의, 경제적인; 경제학의 (economics n. 경제학)
Economic means concerned with the organization of the money, industry, and trade of a country, region, or society.

fingerprint
[fiŋgərprint]

n. 지문
Fingerprints are marks made by a person's fingers which show the lines on the skin. Everyone's fingerprints are different, so they can be used to identify criminals.

suite^{복습}
[swi:t]

n. 호텔의 스위트 룸; (물건의) 한 벌
A suite is a set of rooms in a hotel or other building.

trace*
[treis]

n. 자취, 흔적; 발자국; 기미, 기색; v. 자국을 더듬다, 추적하여 알아내다
A trace is a sign which shows you that someone or something has been in a place.

prior^{복습}
[práiər]

a. 전의, 먼저의; 더 중요한, 우선하는
You use prior to indicate that something has already happened, or must happen, before another event takes place.

criminal^{복습}
[krímənl]

a. 범죄의; n. 범죄자, 범인
Criminal means connected with crime.

argue^{복습}
[ά:rgju:]

v. 논쟁하다; 주장하다 (argument n. 논쟁, 논의)
If one person argues with another, they speak angrily to each other about something that they disagree about.

jury*
[dʒúəri]

n. 배심, 심사원; vt. 심사하다
In a court of law, the jury is the group of people who have been chosen from the general public to listen to the facts about a crime and to decide whether the person accused is guilty or not.

vote^{복습}
[vout]

v. 투표하다; n. 투표, 투표권
When you vote, you indicate your choice officially at a meeting or in an election.

226

convict[*]
[kənvíkt]

vt. ~에게 유죄를 입증하다, 유죄를 선고하다
If someone is convicted of a crime, they are found guilty of that crime in a law court.

assure[복습]
[əʃúər]

vt. 단언하다, 보증하다
If you assure someone that something is true or will happen, you tell them that it is definitely true or will definitely happen, often in order to make them less worried.

fake[복습]
[feik]

v. 가장하다, 꾸며내다, 위조하다; a. 가짜의, 위조의
If someone fakes something, they try to make it look valuable or genuine, although in fact it is not.

seizure[복습]
[síːʒər]

n. (병의) 발작; 잡기, 체포; 압수
If someone has a seizure, they have a sudden violent attack of an illness, especially one that affects their heart or brain.

investigate[복습]
[invéstəgèit]

v. 조사하다, 수사하다; 연구하다
If someone, especially an official, investigates an event, situation, or claim, they try to find out what happened or what is the truth.

envelope[복습]
[énvəlòup]

n. 봉투, 봉지
An envelope is the rectangular paper cover in which you send a letter to someone through the post.

frame[복습]
[freim]

n. 뼈대, 골조; (안경) 테, 액자, 테두리; v. 테를 두르다; 세우다, 고안하다; 모함하다
The frame is the way someone thinks or feels about something at a particular time.

obvious[복습]
[ábviəs]

a. 명백한, 분명한
If something is obvious, it is easy to see or understand.

subtle[*]
[sʌtl]

a. 교묘한, 교활한; 솜씨 좋은; 미묘한, 미세한
A subtle person cleverly uses indirect methods to achieve something.

mull
[mʌl]

v. 숙고하다, 곰곰이 생각하다; 엉망으로 만들다, 실패하다; n. 실패, 혼란
If you mull something over, you think about it for a long time before deciding what to do.

verbal[*]
[və́ːrbəl]

a. 말의, 구두의
You use verbal to indicate that something is expressed in speech rather than in writing or action.

persuade[**]
[pərswéid]

vt. 설득하여 ~하게 하다, 확신시키다 (persuasion n. 설득)
If you persuade someone to do something, you cause them to do it by giving them good reasons for doing it.

stuffed[복습]
[stʌft]

a. 속을 채운; 배가 너무 부른 (stuffed animal n. 봉제 동물인형)
Stuffed animals are toys that are made of cloth filled with a soft material and which look like animals.

evidence[복습]
[évədəns]

n. 증거, 증언; 근거, 증명; vt. 증거가 되다, 입증하다
Evidence is the information which is used in a court of law to try to prove something.

premeditation
[priːmedətéiʃən]

n. [법률] 예모(은밀하게 계획을 세움); 미리 계획함
Premeditation is thinking about something or planning it before you actually do it.

murder [복습]
[mə́:rdər]

v. 죽이다, 살해하다; n. 살인, 살해
To murder someone means to commit the crime of killing them deliberately.

confess**
[kənfés]

v. 자백[고백]하다, 인정하다
If someone confesses to doing something wrong, they admit that they did it.

trial*
[tráiəl]

n. 재판; 시도, 시험; 시련, 고난
A trial is a formal meeting in a law court, at which a judge and jury listen to evidence and decide whether a person is guilty of a crime.

district [복습]
[dístrikt]

n. 구역, 지역
A district is a particular area of a town or country.

attorney [복습]
[ətə́:rni]

n. 변호사; 대리인
An attorney or attorney at law is a lawyer.

steam [복습]
[sti:m]

v. (식품 등을) 찌다; 증기가 발생하다; n. 증기
If you steam food or if it steams, you cook it in steam rather than in water.

bun [복습]
[bʌn]

n. (작고 둥글납작한) 빵
Buns are small bread rolls. They are sometimes sweet and may contain dried fruit or spices.

get in touch [복습]

idiom ~와 연락을 하다
If you get in touch with someone, you make contact with them by phone, letter, or visit.

ungrateful
[ʌ́ngréitfəl]

a. 감사할 줄 모르는, 배은망덕한
If you describe someone as ungrateful, you are criticizing them for not showing thanks or for being unkind to someone who has helped them or done them a favor.

go through [복습]

idiom 겪다; 자세히 검토하다; 통과하다
If you go through an event or a period of time, you pass through it from the beginning to the end.

wreck*
[rek]

n. 만신창이; 파손, 파괴, 난파; v. 난파시키다; 망가뜨리다, 파괴하다
(train wreck n. 건강이 완전히 망가진 사람)
A wreck is something such as a ship, car, plane, or building which has been destroyed, usually in an accident.

reimburse [복습]
[rì:imbə́:rs]

vt. 배상하다, 변상하다
If you reimburse someone for something, you pay them back the money that they have spent or lost because of it.

broke**
[brouk]

a. 파산한, 무일푼의
If you are broke, you have no money.

accountant*
[əkáuntənt]

n. 회계사; 회계원, 경리 사무원
An accountant is a person whose job is to keep financial accounts.

arrest [복습]
[ərést]

vt. 체포하다, 저지하다; (주의 · 이목 · 흥미 등을) 끌다; n. 체포, 검거, 구속
If the police arrest you, they take charge of you and take you to a police station, because they believe you may have committed a crime.

228

detective^{복습}
[ditéktiv]

n. 형사, 수사관; 탐정
A detective is someone whose job is to discover what has happened in a crime or other situation and to find the people involved.

airline^{복습}
[éərlain]

n. 항공 노선; (pl.) 항공 회사
An airline is a system or organization that provides scheduled flights for passengers or cargo.

1분에 몇 단어를 읽는지 리딩 속도를 측정해보세요.

$$\frac{501 \text{ words}}{\text{reading time ( ) sec}} \times 60 = (\quad) \text{ WPM}$$

Build Your Vocabulary

disguise*
[disgáiz]

n. 변장, 위장; v. 변장하다, 위장하다
If you are in disguise, you are not wearing your usual clothes or you have altered your appearance in other ways, so that people will not recognize you.

recognize^{복습}
[rékəgnaiz]

vt. 인지하다, 알아보다
If you recognize someone or something, you know who that person is or what that thing is.

fragile*
[frǽdʒəl]

a. 부서지기[깨지기] 쉬운
Something that is fragile is easily broken or damaged.

note^{복습}
[nout]

n. (악기의) 음; (짧은) 기록; 짧은 편지; v. 주목하다, 알아채다; 메모하다
In music, a note is the sound of a particular pitch, or a written symbol representing this sound.

elaborate*
[ilǽbərət]

a. 정교한, 공들인, 복잡한; v. 애써 만들다, 고심하여 만들다; 상세히 말하다
You use elaborate to describe something that is very complex because it has a lot of different parts.

instrument^{복습}
[ínstrəmənt]

n. 악기; 기구, 도구 (instrumentation n. 기악 편성[연주]법)
A musical instrument is an object such as a piano, guitar, or flute, which you play in order to produce music.

pull oneself together

phrasal v. 기운[침착]을 되찾다, 회복하다
If you pull yourself together, you force yourself to stop behaving in a nervous, frightened, or uncontrolled way.

clue^{복습}
[kluː]

n. 실마리, 단서; vt. 암시를 주다, 귀띔하다
A clue to a problem or mystery is something that helps you to find the answer to it.

lump*
[lʌmp]

n. 덩어리, 한 조각; v. 한 덩어리로 만들다
(have a lump in throat idiom 목이 메다)
A lump of something is a solid piece of it.

throat^{복습}
[θrout]

n. 목구멍, 목
Your throat is the back of your mouth and the top part of the tubes that go down into your stomach and your lungs.

stain^{복습}
[stein]

n. 얼룩, 오염; v. 얼룩지(게 하)다, 더러워(지게 하)다
A stain is a mark on something that is difficult to remove.

230

splatter^{복습}
[splǽtə:r]

v. 튀다, 튀기다; n. 튀기기; 철벅철벅 소리
If a thick wet substance splatters on something or is splattered on it, it drops or is thrown over it.

cope[*]
[koup]

v. 맞서다, 대처하다
If you cope with a problem or task, you deal with it successfully.

permanent^{복습}
[pə́:rmənənt]

a. 영구적인, 불변의 (permanently ad. 영구히)
Something that is permanent lasts forever.

rush^{복습}
[rʌʃ]

v. 급히 움직이다, 서두르다, 돌진하다
If you rush something, you do it in a hurry, often too quickly and without much care.

hand in hand

idiom 손에 손을 잡고
Hand in hand means holding each other's hand.

inspire^{복습}
[inspáiər]

vt. 영감을 주다, 고무하다, 불어넣다
If someone or something inspires you, they give you new ideas and a strong feeling of enthusiasm.

revolve^{복습}
[riválv]

v. 회전하다, 빙빙 돌다 (revolve around phrasal v. ~을 중심으로 돌아가다)
To revolve around someone or something means to have them as the main subject or interest.

graduate^{복습}
[grǽdʒueit]

vi. 졸업하다; n. 졸업생; 대학원생
When a student graduates, they complete their studies successfully and leave their school or university.

community^{**}
[kəmjú:nəti]

n. 지역 공동체[사회], 일반 사회
The community is all the people who live in a particular area or place.

transfer[*]
[trænsfə́:r]

v. 옮기다, 전학하다; 양도하다; n. 이전, 이적; 양도
If you are transferred, or if you transfer, to a different job or place, you move to a different job or start working in a different place.

major^{**}
[méidʒər]

vi. 전공하다; n. 전공 과목; a. 중요한; 많은 쪽의
If a student at a university or college majors in a particular subject, that subject is the main one they study.

landscape^{복습}
[lǽndskeip]

n. 풍경, 경치, 조망; v. (나무를 심거나 지형을 바꾸어) 미화[조경]하다
The landscape is everything you can see when you look across an area of land, including hills, rivers, buildings, trees, and plants.

architecture[*]
[á:rkətèkʧər]

n. 건축학[술], 건축; 구조, 구성 (landscape architecture n. 환경 설계)
Architecture is the art of planning, designing, and constructing buildings.

consider^{복습}
[kənsídər]

v. 고려하다, 숙고하다
If you consider something, you think about it carefully.

occupation[*]
[àkjupéiʃən]

n. 직업, 업무, 일; 점유, 이용 (occupational a. 직업의)
Your occupation is your job or profession.

therapy^{복습}
[θérəpi]

n. 치료, 요법
Therapy is the treatment of someone with mental or physical illness without the use of drugs or operations.

수고하셨습니다!

드디어 끝까지 다 읽으셨군요! 축하드립니다! 여러분은 이 책을 통해 총 48,447개의 단어를 읽으셨고, 1,000개 이상의 어휘와 표현들을 익히셨습니다. 이 책에 나온 어휘는 다른 원서를 읽을 때에도 빈번히 만날 수 있는 필수 어휘들입니다. 이 책을 읽었던 경험은 비슷한 수준의 다른 원서들을 읽을 때 큰 도움이 될 것입니다. 이제 자신의 상황에 맞게 원서를 반복해서 읽거나, 오디오북을 들어 볼 수 있습니다. 혹은 비슷한 수준의 다른 원서를 찾아 읽는 것도 좋습니다. 일단 원서를 완독한 뒤에 어떻게 계속 영어 공부를 이어갈 수 있을지, 도움말을 꼼꼼히 살펴보고 각자 상황에 맞게 적용해 보세요!

리딩(Reading)을 확실하게 다지고 싶다면? 반복해서 읽어 보세요!

리딩 실력을 탄탄하게 다지고 싶다면, 같은 원서를 2~3번 반복해서 읽을 것을 권합니다. 같은 책을 여러 번 읽으면 지루할 것 같지만, 꼭 그렇지도 않습니다. 반복해서 읽을 때 처음과 주안점을 다르게 두면, 전혀 다른 느낌으로 재미있게 읽을 수 있습니다.

처음 원서를 읽을 때는 생소한 단어들과 스토리로 인해 읽으면서 곧바로 이해하기가 매우 힘들 수 있습니다. 전체 맥락을 잡고 읽어도 약간 버거운 느낌이지요. 하지만 반복해서 읽기 시작하면 달라집니다. 일단 내용을 파악한 상황이기 때문에 문장 구조나 어휘의 활용에 더 집중하게 되고, 조금 더 깊이 있게 읽을 수 있습니다. 좋은 표현과 문장을 수집하고 메모할 만한 여유도 생기게 되지요. 어휘도 많이 익숙해졌기 때문에 리딩 속도에도 탄력이 붙습니다. 처음 읽을 때는 '내용'에서 재미를 느꼈다면, 반복해서 읽을 때에는 '영어'에서 재미를 느끼게 되는 것입니다. 따라서 리딩 실력을 더욱 확고하게 다지고자 한다면, 같은 책을 2~3회 정도 반복해서 읽을 것을 권해 드립니다.

리스닝(Listening) 실력을 늘리고 싶다면?
귀를 통해서 읽어 보세요!

많은 영어 학습자들이 '리스닝이 안 돼서 문제'라고 한탄합니다. 그리고 리스닝 실력을 늘리는 방법으로 무슨 뜻인지 몰라도 반복해서 듣는 '무작정 듣기'를 선택합니다. 하지만 뜻도 모르면서 무작정 듣는 일에는 엄청난 인내력이 필요합니다. 그래서 대부분 며칠 시도하다가 포기해 버리고 말지요.

따라서 모르는 내용을 무작정 듣는 것보다는 어느 정도 알고 있는 내용을 반복해서 듣는 것이 더 효과적인 듣기 방법입니다. 그리고 이런 방식의 듣기에 활용할수 있는 가장 좋은 교재가 오디오북입니다.

리스닝 실력을 향상하고 싶다면, 이 책에서 제공하는 오디오북을 이용해서 듣는 연습을 해 보세요. 활용법은 간단합니다. 일단 책을 한 번 완독했다면, 오디오북을 통해 다시 들어 보는 것입니다. 휴대 기기에 넣어 시간이 날 때 틈틈이 듣는 것도 좋고, 책상에 앉아 눈으로는 텍스트를 보며 귀로 읽는 것도 좋습니다. 이미 읽었던 내용이라 이해하기가 훨씬 수월하고, 애매했던 발음들도 자연스럽게 교정할 수 있습니다. 또 성우의 목소리 연기를 듣다 보면 내용이 더욱 생동감 있게 다가와 이해도가 높아지는 효과도 거둘 수 있습니다.

반대로 듣기에 자신 있는 사람이라면, 책을 읽기 전에 처음부터 오디오북을 먼저 듣는 것도 좋은 방법입니다. 귀를 통해 책을 쭉 읽어보고, 이후에 다시 눈으로 책을 읽으면서 잘 들리지 않았던 부분들을 보충하는 것이지요.

중요한 것은 내용을 따라가면서, 내용에 푹 빠져서 반복해 들어야 한다는 것입니다. 이렇게 연습을 반복해서 눈으로 읽지 않은 책이라도 '귀를 통해' 읽을 수 있을 정도가 되면, 리스닝으로 고생하는 일은 거의 없을 것입니다.

 왼쪽의 QR 코드를 인식하여 정식 오디오북을 들어 보세요!
더불어 롱테일북스 홈페이지(www.longtailbooks.co.kr)에서도
오디오북 MP3 파일을 다운로드 받을 수 있습니다.

스피킹(Speaking)이 고민이라면? 소리 내어 읽어 보세요!

스피킹 역시 많은 학습자들이 고민하는 부분입니다. 스피킹이 고민이라면, 원서를 큰 소리로 읽는 낭독 훈련(Voice Reading)을 해 보세요!

'소리 내어 읽는 것이 말하기에 정말로 도움이 될까?'라고 의아한 생각이 들 수도 있습니다. 하지만 인간의 두뇌 입장에서 봤을 때, 성대 구조를 활용해서 '발화'한다는 점에서는 소리 내어 읽기와 말하기에 큰 차이가 없다고 합니다. 소리 내어 읽는 것은 '타인의 생각'을 전달하고, 직접 말하는 것은 '자신의 생각'을 전달한다는 차이가 있을 뿐, 머릿속에서 문장을 처리하고 조음기관(혀와 성대 등)을 움직여 의미를 만든다는 점에서 같은 과정인 것이지요. 따라서 소리 내어 읽는 연습을 꾸준히 하는 것은 스피킹 연습에 큰 도움이 됩니다.

소리 내어 읽기를 하는 방법은 간단합니다. 일단 오디오북을 들으면서 성우의 목소리를 최대한 따라 하며 같이 읽어 보세요. 발음뿐 아니라 억양, 어조, 느낌까지 완벽히 따라 한다고 생각하면서 소리 내어 읽습니다. 따라 읽는 것이 조금 익숙해지면, 옆의 누군가에게 이 책을 읽어 준다는 생각으로 소리 내어 계속 읽어 나갑니다. 한 번 눈과 귀로 읽었던 책이기 때문에 보다 수월하게 진행할 수 있고, 자연스럽게 어휘와 표현을 복습하는 효과도 거두게 됩니다. 또 이렇게 소리 내어 읽은 것을 녹음해서 들어 보면 스스로에게도 좋은 피드백이 됩니다.

최근 말하기가 강조되면서 소리 내어 읽기가 크게 각광을 받고 있기는 하지만, 그렇다고 소리 내어 읽기가 무조건 좋은 것만은 아닙니다. 책을 소리 내어 읽다 보면, 무의식적으로 속으로 발음을 하는 습관을 가지게 되어 리딩 속도 자체는 오히려 크게 떨어지는 현상이 발생할 수 있습니다. 따라서 빠른 리딩 속도가 중요한 수험생이나 고학력 학습자들에게는 소리 내어 읽기가 적절하지 않은 방법입니다. 효과가 좋다는 말만 믿고 무턱대고 따라 하기보다는 자신의 필요에 맞게 우선순위를 정하고 원서를 활용하는 것이 좋습니다.

라이팅(Writing)까지 욕심이 난다면? 요약하는 연습을 해 보세요!

원서를 라이팅 연습에 직접적으로 활용하는 데에는 한계가 있지만, 적절히 활용하면 원서도 유용한 라이팅 자료가 될 수 있습니다.

특히 책을 읽고 그 내용을 요약하는 연습은 큰 도움이 됩니다. 요약 훈련의 방식도 간단합니다. 원서를 읽고 그날 읽은 분량만큼 혹은 책을 다 읽고 전체 내용을 기반으로, 책 내용을 한번 요약하고 나의 느낌을 영어로 적어보는 것입니다.

이때 그 책에 나왔던 단어와 표현을 최대한 활용하여 요약하는 것이 중요합니다. 영어 표현력은 결국 얼마나 다양한 어휘로 많은 표현을 해 보았느냐가 좌우하게 됩니다. 이런 면에서 내가 읽은 책을, 그 책에 나온 문장과 어휘로 다시 표현해 보는 것은 매우 효율적인 방법입니다. 책에 나온 어휘와 표현을 단순히 읽고 무슨 말인지 아는 정도가 아니라, 실제로 직접 활용해서 쓸 수 있을 만큼 확실하게 익히게 되는 것이지요. 여기에 첨삭까지 받을 수 있는 방법이 있다면 금상첨화입니다.

이러한 '표현하기' 연습은 스피킹 훈련에도 그대로 적용될 수 있습니다. 책을 읽고 그 내용을 3분 안에 다른 사람에게 영어로 말하는 연습을 해 보세요. 순발력과 표현력을 기르는 좋은 훈련이 될 것입니다.

꾸준히 원서를 읽고 싶다면? 뉴베리 수상작을 계속 읽어 보세요!

뉴베리 상이 세계 최고 권위의 아동 문학상인 만큼, 그 수상작들은 확실히 완성도를 검증받은 작품이라고 할 수 있습니다. 특히 '쉬운 어휘로 쓰인 깊이 있는 문장'으로 이루어졌다는 점이 영어 학습자들에게 큰 호응을 얻고 있습니다. 이렇게 '검증된 원서'를 꾸준히 읽는 것은 영어 실력 향상에 큰 도움이 됩니다.

아래에 수준별로 제시된 뉴베리 수상작 목록을 보며 적절한 책들을 찾아 계속 읽어 보세요. 꼭 뉴베리 수상작이 아니더라도 마음에 드는 작가의 다른 책을 읽어 보는 것 또한 아주 좋은 방법입니다.

• 영어 초보자도 쉽게 읽을 만한 아주 쉬운 수준. 소리 내어 읽기에도 아주 적합.
Sarah, Plain and Tall*(Medal, 8,331단어), The Hundred Penny Box (Honor, 5,878단어), The Hundred Dresses*(Honor, 7,329단어), My Father's Dragon (Honor, 7,682단어), 26 Fairmount Avenue (Honor, 6,737단어)

영어원서 읽기 TIPS

- 중 · 고등학생 정도 영어 학습자라면 쉽게 읽을 수 있는 수준. 소리 내어 읽기에도 비교적 적합한 편.

Because of Winn-Dixie★(Honor, 22,123단어), What Jamie Saw (Honor, 17,203단어), Charlotte's Web (Honor, 31,938단어), Dear Mr. Henshaw (Medal, 18,145단어), Missing May (Medal, 17,509단어)

- 대학생 정도 영어 학습자라면 무난한 수준. 소리 내어 읽기에 적합하지 않음.

Number The Stars★(Medal, 27,197단어), A Single Shard (Medal, 33,726단어), The Tale of Despereaux★(Medal, 32,375단어), Hatchet★(Medal, 42,328단어), Bridge to Terabithia (Medal, 32,888단어), A Fine White Dust (Honor, 19,022단어), Jennifer, Hecate, Macbeth, William McKinley and Me, Elizabeth (Honor, 23,266단어)

- 원서 완독 경험을 가진 학습자에게 적절한 수준. 소리 내어 읽기에 적합하지 않음.

The Giver★(Medal, 43,617단어), From the Mixed-Up Files of Mrs. Basil E. Frankweiler (Medal, 30,906단어), The View from Saturday (Medal, 42,685단어), Holes★(Medal, 47,079단어), Criss Cross (Medal, 48,221단어), Walk Two Moons (Medal, 59,400단어), The Graveyard Book (Medal, 67,380단어)

뉴베리 수상작과 뉴베리 수상 작가의 좋은 작품을 엄선한 「뉴베리 컬렉션」에도 위 목록에 있는 도서 중 상당수가 포함될 예정입니다.

★ 「뉴베리 컬렉션」으로 이미 출간된 도서

어떤 책들이 출간되었는지 확인하려면, 지금 인터넷 서점에서
뉴베리 컬렉션을 검색해 보세요.

236

뉴베리 수상작을 동영상 강의로 만나 보세요!

영어원서 전문 동영상 강의 사이트 영서당(yseodang.com)에서는 뉴베리 컬렉션 『Holes』, 『Because of Winn-Dixie』, 『The Miraculous Journey of Edward Tulane』, 『Wayside School 시리즈』 등의 동영상 강의를 제공하고 있습니다. 뉴베리 수상작이라는 최고의 영어 교재와 EBS 출신 인기 강사가 만난 명강! 지금 사이트를 방문해서 무료 샘플 강의를 들어 보세요!

'스피드 리딩 카페'를 통해 원서 읽기 습관을 길러 보세요!

일상에서 영어를 한마디도 쓰지 않는 비영어권 국가에서 살고 있는 우리가 영어 환경에 가장 쉽고, 편하고, 부담 없이 노출되는 방법은 바로 '영어원서 읽기'입니다. 언제 어디서든 원서를 붙잡고 읽기만 하면 곧바로 영어를 접하는 환경이 만들어지기 때문이지요. 하루에 20분씩만 꾸준히 읽는다면, 1년에 무려 120시간 동안 영어에 노출될 수 있습니다. 이러한 이유 때문에 영어 교육 전문가들이 영어 원서 읽기를 추천하는 것이지요.

하지만 원서 읽기가 좋다는 것을 알아도 막상 꾸준히 읽는 것은 쉽지 않습니다. 그럴 때에는 13만 명 이상의 회원을 보유한 국내 최대 원서 읽기 동호회 〈스피드 리딩 카페〉(cafe.naver.com/readingtc)를 방문해 보세요.

원서별로 정리된 무료 PDF 단어장과 수준별 추천 원서 목록 등 유용한 자료는 물론, 뉴베리 수상작을 포함한 다양한 원서의 리뷰와 정보를 무료로 확인할 수 있습니다. 특히 함께 모여서 원서를 읽는 '북클럽'은 중간에 포기하지 않고 원서 읽기 습관을 기르는 데 큰 도움이 될 것입니다.

chapters one & two

1. C　He worked for Raincreek Irrigation and Landscaping. He was in the process of digging a trench along the side yard of a house that belonged to the mayor of Austin, a woman with the unusual name of Cherry Lane.

2. A　During his first week at Camp Green Lake, close to three years before, a scorpion had stung him on the arm, and the pain had traveled upward and settled in his armpit. The pain eventually went away, but the name stuck.

3. D　1. Graduate from high school. 2. Get a job. 3. Save his money. 4. Avoid situations that might turn violent. And 5. Lose the name Armpit.

4. B　They had met each other at Camp Green Lake.

5. C　"Here's the deal. They just added Austin to her tour because of some kind of screwup in San Antonio. Tickets go on sale day after tomorrow. Fifty-five dollars a pop."

6. A　The first person she'd fire would be El Genius. He was her business manager and agent, and also happened to be married to her mother. They had gotten married shortly before the tour. His real name was Jerome Paisley, but he actually wanted people to call him El Genius.

7. D　Fred carefully put the letter and the photograph in a plastic bag. "What are you doing that for?" "FBI."

chapters three & four

1. B　Armpit's home was in east Austin. The house was a duplex, with two identical front doors that faced each other across a wide front porch, 141A and 141B. Armpit's family lived in 141B. It was just him and his parents.

2. C　But as much as Armpit helped her, she helped him even more. She gave his life meaning. For the first time in his life, there was someone who looked up to him, who

cared about him.

3. B   After he returned from Camp Green Lake, his parents bought a home drug-testing kit. They weren't going to stand by and let him ruin his life, like his brother.

4. A   He didn't have a problem with foot odor, but when your name was Armpit you had to be extra careful.

5. C   Most of the class period was spent discussing the next major assignment. Everyone had to bring a stuffed animal to school and give a campaign speech for it.

6. D   "No, I just wanted Coach Simmons to think that. He gives better grades to football players."

7. A   "I planted that story," he boasted. "You didn't even sell out in Philly." He pointed to his big, fat head and said, "El Genius at work."

chapters five & six

1. C   Armpit brought his economics book along. He knew he'd probably miss speech, but there was a test in econ and he couldn't afford to miss that.

2. C   The mystery of who they were was solved shortly after seven-thirty, when the guys who were paying them showed up. One was a fast-talking, skinny white guy. With him was a big dude wearing a cowboy hat and boots. . . . "You just hand it to the ticket agent and ask for six tickets. You then give the tickets to Moses, and he will pay you twenty-five dollars."

3. A   "Tell you what. I'll give you seventy bucks for each ticket. That's fifteen more than face value. Times twelve, you'll make a hundred and eighty dollars. Ninety bucks each."

4. D   As he was getting out of the car, X-Ray said, "By the way. I'm going to need thirty bucks to put an ad in the paper."

5. B   He'd gotten a ninety on his economics test, thanks to Felix. He'd learned more in the parking lot of the Lonestar Arena than he had learned all year in class.

6. D   "So is there something wro—" He caught himself. "Does Coo have a disability?" he asked.

7. A   "I think Coo's great," Armpit assured her. "I just don't want to take your favorite. It's just a stupid speech. What if something happens?" "Coo isn't scared," said Ginny. "He is always strong and brave. H-he will be the b-best ruler of the w-w-world!"

1. D   When the door opened, he took three copies of the Austin American Statesman, just to get even, and left two of them on top of the machine.

2. B   "I told you to keep the price low."

3. A   But he felt good. He had a feeling of satisfaction that he could never explain to X-Ray. It was good clean work. Scalping tickets felt dirty in comparison.

4. C   "You know, you didn't stutter at all when you were adding," he pointed out. "I only stutter when I t-t-t-talk."

5. B   "They were two big white guys. And there won't be too many people around at ten o'clock. I just think it's a good idea to have some backup."

6. A   But Armpit knew he wasn't good at making jokes, and if he didn't write his speech down, he would just stand there, sweating and babbling nervously. Besides, he really wanted Coo to win, for Ginny's sake.

7. D   "Our respect is worth a lot more than that," said X-Ray. "Who do they think they are?" "If you don't sell the tickets, I'm going to kill you," Armpit warned him

1. A   "Hey, Armpit, want a ride?" He glanced over to see a yellow Mustang slowly moving along beside him.

2. B   It wasn't that they were cruel. All the other speeches had been humorous and they expected more of the same. The sight of Armpit, the biggest and toughest kid in class, holding the little baby toy just added to the comedy, and it took a while for what he was saying to sink in.

3. B   "Those clowns? Hell no! A lady called me this morning. Wanted four tickets for her kid's birthday."

4. D   Kaira was sick of being alone and so had asked the guys in the band if she could ride with them.

5. C   "I'm all right," he said, getting back to his feet, then made his way to the CD rack. "Hey, Kaira, you ever heard of Janis Joplin?"

6. D   "All I'm saying," said Billy, "is your mama would be better off if she kept one eye on her husband and one eye on Aileen."

7. C   Aileen always registered Kaira under an assumed name so she wouldn't be hassled by fans. Aileen chose characters from old TV shows, but Kaira hadn't been

stumped yet.

1. B   "Said he couldn't get away. Works from six in the morning until midnight." Armpit thought that sounded a little suspicious.

2. A   "Well, I don't know about that," said Murdock. "But I only get to see my daughter one weekend a month, so I gotta make the most of it. When she heard Kaira DeLeon was going to be playing, it was all she could talk about."

3. A   "Can I get you something to eat?" Murdock asked. "On the house."

4. B   Joe the Armadillo won, and Dumbo was elected vice ruler of the world. If for any reason Joe was unable to fulfill his obligations, Dumbo would take over. Armpit tried not to let his disappointment show. After all, it was just a stupid assignment, and people just voted for the only ones they could remember.

5. C   "You want to go to the concert on Saturday?" She bit her lip. "You mean with you?" "Yeah." "Yeah."

6. C   By the time economics was over, Armpit had convinced himself that X-Ray had already sold the last two tickets and that he was going to have to buy two from a scalper for fifteen hundred dollars.

7. B   "Man, that girl's really gotten to you," said X-Ray. "Look, they're your tickets. You don't have to buy them twice!"

1. C   "How do I look?" "All dreamy-eyed." She giggled some more. "What's her name?" she asked in a teasing kind of voice.

2. D   "He is kind of dangerous," said Claire. "Maybe that's what she likes about him," said Roxanne. "The danger!" "He's a nice guy," said Tatiana. "He's sweet." "Sweet? He almost killed two people, girl!" Roxanne reminded her.

3. B   Her father had left home when she was a baby. "He l-left because of m-me. B-because of my disa-b-bbility."

4. A   "I'm really sorry. There's this family thing I got to do. I forgot all about it. They won't let me out of it. My parents have this thing about family time!"

5. C   He shook his head. X-Ray had said people were still calling about the tickets,

so maybe it wasn't too late. If nothing else, they could go to the Lonestar and try to sell them at the door. But now another thought came to him. "So, Ginny," he said. "You want to go to the concert with me?"

6. B   "Ginny? Are you outta your gourd? Have you completely lost your mind?" "Look, she had a really bad day. Just bring the tickets over here. I want to get an early start so we can beat the crowds." "We're talking three hundred dollars!"

7. A   He would be driving Ginny's mother's car. She insisted on it, which was fine with him, because if he took the X-Mobile they'd have to first take X-Ray home and they were running out of time.

chapters fifteen & sixteen

1. D   "You know, you don't stutter at all when you sing," Armpit pointed out.

2. A   "Counterfeit tickets," said the security guard. "He refuses to leave." "What?" Armpit exclaimed, reaching for the tickets. "Let me see . . ." An officer grabbed his arm and twisted it behind his back, spinning him around.

3. D   His head was lifted off the floor by his hair and a police officer shouted in his face. "What's she on?" "What'd you give her?" shouted the other officer.

4. C   "Let him go!" ordered the mayor. "I don't think that's a good idea." "You let him go right now, unless you want to spend the next ten years walking up and down Lamar Boulevard."

5. C   "Funniest thing I ever saw!" laughed Jerome Paisley as he returned to the backstage area. "This little bit of a girl, wriggling around on the floor, drooling all over herself. She looked like a goldfish that fell out of its bowl. You know how they flop around until they die?"

6. B   "I heard there was a problem with some tickets," the girl said. She sat on the cot next to Armpit and asked Ginny her name. . . . That made Kaira smile. "You seem okay now," she said. "Would you like to come backstage and watch the concert from there?"

7. D   The crowd shouted for more, Ginny and Armpit right along with them. The lights remained dark. After about five minutes they came back out and did "Just Hold On a Little Longer." On the last line, ". . . And then I'll be on my way," Kaira blew a kiss to the crowd and once again left the stage.

1. B "... could have been your best performance," the man was saying, "but you know what the critics are going to write? 'She's no Janis Joplin.' All they're going to talk about is how you butchered her classic song!"

2. C "It's chocolate chip," she told Armpit. "Is that okay?"

3. C "These are my friends, Ginny and Theodore. This is Cotton, our drummer." "Well, not anymore," said Cotton. "Your dad just fired me. I just wanted to stop in and say good-bye."

4. D "A hint? What kind of a hint?" "I said it was a p-part of the b-body."

5. A He had just come from Ginny's mother, who was delighted that Ginny had had such a wonderful time.

6. B "... And then I made some copies—but just to see how they'd look, I swear! I wasn't planning to do anything with them."

7. C "We don't have to leave for Dallas until one. You want to get together and have breakfast or something?"

1. A A family of four came out of the elevator and headed in his direction. ... "Excuse me," Armpit said. "You ever watch the show Bewitched?" He knew he must have sounded crazy.

2. C "Thanks." Armpit picked up the phone and asked the operator for Samantha Stevens.

3. A "My manager tells me I need to take big steps," she said. "I have to grab for everything I can get right now, because in a few years I could be all washed up."

4. C "Whatever my name is, you have to touch me there."

5. D "So you d-didn't kiss her?" "I couldn't. Not with her bodyguard right there."

6. B "I'm Detective Debbie Newberg from the Austin Police Department." She opened the wallet, showing them her badge. "I wanted to talk to you about the concert tickets."

7. D As he watched her drive away, he felt bad about having to lie to her. She was nice. She had a sweet smile. It was hard to imagine her out in the world, fighting criminals. He worried she might get hurt.

1. B   "We got nothing to worry about," he said. "Nothing to worry about. The police have better things to do than to launch a big investigation over a couple of phony tickets."

2. C   On the back of their souvenir T-shirts was a list of the fifty four cities on the tour. Ginny and Armpit looked at them every day for the next week and a half and tried to predict where Kaira was.

3. D   How could he explain it was all because a Kaira DeLeon song came on the radio?

4. A   "How about Armpit?" He almost dropped the phone.

5. B   It's just that you and Ginny are really my only friends. Is that pathetic or what? I don't mean you and Ginny are pathetic. I'm the one who's pathetic!

6. C   I'm so mad Dr. Doofus showed up when he did. That's my new name for him. He's a doctor of doofology.

7. A   When I sing love songs, it helps for me to picture someone in my mind. . . . Anyway, now, when I sing those songs, I picture you.

1. A   "We've got a suspect down at the station. I'd like you to be here while I question him."

2. D   "No, it's a two-way mirror. Behind it is an expert criminal psychologist. He's watching and listening to everything you say. He knows when you're lying just by your body language, and by the infection of your voice."

3. B   "Felix called him Armpit. I never even saw the dude until that day in line."

4. A   X-Ray called him later and told him he'd had a nice chat with Debbie Newberg and that everything was cool now, but just in case, it might be a good idea if they stayed away from each other for a while.

5. C   "You are so . . . I don't know. Other guys would be all braggy about it. You're just so real. So down-to-earth. I feel like a big phony whenever I talk to you."

6. B   "Okay, this is really embarrassing, but you asked for it. Every time I hear the song, it sounds like you're singing, 'Armpit. Save me, Armpit. A damsel in distress.' "

7. A   "Three days in San Francisco. Just you and me. What do you say?"

chapters twenty-five & twenty-six

1. D   She sounded incredibly efficient.
2. C   So far, with the help of Jerome, she had managed to extract nearly three million dollars from Kaira's trust account.
3. B   However, if, for example, somebody like Billy Boy killed Kaira before she turned eighteen, then her mother would inherit all her money. Jerome, her mother's husband, would continue to oversee all the financial matters.
4. A   And he was just about to do that when a mountain laurel planted near the corner of the house caught his attention.
5. B   X-Ray had a large bruise on his right cheek, and he wasn't wearing his glasses. His shirt was ripped.
6. C   "Kaira DeLeon's letter. I'll pay you a hundred and fifty dollars for it."
7. B   "You wouldn't like a job, would you? Six-fifty an hour?" "Sounds good," X-Ray said, much to Armpit's surprise.

chapters twenty-seven & twenty-eight

1. B   Armpit figured that Felix would probably sell the letter on eBay.
2. A   And so he remained, paralyzed by indecision, a donkey between two haystacks.
3. D   "I want the letter now," said Felix.
4. A   A horn sounded from the street, and Armpit looked up to see a long white limousine stopped in the middle of the road. "I called the police!" the driver shouted, pointing to his cell phone.
5. C   The white limo was now parked in front of his house. The driver stood beside it, but when he saw Armpit, he got back inside and locked the doors.
6. C   The cowboy hat lay on the ground, white with a brown band. Armpit, remembering X-Ray's glasses, stepped on it.
7. A   There was no time to shower.

chapters twenty-nine & thirty

1. C   It was like the whole city was air-conditioned. There was also a freshness to the air that he didn't get in Texas, where it seemed that the same hot and humid air stayed in

one place all summer long, becoming more stale and stagnant by the minute.

2. B   The suite was identical to Armpit's. Kaira's stepfather slid open a closet door and pulled out a baseball bat, holding it by fat end. "Take a look at this baby!"

3. A   He went right to Kaira, grabbed her, and kissed her on the lips.

4. D   He returned to the sweatshirts even though Kaira told him not to worry about the price. "You just charge it to your room. The tour will pay for it."

5. B   "Okay, here's the deal," she told the driver, handing him Armpit's fifty. "The guy following us is a total doofus. As soon as you can ditch him, let us out, then keep on going to the bridge."

6. D   Before leaving, he took the knife from the fruit and cheese plate.

7. A   He ended up buying Ginny a silk scarf that showed the Golden Gate Bridge stretching across a background of blue sky and green ocean.

chapters thirty-one & thirty-two

1. D   The crowds of people and the strong smells of Chinatown had gotten to her. "I could kill for a cup of coffee."

2. C   "You could be my guitar player!" "That'd be great," Armpit agreed. "Except I don't know how to play the guitar."

3. A   "I dread it," said Kaira. "I know, that makes me sound like an awful person, but I just get creeped out being around someone like that. . . ."

4. A   He handed her a napkin. "Would you mind?" Kaira showed him her empty hands, but he gave her a pen. She signed the napkin.

5. B   She picked up her cup and tossed the contents at him, splattering him with coffee and cream.

6. A   There was something special about being in a strange place, all alone in a mass of people, even if you had just screwed up your life, or perhaps especially if you had just screwed up your life.

7. D   His face had the look of pained urgency. He had never lost Kaira before.

chapters thirty-three & thirty-four

1. C   Armpit was winded when returned to the hotel. He had always thought the hills in Austin were steep, but they were nothing compared to where he'd just been.

246

2. D   She dropped the towel on the floor, opened the bathroom door, and took one step into the bedroom. Jerome Paisley closed his eyes as he swung. The bat caromed off her shoulder, then slammed against her throat.

3. C   Fred remained on the floor. Sticking into his stomach was the knife from Armpit's fruit and cheese plate.

4. B   Using every last bit of strength she had left, she pulled the cord. The lamp came down with a crash.

5. D   Nancy Young suggested, only somewhat tongue-in-cheek, that Armpit might want to leave now, before he got stuck with the bill.

6. B   It was impossible for them to take their usual walk. The street was filled with news vans and camera crews.

7. B   "I just wanted to let you know I've been assigned to another case. I told my superiors that all my leads had dried up. And really, for just two counterfeit tickets, it isn't worth the resources."

chapters thirty-five & thirty-six

1. B   His fingerprints were on the bat. The knife came from his room. Her room key was found in his hotel suite. Traces of his blood and hair would be discovered in the next letter from Billy Boy. Then there was his prior criminal history, and the very public argument at the coffeehouse.

2. A   "You should be a lawyer," said Ginny.

3. C   Armpit had been a little disappointed when the San Francisco district attorney told him that. If there were a trial then he'd get to go back to San Francisco and see Kaira again.

4. B   That woman Aileen had stolen most of the money from the concert tour, and there were still many people who needed to be paid and ticket holders who needed to be reimbursed. According to the newspapers, Kaira was broke.

5. D   The doctors said she might never be able to sing again.

6. C   Her voice sounded fragile, like fine crystal that might break at any moment, but each note was true and clear.

7. D   Anyway, he couldn't let his life revolve around Kaira DeLeon. He had his own set of small steps to take.

SMALL STEPS

1판 1쇄 2012년 10월 8일
2판 2쇄 2024년 4월 22일

지은이 Louis Sachar
기획 김승규
책임편집 김보경 차소향
콘텐츠제작및감수 롱테일 교육 연구소
저작권 명채린
디자인 김수진
마케팅 두잉글 사업 본부

펴낸이 이수영
펴낸곳 롱테일북스
출판등록 제2015-000191호
주소 04033 서울특별시 마포구 양화로 113, 3층(서교동, 순홍빌딩)
전자메일 help@ltinc.net

ISBN 979-11-91343-92-2 14740